Reshaping the University

SRHE and Open University Press Imprint

Current titles include:

Catherine Bargh *et al.*: *University Leadership*
Ronald Barnett: *Beyond all Reason*
Ronald Barnett: *Higher Education: A Critical Business*
Ronald Barnett: *Realizing the University in an age of supercomplexity*
Ronald Barnett & Kelly Coate: *Engaging the Curriculum in Higher Education*
Tony Becher and Paul R. Trowler: *Academic Tribes and Territories (2nd edn)*
John Biggs: *Teaching for Quality Learning at University (2nd edn)*
Richard Blackwell & Paul Blackmore (eds): *Towards Strategic Staff Development in Higher Education*
David Boud *et al.* (eds): *Using Experience for Learning*
David Boud and Nicky Solomon (eds): *Work-based Learning*
Tom Bourner *et al.* (eds): *New Directions in Professional Higher Education*
Anne Brockbank and Ian McGill: *Facilitating Reflective Learning in Higher Education*
Stephen D. Brookfield and Stephen Preskill: *Discussion as a way of teaching*
Ann Brooks and Alison Mackinnon (eds): *Gender and the Restructured University*
Sally Brown and Angela Glasner (eds): *Assessment Matters in Higher Education*
Burton R. Clark: *Sustaining Change in Universities*
James Cornford & Neil Pollock: *Putting the University Online*
John Cowan: *On Becoming an Innovative University Teacher*
Sara Delamont, Paul Atkinson and Odette Parry: *Supervising the Doctorate 2/e*
Sara Delamont & Paul Atkinson: *Successful Research Careers*
Gerard Delanty: *Challenging Knowledge*
Chris Duke: *Managing the Learning University*
Heather Eggins (ed): *Globalization and Reform in Higher Education*
Heather Eggins & Ranald Macdonald (eds): *The Scholarship of Academic Development*
Gillian Evans: *Academics and the Real World*
Merle Jacob and Tomas Hellström (eds): *The Future of Knowledge Production in the Academy*
Peter Knight: *Being a Teacher in Higher Education*
Peter Knight and Paul Trowler: *Departmental Leadership in Higher Education*
Peter Knight and Mantz Yorke: *Assessment, Learning and Employability*
Ray Land: *Educational Development*
John Lea *et al. Working in Post-Compulsory Education*
Mary Lea and Barry Stierer (eds): *Student Writing in Higher Education*
Dina Lewis and Barbara Allan: *Virtual Learning Communities*
Ian McNay (ed.): *Beyond Mass Higher Education*
Elaine Martin: *Changing Academic Work*
Louise Morley: *Quality and Power in Higher Education*
Lynne Pearce: *How to Examine a Thesis*
Moira Peelo and Terry Wareham (eds): *Failing Students in Higher Education*
Craig Prichard: *Making Managers in Universities and Colleges*
Stephen Rowland: *The Enquiring University Teacher*
Maggi Savin-Baden: *Problem-based Learning in Higher Education*
Maggi Savin-Baden: *Facilitating Problem-based Learning*
Maggi Savin-Baden and Kay Wilkie: *Challenging Research in Problem-based Learning*
David Scott *et al.: Professional Doctorates*
Peter Scott: *The Meanings of Mass Higher Education*
Michael L Shattock: *Managing Successful Universities*
Maria Slowey and David Watson: *Higher Education and the Lifecourse*
Colin Symes and John McIntyre (eds): *Working Knowledge*
Richard Taylor, Jean Barr and Tom Steele: *For a Radical Higher Education*
Malcolm Tight: *Researching Higher Education*
Penny Tinkler and Carolyn Jackson: *The Doctoral Examination Process*
Susan Toohey: *Designing Courses for Higher Education*
Melanie Walker (ed.): *Reconstructing Professionalism in University Teaching*
Melanie Walker and Jon Nixon (eds): *Reclaiming Universities from a Runaway World*
Diana Woodward and Karen Ross: *Managing Equal Opportunities in Higher Education*
Mantz Yorke and Bernard Longden: *Retention and Student Success in Higher Education*

Reshaping the University

New Relationships between Research, Scholarship and Teaching

edited by Ronald Barnett

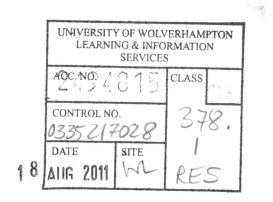
Society for Research into Higher Education
& Open University Press

Open University Press
McGraw-Hill Education
McGraw-Hill House
Shoppenhangers Road
Maidenhead
Berkshire
England
SL6 2QL

e-mail: enquiries@openup.co.uk
world wide web: www.openup.co.uk

and Two Penn Plaza, New York, NY 10121–2289, USA

First published 2005
Reprinted 2006.

A catalogue record of this book is available from the British Library

ISBN-13: 978 0335 21701 X (pb)   978 0335 21702 8 (hb)
ISBN-10 0335 21701 X (pb)   0335 21702 8 (hb)

Library of Congress Cataloging-in-Publication Data
CIP data has been applied for

Typeset by RefineCatch Limited, Bungay, Suffolk
Printed in Great Britain by the Cromwell press, Trowbridge, Wiltshire.

For Tony Becher
who was the first to teach so many of us about the shapes of higher education

Contents

Introduction

Ronald Barnett

Beginnings

The debate as to the relationship between teaching and research is surely already becoming tired, if not tiresome. Opponents barely confront each other's arguments, tending rather to speak past each other. One view holds to the idea of there being a necessarily close and positive relationship between teaching and research; an opposite view contends that teaching and research are quite distinct activities – indeed, almost logically different kinds of activity – and alleges as well (as if this extra point was then relevant) that there is little, if any, empirical evidence to back up the assertion of a 'close and positive relationship'. In all this, of course, facts, values *and* hopes become inextricably interwined. That the parties talk past each other partly because they are speaking from different value positions is hardly noticed.

Of course, there are more nuanced voices. The nuances to which we are drawn are variants of the point that 'it all depends'. On the one hand, it all depends on the subject; on the other hand, and perhaps more sinisterly, it all depends on the kind of institution one has in mind. Others suggest that it all depends on the level of study. But even with nuances, we run into difficulties for there is often difference of view as to the extent or even the presence of relationships between teaching and research. Is an institution's research strategy *really* supportive of its learning and teaching strategy? There are differences of view even among the members of the senior management team on the matter.

Partly, no doubt, we can account for the differences of view through an understanding of the different interests at work: the political sphere, vice-chancellors, pro-vice-chancellors; research-oriented academics and academic staff developers can be forgiven if they emerge with weighted views, tipping the balance of perspective or even judgement in one direction or another. But a consequence of the partiality of many of the views on offer is that opportunities for conceiving of new relationships between and in and around teaching and research go unexplored.

Even the term 'relationships', open-ended as it may seem, comes with its own presuppositions. Often, its user invites us to have in mind a single individual and his/her teaching, and the dominant issue that is implicitly put before us is the extent to which *that* teaching – of this lone individual – draws on her or his own research. This I take to be the dominant paradigm for this debate. Other 'relationships' are certainly present but they are less evident; for example, whether the individual's research may draw on her teaching or whether the teaching in our individual's department is influenced by that department's research. Even less evident are the possibilities that our individual might draw on research conducted elsewhere or that her department may be managed in such a way as to prompt and encourage its staff to place their teaching in the context of research conducted by researchers around the world. And virtually absent from the connotations of 'relationships' is the conjecture that all manner of relationships – positive, neutral and antipathetic – may be found simultaneously not only in a single institution but even in a single department.

So the very term 'relationships' is not neutral; it brings in its wake certain promptings, erasures and even censures. This is far from a pedantic point for on it turn major matters of policy and resource allocation. There is much water between, on the one hand, the sense that, as a university teacher, I should myself both conduct research and bring it into a close and productive relationship with my teaching and, on the other hand, the sense that my teaching should draw upon the research conducted by others, even around the world. If we are not careful, therefore, an inquiry into the 'relationships' between research and teaching may open up some policy options but it may also close off others.

This, then, is the main aim of this volume: to inquire into the relationships between research and teaching in a reasonably disinterested way and, on that basis, to see if some new relationships, some new possibilities, might be glimpsed.

Shapes and spaces

Not only do universities exhibit diversity between themselves, with their contrasting missions and internal characteristics, but they are supremely dynamic institutions. They move; their shape changes, as – for instance – their disciplinary base shifts or their interventions with the wider society take on new forms or their priorities alter and, in the process, the balance of their activities may even be transformed. Universities have, as we may term it, an architecture, with their activities taking up shapes and forming patterns, and those shapes and patterns are all the time changing.

A related matter is that of space. If the key activities of the university – research, teaching, management – may be considered as so many shapes forming patterns, different possibilities present themselves so far as space is concerned. It may be said that the history of the university has been the successive introduction of new spaces. To teaching has been added over the years successively systematic scholarship, research, administration, outreach activities, management, exploitation and application of knowledge and perhaps most recently an agenda of 'participation and inclusion'.

It is as if the university is infinitely extendable; space it seems, can always be found for new activities, for new agendas and even new discourses. But the matter of possibilities also presses itself. On the one hand, there may be a sense that at any one time, the university is chockfull of activities piled on top of each other that fill out the university; and even literally, as the estates office struggles to accommodate all the growing activities of a university. On the other hand, it is just possible that opportunities to breathe may be glimpsed: however hard pressed the staff – and even the students – feel themselves to be, and even while they may feel themselves to be suffocating with the press of contemporaneous demands, it may be possible to let in air.

The basic metaphor, then, the discursive hook (as we might term it), underlying and fuelling this volume is that of shapes and spaces. If we conceive of research and teaching as occupying spaces in the university, then we can ask questions of the following kind: What are the spaces that these activities occupy? How are they shaped? How do these spaces stand in relationship with each other? What is their configuration? Are there spaces for other activities? Are the spaces genuinely open or are they actually closed in some way (by virtue of the ideologies they represent or the resources they demand for their occupation)? Do the actors in those spaces feel that the spaces are theirs to a certain extent? Can new spaces open up within the activities themselves?

Space is at least three-dimensional so that reflection invites yet further questions: are some activities and discourses being occluded, being hidden from view and even being submerged so that they are not really active? Is, for instance, teaching in danger – in some institutions, in some departments – of being just such an occluded activity? Is research so dominating teaching that research is suffocating teaching or enlarging it? Can teaching be reconfigured? Is research itself too narrowly drawn? Might scholarship offer the prospect of a new arena, in which, say, writing itself can take on new forms and so inject new light on dusty areas of academic life?

To ask these questions invites an immediate qualification for such a metaphor – of spaces and shapes – can illuminate the totality of a university's activities and its relationships with the wider society. Then, shapes that are already indistinct and contentious within the university would become even more blurred as our gaze shifted to the – probably fast-dissolving – border between the university and its host society. We would certainly want to resort, surely, to Peter Scott's term of 'transgressivity': the wider society transgresses, it might be said, on the space that was the university's. But the traffic is not all one way: the university is becoming ever more active in society and could equally be said to be transgressing on society. Or perhaps the idea of 'transgression' is too negative; instead, alternative and more neutral if not more positive terms of 'interchange' and 'collaboration' might be called up.

Some of that wider story will come into view in this volume. We cannot hope to understand the shapes and patterns of the contemporary university unless we also bring into view that wider societal and, indeed, policy context. If we want to see if there are opportunities for new spaces to emerge in or be inserted into the university, then we need to take account of any forces at work that might be distorting the university in some way. Admittedly, the idea of 'distortion' is value laden: it suggests not merely a change in shape but that the change in question is damaging or corrupting the university itself. There are contributors to this volume – notably Peters and Olssen on the one hand and Naidoo on the other – who want to make just such a claim. The argument is that the 'neo-liberal' forces that are confronting the university are distorting its fundamental activities – teaching and research – and their relationships.

It is all too easy, within such a context of large and even global socio-economic forces bearing in on the university, to imagine the university is 'in ruins' (Readings 1996). The general tone and force of the contributions here suggest that such an interpretation would be premature and that, despite the considerable challenges that face the university, it is possible – with imagination and energy – to insert new spaces either for reconstructing existing activities or their interrelationships *or* even for opening the prospect of new activities. Such creative possibilities imply that, almost whatever the general shape of a system and its individual institutions, possibilities exist for doing some justice to the university and to its sense of itself as a coherent institution. There are many spaces in the university for many different kinds of activity and some of those spaces have their own integrity but, even so, they also have interesting interrelationships. There is even light shining through and illuminating those spaces such that they can be seen in new ways.

Relating research and teaching

The dominant issue in this volume is that of the relationships between teaching and research but, as we shall see, that matter cannot be explored seriously without bringing into view a large hinterland of contiguous issues that include those just identified and others as well. For example, present in more than one of the chapters is the matter of disciplinary inquiry: does it take the same shape both in the context of research and in the context of teaching? Could it form a bridge between research and teaching: could the two spaces be connected in that way? A further example – taken up in this volume – is that of 'scholarship': can scholarship be taken seriously in the contemporary university, or do the contemporary discourses and ideologies of the university squeeze it out?

It remains the case, however, that while the shape of the university changes – as room is found to add new activities and discourses (especially, in a 'neo-liberal' climate, those associated with markets and income-generation) – research and teaching remain the domain activities in the university.

Research and teaching not only are large sets of activity in themselves – and so issues as to their interrelationships naturally arise – but being so large, they also structure to some degree other potential sources of energy and development. Opportunities for so-called third stream (or income generation) activities are weighed in part in terms of their research potential or even possibilities for carry-over into teaching situations.

In the total space that is the university, therefore, the dominant shapes are those occupied by teaching and research and, in considering possibilities for reshaping the university, it is right that we should focus our attention on those two domains. Is there daylight between them? Are they pulling away from each other? Are their interrelationships wholly different in some parts of the university (such that the different wings of the university inhabit almost different universities)? If there are different relationships between research and teaching, how do we understand the structuring principles at work? Are the main structural features here those of disciplines or are they those of staff? And if the latter, how might we understand that? Is it that staff as individuals simply take up different attitudes in the significance that they attach to their teaching and to their research *or* are there present some further underlying forces at work? Is it, for instance, the case that there is a management strategy to identify individual members of staff as 'research active' or is it that some academic fields – as perhaps in the newer professional areas – are both more practically oriented and are in the early stages of establishing a research base?

It is apparent, therefore, that perceptions of the interrelationships between teaching and research can be held at different levels: we can look at the large structures of the building that is the university and we can look at the interstices of those structures. Quite different patterns might emerge from those surveys. A macro-study in a single university might reveal, for instance, that research and teaching had taken on somewhat different patterns, in their distribution across the institution. Contrasting profiles could be imagined. Rather than research and teaching being found evenly, it might be that in a university, say, with a considerable degree of involvement with professions and practical settings, a significant minority of staff would be focusing their energies on teaching, while a large proportion would be engaged – doubtless to varying degrees – in both research and teaching, while a proportion (possibly even a significant proportion) would be permitted, for various reasons, to devote themselves more or less solely to research. Yet others, in that same institution, would have hybrid academic lives, in which their involvement in professional activities as such formed a significant part of their portfolios. Such a range of contrasting relationships might even be observed within a single department.

Apart from their *distribution*, questions would arise as to the *relationships* between teaching and research. In our hypothetical example, for those staff engaged both in teaching and research, we can anticipate close and positive relationships between their two activities (although whether their teaching was research-led or merely research-informed would be a matter of investigation (see Mick Healey's chapter here)). For those staff engaged only in teaching, their teaching would be likely to exhibit at best only indirect relationships, while for those engaged only in research, no question arises at all as to the relationship between research and their teaching.

But further questions arise as to the direction of the relationships between research and teaching in our hypothetical university. Do its research strategy, its learning and teaching strategy and its human resources strategy work in concert with each other or are they pulling against each other? While the vice-chancellor and the other members of the senior team declare that there is a close (and an implied positive) relationship between research and teaching, are the university's strategies actually acting *de facto* to set research and teaching against each other? Are the criteria for academic titles based solely on individuals' research performance? Are staff who are devoting their efforts largely to teaching marginalized in the university's culture? Are 'research-active' staff encouraged to 'buy themselves out' of teaching?

To pick up our spatial metaphor, research and teaching can be regarded as tectonic plates in the total space that is the university. As such, they are never still. They may be drifting apart, at least for a large portion of a university's staff; or they may be coming closer together and even overlapping each other. And both kinds of movement may be observed, we may anticipate, in the same institution. For some departments, or for courses, the forces and policies at work may be such that relationships between research and teaching may be pulling apart while for other departments, the two domains may be coming into closer and more vibrant company. Again, such counter movements might even be observed in the same department.

Reshaping the university

We may consider research and teaching as conversations. Clearly, the form of those conversations varies substantially, even within research on the one hand and teaching on the other hand. The conversations that historians have with each other are not identical to those that physicists have with each other. Characteristically, for example, more people take part at any one time in the conversations of natural science compared with those in the humanities (as reflected in the numbers of names on single papers in the academic journals). We could say that considered as spaces, disciplinary conversations are more or less permissive, with – in our example – the one being more expansive and more multi-vocal than the other.

Several contributors to this volume open the possibility that higher education is not a commodity but is an experience framed in large part by the students themselves and that the university is not merely an organization but is a community. On either consideration – education as a particularly personal experience or as part of a collective experience – some kind of open space is implied.

Many universities have a 'Senate' but the senate is Roman in origin. The question that this reflection opens up is the following: are universities too much like senates? While things could get heated, senates were relatively ordered affairs, having their rules over turn-taking, rhetorical gambits and the range of what could be said. It may be that, in the 'internet university' of the twenty-first century (cf., Robins and Webster 2002), we should abandon the senate as the ideal of conversational space and replace it with the earlier Greek idea, that of the *agora*. It just may be that the agora offers us ideas as to teaching and research as conversational and relatively open discursive spaces and, thereby, new relationships between them. And it just may be that some of those spaces will even be in productive tension with each other.

We can press these thoughts a little further and make them a little down-to-earth through a conceptualization of the project that forms this volume. The chapters taken together could be said to constitute an exploration of three kinds of space in the university:

- *Pedagogical and curricula space* Pedagogical space and curricula space *are* different kinds of space but we may legitimately put them together. In *pedagogical space*, the key issues are just two: what space do tutors and course teams have in order to attempt new pedagogies, with alternative kinds of pedagogical relationships? And, in those pedagogies, just what spaces are to be accorded to students such that they may strive and struggle to become authentically their own persons? In *curricula space*, there is but one dominant question: what space do course teams have themselves to initiate new kinds of course, free from ideological or discursive constraint (undictated by frozen ideas of 'skills' or 'outcomes')? These two spaces – pedagogical and curricula – should be considered together since their realization is, to an extent, intertwined. In the end, adventurous curricula will be brought off through daring pedagogies and, in turn, imaginative pedagogies will ultimately point to a transformation in curricula.
- *Scholarly space* By scholarly space, I have in mind the space available to academic staff to pursue their own research interests in their own way. Two of the chapters in Part 1 point to the distortions that the UK's Research Assessment Exercise has wrought on research itself. The evaluation instruments are not neutral in their effects, whatever their intent. More broadly, as universities find themselves to be part of a neo-liberal project (aimed at 'public' services in general), space for untrammelled research shrinks: now knowledge has to perform and to show a return on the investment. Certainly, the return on the investment may be indirect – 'impact' in the wider community – and may have scholarly trappings, such as output in the academic literature. In such a setting, the space for scholarly research may even be said to grow, as opportunities for new kinds of knowledge production emerge (so-called Mode 2 knowledge). But questions arise, or should do so, as to the extent to which such scholarly space is constrained – by local interests, by financial return – even as the space could formally be said to be expanding.

- *Intellectual and discursive space* By intellectual and discursive space, I have in mind that space accorded to the academic community to make its contribution to social discourse and the wider public sphere. Societies differ in the regard with which they hold the intellectual life to be valuable and, indeed, this regard can change within a single society. But academics may come to construct themselves in somewhat narrow ways, coming – for instance – to place undue value on their own immediate research and scholarly interests and so fail to take advantage of the space available to them.

Through perceiving these spaces as major constituents of the spaces that form the university – pedagogical/curricula; scholarly; intellectual/discursive – we may see the debate over the relationships between teaching and research in a somewhat different way than is customary. For that debate is characteristically drawn rather narrowly. First, it tends to focus on the activities of academics as if they were only the preserve of academics. Second, self-evidently, the interrelationships between research and teaching come into view but those relationships are typically construed as if research and teaching filled out the university. Understanding the university as a complex of large spaces in a dynamic relationship with each other, in which some spaces may be closed off and yet others may open, surely allows us imaginative possibilities that the contemporary debate over the relationships between research and teaching rather eschews.

This volume should be seen, therefore, as an attempt to help to open up the contemporary university. It shows that, while there are pressures that would close off the spaces that constitute the university, if we are sufficiently imaginative, new spaces and new relationships may be opened. The university can be reshaped after all.

Part 1

Myths and Distortions

Overview

The story of this first part of the book is that the relationships between teaching and research are being misshapen due to two sets of forces: we may understand these two sets of forces as belief systems on the one hand, and societal on the other hand.

In the opening chapter, by Mark Hughes, we are directed to the first set of forces, that of belief systems, and the claim being made is that the relationships between teaching and research are subject to widespread misinterpretation: there are a number of *myths* in general circulation. Mark Hughes points to five such myths:

1. The myth of the mutually beneficial relationship between research and teaching;
2. The myth of a generalizable and static relationship;
3. The myth that scholarship is separate from research and teaching;
4. The myth of the superiority of the lecturer as researcher;
5. The myth of disinterested research into the relationship between research and teaching.

Myths such as these have two kinds of distorting effects. First, having become pervasive, they come, in the process, to exert an undue grip on collective perceptions of the relationships between research and teaching. They become a discourse, in which understandings of the matter take on a given character: there emerges a ready-made framework of collective assumptions that hardly brooks much in the way of critical reflection. Second, and partly as a result of the first aspect, these myths come to affect dispositions to act. Social practices in and around higher education can lean on them as a justification in a largely unreflective way.

This phenomenon of myths in higher education calls into view a paradox that a number of scholars have observed for quite some time. It is that the very institution that forms its collective identity around the idea, indeed the virtue, of critical self-reflection, seems at times singularly to exhibit just its opposite, namely a level of 'blankness' – as Leavis might have put it – about its own collective beliefs and practices. Such a lack of reflexivity – as we should perhaps term it these days – might be tolerable if the myths in question are about marginal matters in academic life but the myths in question here – being focused on research, scholarship and teaching – are concerned with perhaps the dominant activities to be found in universities (even today). Accordingly, these myths come to have a disproportionate effect on the character and the shape of academic life itself.

We can, and perhaps should, observe something else about the myths identified by Mark Hughes. It is that the five myths, in their being held together, constitute an academic ideology. Collectively, the myths not only hold to an assumption that research and teaching stand in a mutually bene-ficial interrelationship (myth 1) but that research is superior to teaching (4) and that this is a fixed relationship (2). When coupled with the assumption that research into the teaching–research relationship is disinterested (5), we have here surely a collective self-image of academic life that justifies claims for research as such. The myths act collectively to sustain research and to give it priority in higher education policy. It is a research ideology masquerading as an informed belief. Moreover, it acts to thwart creative thinking that, (3) for instance, could open up through reconceiving the potential relation-ships between scholarship, teaching and research. The five myths constitute an ideology that, as is the case with ideologies in general, acts to freeze the configuration of spaces that make up the university. The myths are pernicious, through and through.

The two chapters by Rajani Naidoo on the one hand and Michael Peters and Mark Olssen on the other hand come at the matter in hand from a separate perspective. Whereas Hughes is alerting us to distortions on the level of ideas and presuppositions, and ultimately to discourse, Naidoo and Peters/Olssen point us to the large societal and global shifts that, in turn, are effecting distortions in academic institutions.

The fundamental distortion to which both chapters allude is that wrought by a policy framework that has placed higher education in a market situation (albeit a quasi-market situation). In such a setting, *both* teaching and research are liable to be corrupted: on the one hand, the pedagogical rela-tionship comes to be 'commodified' as it takes on a market transaction and, on the other hand, research, in the 'learning economy' comes to be struc-tured through its results, rather than its inherent truth value. (Naidoo's chapter focuses more on the teaching side; Peters and Olssen focus more on research.) At the same time, too, the relationship between teaching and research becomes distorted, as the two activities, now driven by somewhat separate interests, split apart.

Both chapters offer an insight into a complex array of forces at work and their impact on academic life. What is striking for our purposes here, however, are two things. First, even if they are working at a different level from Mark Hughes's chapter, both chapters are in effect telling a story with a striking parallel to Hughes's chapter. The parallel lies precisely in the presence of ideology. Here, Naidoo and Peters/Olssen are demonstrating the impact of the neo-liberal turn that, worldwide, higher education is undergoing; but neo-liberalism at least has many characteristics of ideology and may even be judged an ideology in its own right. It has a head of steam behind it, it reflects certain powerful interests (those of economic development and the corporate world) and seeks to carry all before it. Activities and institutions – and ultimately individuals – are tacitly (or not so tacitly) encouraged to adopt its way of comprehending the world; its *Weltanschauung*.

Here, too, therefore, in parallel to the spell of myths, we see large societal and global forces leading to deformations in the activities that make up the university. A key issue that all three chapters open up – and which Peters/ Olssen raise explicitly – is that of the space left to the academy to pursue more disinterested goals. Is there, indeed, room still left to the academy to reshape the academy in creative ways, ways that fulfil wider or even more virtuous ends than those that are currently dominant? To ask such a question admittedly begs a prior question: even if there is such a space still available, is the academic community seriously interested in working to open it up? Is the academy really interested in acting in the wider interests of society and the public good? In order to answer this set of questions, we first need to try to understand the emerging configuration of the university: in particular, just what shape are research and teaching taking and how are their interrelationships faring? Before we try to sketch out creative possibilities for *reshaping* (Part 3), we need to understand its *current* shape (Part 2); but before we do even that, we should try to identify any major current *constraints* on the university; and it is this matter that, therefore, occupies us in Part 1.

1

The Mythology of Research and Teaching Relationships in Universities

Mark Hughes

Introduction

The debate about research and teaching relationships is neither new nor UK-specific. However, the debate has come to have significant implications in terms of research and teaching policy making at both national and institutional level. If research does inform teaching and, more specifically, has a positive impact upon the quality of teaching, then this may be used as an argument for increasing the funding of research. If the opposite is true, then there may be a case for diverting funding from research to teaching. Similarly, relationships between teaching and research have implications in terms of organization of universities and their departments. Evidence of a relationship between research and teaching would suggest the need to locate research and teaching closely together, whereas evidence of a lack of a relationship would support the notion of research-only and teaching-only institutions.

Ramsden and Moses (1992: 273) suggested that 'few beliefs in the academic world command more passionate allegiance than the opinion that teaching and research are harmonious and mutually beneficial'. While they remain sceptical and even offer empirical evidence to challenge this belief, interest in research and teaching relationships continues 'fuelled [in the UK] by factors such as changes in central funding policy, the performance appraisal of academic staff, the role of the "new" universities, and the pressures created by the Research Assessment Exercise' (Breen and Lindsay 1999: 75).

To inform this chapter, I reviewed some of the recent literature to establish what is known about relationships between teaching and research in higher education, by focusing mainly upon papers published in four leading higher education refereed journals: *Higher Education, Higher Education Quarterly, Higher Education Review* and *Studies in Higher Education*. These particular journals were chosen because 'they are, arguably the most prestigious specialist journals for those academics writing on higher education that are seeking to publish, and be read, in the United Kingdom' (Tight 1999: 28). All issues from 1990 to 2002 were reviewed in order to inform understanding about research and teaching relationships in higher education.

Overall, the relatively limited amount of empirical work undertaken with regards to relationships between research and teaching is surprising. In the refereed journals, papers were often based upon the author's reflections and casual observations rather than new empirical material or systematic literature reviews. When original empirical work had been undertaken, it was small-scale (such as a single department or departments in an institution).

What emerges from this literature is a sense that the anticipated empirical evidence to support the existence of teaching and research relationships does not exist (see Table 1.1).

There were signs that, in the mid-to-late nineties, the focus of the debate was shifting: rather than thinking in terms of a universal relationship between research and teaching, there are a series of context specific relationships between research and *learning*. Brew and Boud (1995b) and Brew (1999a) have done much to reorientate the debate and their ideas are explored later in the chapter.

The intention here is neither to repeat that literature, which has been effectively documented in earlier papers (see Jenkins *et al.* 1998 and Lindsay *et al.* 2002 for good overviews of this literature) nor to offer new empirical material (see Coate *et al.* 2001 for a summary of findings from a recent major research project). However, arising from this literature, an enduring mythology of the research and teaching relationship can be identified. The intention, therefore, is to contribute to the ongoing debate about research and teaching relationships through the concept of myth. While the idea of research and teaching myths is not new (see for example, Barnett 1992; and Terenzini and Pascarella 1994), the explanations for these myths offer

Table 1.1 Questioning the relationship between research and teaching

---

. . . White says that 55 per cent of the studies she looked at contained 'irregular' remarks – statements that overemphasised the importance of the relationship between research productivity and teaching effectiveness, even when the results did not indicate such an association. (Ramsden and Moses 1992: 277 citing White 1986)

Investigations of the links between teaching and research, of which there have been a large number, have failed to establish the nature of the connection between the two or, indeed, whether there is one. It is not that results are conflicting but they are inconclusive. (Brew and Boud 1995b: 261)

Much of the research literature questions the positive impact of staff research on quality teaching. (Jenkins *et al.* 1998: 128)

This developing literature is strong on rhetoric and light on the empirical nature of the relationship between teaching and research. (Coate *et al.*, 2001: 159)

---

a critical and challenging perspective on the research and teaching relationships debate.

The mythology may be explained in terms of the misinterpretation of the available evidence, mystification of the debate and mischief of the protagonists. Five such myths may be identified:

1. The myth of the mutually beneficial relationship between research and teaching;
2. The myth of a generalizable and static relationship;
3. The myth that scholarship is separate from research and teaching;
4. The myth of superiority of the lecturer as researcher;
5. The myth of disinterested research into the relationship between research and teaching.

We shall look in turn at each of these myths. Then, in the final section of this chapter, conclusions are drawn in terms of challenging the myths and the implications of such challenges.

1. The myth of the mutually beneficial relationship between research and teaching

The essence of this myth is that there is an empirically proven, mutually beneficial relationship between research and teaching. In understanding this myth, it is necessary to understand the centrality of research and teaching in universities. Content analysis of UK university mission statements highlights the espoused centrality of the activities of research and teaching (Davies and Glaister 1996: 281). However, while the activities of research and teaching are believed to be central to universities, this does not mean that they are mutually harmonious. The following discussion will consider the endurance of the myth in terms of learning, reification, intangibility and misinterpretation.

In Table 1.1, the relationship between research and teaching was questioned, particularly in terms of the lack of empirical evidence. Brew and Boud (1995b: 261) suggest that the fact that further studies continue to be undertaken indicates an unwillingness to accept that there is very little correlation between research and teaching. They (1995: 262) cite Centra (1983) and Neumann (1992) suggesting that 'the belief that there is a link is stronger than present evidence for the link'. The search for a positive relationship between research and teaching is like the 'holy grail'. Most researchers believe it exists and at regular intervals that belief spurs a new quest to find it. However, in the literature, a recurrent theme is also that of research and teaching as very different activities. The writings of Shore, Barnett, Brew and Boud and Westergaard help to illustrate this point.

Shore *et al.* (1990: 33) highlighted that 'the primary goal of research is to ask questions and create new knowledge. Students spent a lot of time answering questions and mastering old knowledge.' This quotation suggests that in seeking evidence of a relationship between research and teaching, researchers may be comparing knowledge creation with knowledge development, which may never prove fruitful. As Barnett (1992: 623) has warned: 'knowledge in the context of discovery and knowledge in the context of transmission are entirely different enterprises.' Learning may just prove to be the commonality between research and teaching, if indeed there is such a link to be made:

> Learning however is the vital link between research and teaching. It is a shared process in these two enterprises . . . Teaching and research are correlated where they are co-related, i.e. when what is being related are two aspects of the same activity: learning! (Brew and Boud 1995b: 268)

In the literature surveyed for this chapter, the norm was always to write about 'research and teaching' relationships. However, rather than research and teaching relationships as so often previously configured, relationships may exist between research and learning. One important behavioural consequence of emphasizing learning is that 'through the personal learning and growing in which they engage . . . researchers are able to identify with their students' (Brew and Boud 1995b: 270). If we think of research as a learning process on the one hand and the process of student learning on the other hand, then they do share a common context in discovery. Similarly, Westergaard (1991: 27) suggested: 'higher education must, for students no less than for staff, be investigative and exploratory, sceptical and critical.' Again, in this quotation, the common ground between the different activities of research and teaching is learning.

The concept of reification offers another explanation for the enduring myth of the mutually beneficial relationship between research and teaching. Hughes and Tight (1995: 61) note strong correlations between grades in the (UK's) Research Assessment Exercise and grades for teaching quality in the Teaching Quality Assessment but acknowledge that this does not prove that there is a relationship. An explanation as to why the belief in strong and positive research and teaching relationships persists despite the lack of empirical evidence may be in terms of reification. If reification involves the treatment of an abstract notion as if it were a thing, then the research and teaching relationship may have become reified to such an extent that its existence is taken for granted in a manner similar to the way we take the existence of an 'organization' or 'society' for granted.

Another explanation for the myth of the mutually beneficial relationship between research and teaching is in terms of references to the intangible/indirect nature of the relationship. Examples from the literature may help to explain this point. Neumann (1992), in researching the perceptions that senior academic administrators hold on the relationship between research and teaching, identified three broad types of connection; the tangible connection; the intangible connection; the global connection. The second of these connections is described by Neumann as follows: 'The intangible connection relates (a) to the development in students of an approach and attitude towards knowledge, and (b) provides a stimulating and rejuvenating milieu for academics.' The words 'stimulating and rejuvenating milieu for academics' are wonderfully ambiguous and indicative of this form of the myth. Similarly, Hughes and Tight (1995: 53–62) identified five alternative relationships:

- no necessary relation;
- direct relationship;
- indirect relationship mediated through scholarship;
- indirect relationship mediated through the department, discipline or profession rather than through the individual;
- indirect linkage mediated through development activities.

No less than three of these relationships are described as 'indirect', but it is difficult to challenge or test the position that research and teaching are *indirectly* related.

A more troubling explanation for the enduring myth of the mutually beneficial relationship between research and teaching is misinterpretation of the evidence. Indications of misinterpretation are evident in White's (1986) work (to which reference is made in Table 1.1 but bears repeating here):

> White says that 55 per cent of the studies she looked at contained 'irregular' remarks – statements that overemphasised the importance of the relationship between research productivity and teaching effectiveness, even when the results did not indicate such an association. (Ramsden and Moses 1992: 277 citing White 1986)

While we might reasonably expect that research into research and teaching relationships would itself exhibit high standards, the fact that this research can be methodologically challenged is ironic. More generally, the conclusions reported in Table 1.1 are disturbing and may be explained in terms of one of the subsequent myths relating to disinterested research into research and teaching relationships.

2. *The myth of a generalizable and static relationship*

The essence of this myth is the assumption that there is a static and generalizable relationship between research and teaching, which could be identified. However, Brew (1999a: 296) has warned that 'relationships between teaching and research are dynamic and context driven'. This means that research and teaching are changing over time and any relationships that do exist between research and teaching will change over time. A significant driver of these changes is change in the context in which research and teaching take place. Rather than searching for evidence about a single relationship between research and teaching, the Brew quotation suggests that there will be many different relationships between research and teaching, which are influenced by the context in which research and teaching takes place.

In Table 1.2 examples of the type of contextual factors, which are likely to impact upon research and teaching, are suggested.

The implication of Table 1.2 is that each of these factors may independently, as well as in their interconnectivity, impact upon relationships between research and teaching. While Table 1.2 is not exhaustive, it does provide an antidote to assumptions that there is a single generalizable relationship between research and teaching in higher education.

As the 'research' and 'teaching' contextual factors in Table 1.2 suggest, even our understanding of what constitutes research and teaching vary considerably. Brew (1999a: 292) cites Shore *et al.* (1990), Elton (1992) and Hattie and Marsh (1996) as suggesting that research on the relationship between teaching and research would gain by consideration of different conceptions or types of research. As Brew and Boud note (1995b: 272), research processes are likely to vary from discipline to discipline; for example, as between natural science research and research in the humanities.

The consideration of contextual factors encourages acknowledgement about the difficulties of comparing different empirical studies into research and teaching relationships. Even if conclusive evidence had been discovered, it would apply to a specific context, rather than all research and teaching. For example, can conclusive empirical evidence about a relationship between research and teaching on a full-time chemistry undergraduate course in Australia be generalized to a part-time postgraduate finance course in Britain?

Table 1.2 Research and teaching contextual factors

Research
i) type of research; ii) level of research; iii) academic discipline

Teaching
i) mode of delivery; ii) learning philosophy; iii) academic discipline

Individual
i) teaching role; ii) scholarship role; iii) research role

Student
i) level of ability; ii) level of study

University
i) type; ii) strategy

National
i) national culture; ii) politics

---

3. The myth that scholarship is separate from research and teaching

The essence of this myth is that in searching for examples of relationships between research and teaching, scholarship has been dealt with as something separate from research and teaching. Elton (1992: 252) has defined scholarship as being broadly characterized 'as consisting of new and critical interpretations of what is already known . . . an activity that is necessary as a precondition for both good research and good teaching'. Although scholarship is a precondition of research and teaching, Elton (1986a: 302) has warned us that scholarship is 'the tenderest plant, since it is never the prime purpose of an institution'. This was evident in the analysis of UK university mission statements cited earlier: such mission statements espouse the centrality of research and teaching, but rarely if ever mention scholarship.

The mediating role of scholarship between research and teaching has been suggested on many occasions (Moses 1990, Westergaard 1991, Hughes and Tight 1995 and Elton 1986a and 1992). There is a danger, however, that in seeking to identify research and teaching relationships, scholarship may be overlooked. In the paper by Jenkins *et al.* (1998), students appear to be referring (at times) to the scholarship of their lecturers, which is used to confirm a relationship between research and teaching. Moses (1990: 352) indeed warns, 'that without the notion of "scholarship", the debate about research and teaching functions will cause more confusion and misconceptions than clarification of the issues'. (Lewis Elton addresses more fully the role of scholarship in the research and teaching nexus in Chapter 6.)

4. The myth of superiority of the lecturer as researcher

The essence of this myth is that lecturers as researchers are superior to lecturers who are not active in research. Debates about research and teaching relationships are often focused at an institutional level, which lead to policy suggestions about research-only and teaching-only institutions. However, this particular myth is concerned with the role of individual lecturers.

Shore *et al.* (1990: 21) cite an extract from the then editor (Scott 1988: 3) of the *Times Higher Education Supplement* suggesting that 'students need to be taught by people who were active players not passive spectators in their disciplines'. Similarly Hughes and Tight (1995: 51) highlight this type of belief:

> Students are seen as short-changed if they are not learning from lecturers working at the 'frontiers of knowledge', while researchers are hardly worth their salt if they are not regularly reporting back on their latest findings to postgraduate and undergraduate seminar groups.

While undertaking their fieldwork, Coate *et al.* (2001: 172) frequently encountered the pervasive belief that good researchers will also be good teachers. The myth of superiority of the lecturer as researcher relates closely to the other myths discussed in this chapter. It may be that empirical evidence will one day confirm the superiority of the lecturer as researcher over the lecturer who is not research-active, but at present this evidence does not exist, as was demonstrated in the earlier discussion about the myth of the mutually beneficial relationship between research and teaching (see Table 1.1).

The myth of the superior lecturer as researcher also draws upon the myth of the generalizable and static relationship between research and teaching. There may well be specific disciplines and levels of education where students benefit from being taught by lecturers as researchers, although this is different from believing that all lecturers as researchers are superior to lecturers who are not research-active (Table 1.2 highlighted potential contextual factors which may influence research and teaching relationships).

Ramsden and Moses (1992: 277) have done much to challenge the myth of the superiority of the lecturer as researcher. However they do acknowledge findings of Feldman (1987: 279) concerning slight positive associations between research and teaching being more likely to occur in the humanities and social sciences than the natural sciences. Coate *et al.* (2001: 167), however, offer a further twist to this story in that the variations across the disciplines may be according to the level of study: it appears that, in the humanities, the links at undergraduate level may be relatively strong but that the links at undergraduate level may be somewhat weaker whereas, in the sciences, these relationships across the levels of study may be reversed (with weaker links at undergraduate level but stronger links at postgraduate level).

The myth of superiority of the lecturer as researcher may be closely related to the structure and even the political economy of academic life. Ramsden and Moses (1992: 275) capture the benefits of being a lecturer as researcher: 'in universities, promotions and salary levels are chiefly determined by research success – perhaps because it is thought to be impossible to identify excellent teaching per se . . .'

5. The myth of disinterested research into the relationship between research and teaching

The essence of this myth is that academics have undertaken such research and scholarship into the relationships between research and teaching without any vested interest in the outcome. There are at least three explanations for this myth: a Machiavellian desire to secure resources; a desire to protect an interesting part of academic work; and self-interest of a small number of unrepresentative academics.

The Machiavellian desire to secure resources is evident in the following quotation: 'the argument that there is a link between teaching and research needs to be sustained until there is convincing recognition and resourcing for good teaching' (Brew and Boud 1995b: 264). The means justifies the ends in terms of obtaining government funding for research which may also benefit teaching. If researchers really believed that research benefited teaching, surely an expectation would be for more research into the student perspective on research and teaching relationships; but this possibility was not evident in the literature review (notable expectations were the work of Jenkins *et al.* 1998, Breen and Lindsay 1999 and Lindsay *et al.* 2002).

In terms of the Machiavellian goal of securing extra funding by emphasizing the benefits of research, Hughes and Tight (1995: 52) warn that British government White Papers have been more 'critical or perhaps realistic' about the relationship between research and teaching, even suggesting that due to their dependence on state funds, 'universities and their staff have responded by modifying their claims for irreducible linkage'.

Another explanation for an emphasis on research and teaching relationships is that it aims to legitimate an interesting part of academic work. Academic activities have traditionally embraced research, teaching and 'study' (Clark 1993: 301). However, increasingly academics have been required to undertake administration. Court (1996: 257) identified an 'increase in administration since the Robbins survey – from 11 to 33 per cent in term-time . . .' Also, he (1996: 258) found that 'Nearly half of personal research and scholarship – vital for achieving academic excellence – is being done outside office hours'.

Academics, in defending their research, may be responding to an increase in administrative work, among other things. The mischief is in emphasizing the research element of the work, potentially in order to reduce the administrative element. Shore *et al.* (1990: 22) cite Webster (1984) effectively caricaturing the legitimization of research as informing teaching.

> We find it more fun, more exciting, more rewarding, and less constraining . . . we argue that we should do research not for real reasons but for one that is more acceptable to the students, parents and legislators who indirectly pay our salaries – the possibly spurious reason that our research will enhance our teaching.

It is difficult to test the validity of this caricature, but what we do know is that there have been studies which found that research does not inform teaching (Shore *et al.* 1990 and Ramsden and Moses 1992) and may, on occasions, have an injurious impact on teaching (Coate *et al.* 2001).

A third explanation relates to the protagonists in the debate. By definition it is going to be the lecturers as researchers who research into research and teaching relationships, rather than lecturers who are not research-active. Similarly, the authors of the influential papers in the refereed journals (the source of findings for this chapter) may be involved in more research than teaching.

There is an issue about the representativeness of the protagonists in the debate. Court (1999: 67) highlighted findings from a survey for the Dearing Report: 'the survey noted that staff in the pre-1992 institutions spent

30 per cent of their time, and staff in the [post] 1992 institutions 10 per cent of their time on research.' While this is another example of the context factors that impact upon research and teaching relationships, it does suggest that in the UK some academics in the post-1992 institutions may have less investment in perpetuating the research and teaching relationship mythology.

While 'research has become part of academic currency, bestowing credibility on those who possess a curriculum vitae listing their research publications' (Barnett 1992: 623), there are signs among the academic community of disillusionment with this arrangement. Court (1999: 65) found that emphasis on research in determining careers has gone too far. Court undertook a self-report questionnaire survey of 561 academic respondents with a balance of academics from pre-1992 and post-1992 institutions, and found that more that half his respondents agreed that appointments and promotion placed too much emphasis upon research. Court (87) concludes his paper on a poignant note.

> Staff assigned more teaching and administration or other tasks because their research profile is modest or non-existent – as envisaged by the Dearing Report – will find it hard not to feel second-class citizens in the more differentiated higher education of the future.

Assessments such as the Research Assessment Exercise (RAE) may polarize such a situation. Talib (2002: 58) has warned that the RAE may potentially reward research – intrinsically and extrinsically – for the research-active at the expense of other activities in universities such as teaching.

Implications

In this chapter, it has surely emerged that empirical work reported in prestigious specialist journals reflects neither the strategic significance for universities, nor the policy significance for government, of potential research and teaching relationships. Much of the work published in the refereed journals in the early 1990s was descriptive and anecdotal. However, from the mid-1990s onwards, there appeared to be a desire to challenge the myths around espoused teaching and research relationships. It is this process of challenging myths that is likely to inform the redefinition of the role, activities and shape of universities.

In this section, I identify some implications arising from the five research and teaching relationship myths that I have examined in this chapter. The essence of each myth is succinctly restated before conclusions are drawn in terms of why the myth should be challenged and the implications of such a challenge.

The myth of the mutually beneficial relationship between research and teaching

The essence of this myth is that there is an empirically proven, mutually beneficial relationship between research and teaching. However, according to Brew and Boud (1995b) 'the belief that there is a link is stronger than present evidence for the link' (see Table 1.1). In challenging the passionate allegiance to the belief, it is necessary to go beyond suggesting that a link between research and teaching is unproven: these two activities are not necessarily comparable (Barnett 1992). Brew and Boud (1995b) believe that the relationship between teaching and research could never be satisfactorily demonstrated; however, learning is a shared process between these two enterprises.

Accordingly, the debate shifted from research and teaching to research and learning in the mid- to late 1990s. It follows that, in more practical terms, policy makers, as well as academics, need to avoid assumptions and assertions that there is an empirically established, mutually beneficial relationship between research and teaching.

The myth of a generalizable and static relationship

The essence of this myth is the assumption that there is a static and generalizable relationship between research and teaching, which can be identified. This myth may be understood in terms of an analogy with the search for the 'Loch Ness Monster': many people would like to believe the monster exists and would support the search, but such support is not verification of the existence of the monster.

Instead of thinking in terms of a single example of a research and teaching relationship we need to acknowledge that any relationships between research and teaching are likely to vary over time and to be informed by different contexts (Brew 1999). The links may be strong or weak, direct or indirect, and positive or negative; or the relationship may be entirely neutral, as where the two activities are entirely independent of each other (notably in those countries where research is conducted mostly in designated research institutes). And we may surmise that this diverse set of relationships is to be found both across disciplines and institutions; and even, on occasions, *within* a single large department. In short, a wide range of relationships may be manifest in a single institution.

There is, then, a need for caution when generalizing from research studies into research and teaching. The experience of a full-time undergraduate on an Australian chemistry course may be very different from the experience of a part-time postgraduate on a British finance course. While all the myths require and encourage further research, there is a particular requirement for context-specific research. Rather than searching for one generalizable instance in which a positive relationship – between research and teaching – can be demonstrated. Many different case studies are required, which might further our understanding about the nature of research and teaching relationships both positive and negative in different contexts.

The myth that scholarship is separate from research and teaching

The essence of this myth is that scholarship is something separate from research and teaching. However, scholarship is an integral element of both research and teaching. Elton (1986a, 1992) has championed the role of scholarship within the research and teaching relationships debate. Scholarship has been characterized 'as consisting of new and critical interpretations of what is already known . . . an activity that is necessary as a precondition for both good research and good teaching' (Elton 1992). The problem with scholarship being a precondition of both good teaching and good research is that its role may be underestimated in understanding the many context-specific relationships that exist between research and teaching. Consequently, institutions both locally and nationally could do more to encourage high-quality scholarship as a means of improving both research and teaching.

The myth of superiority of the lecturer as researcher

The essence of this myth is that lecturers as researchers are superior to lecturers who are not research active. While 'students are seen as short-changed if they are not learning from a lecturer working at the frontiers of knowledge' (Hughes and Tight 1995), the myth relates to the assertion that one category of lecturers is definitely superior to another. In time this may be proved to be true, but until we have empirical evidence of a positive relationship between research and teaching, the assertion is questionable.

The objectionable element of this myth is not the lack of conclusive empirical evidence, which has been a theme of this chapter, but the discriminatory implication that the lecturer as researcher is academically superior to a lecturer who is not research active. The persistence of the myth of the superior lecturer as researcher has implications for the careers, remuneration and advancement of many academics.

The myth of disinterested research into the relationship between research and teaching

The essence of this myth is that academics have undertaken such research and scholarship into the relationships between research and teaching without any vested interest in the outcome. The contemporary debate about research and teaching relationships has been instigated and fuelled by academics themselves, in particular by research-active academics with research and scholarship skills enabling them to gain publication in refereed journals.

In defending his belief in a positive research and teaching relationship, Westergaard (1991) suggested that 'higher education must, for students no less than for staff, be investigative and exploratory, sceptical and critical'. If researchers had applied these criteria to understanding research and teaching relationships, this may have led to the nirvana of research-informed teaching, rather than the misinterpretation, mystification and mischief, which currently clouds the literature.

Conclusion

It is an irony that research into, and reflection on, the relationships between research and teaching in higher education can sometimes fall short of the best standards of research. What we have is a field marked out by a number of myths that are hard to dislodge. A positive relationship between research and teaching is characteristically assumed as a starting point to much of the debate.

An implication is that spaces and shapes of the university are locked tight. It is difficult for them to be prised open, and new spaces found or formed. A way forward, therefore, would surely lie in the presuppositions that inform the myths being set aside, both about what is the case and what might be the case. It may be that a wide variety of relationships between the key activities of the university may be feasible, and even new activities or existing ones reshaped so as to open new spaces, new configurations. For that to happen, we need to face up to and abandon any existing myths as to the shape of the university.

Acknowledgement

I thank Professor Tom Bourner and Professor Ronald Barnett for constructively reviewing earlier drafts of this chapter. Responsibility for the views expressed in this chapter rests solely with the author.

2
Universities in the Marketplace: The Distortion of Teaching and Research

Rajani Naidoo

Governments world-wide have begun to implement funding and governance frameworks based on market principles in an attempt to shift the terms on which fundamental activities such as teaching, learning and research take place in higher education. The expectation is that the implementation of market forces will lead to student empowerment, greater equity and higher quality. This chapter argues that contrary to the intentions of policy makers, attempts to restructure academic cultures to comply with market principles lead to the 'commodification' of academic practices which may deter innovation, promote passive and instrumental attitudes to learning, threaten knowledge creation and entrench academic privilege.

The chapter begins by outlining a socio-political framework to describe current market trends in higher education. In the next section, the work of Bourdieu (1988, 1996) is drawn on to develop an analytical understanding of how market pressures are likely to lead to the increasing commodification of higher education. The extent to which such pressures lead to the deformation of research and teaching and learning is outlined. Finally, the chapter turns to empirical studies conducted in a variety of national settings to explore the potential consequences on constituent elements of higher education including the professional identities of academics; the curriculum; student dispositions to learning; and the nature of research.

Market forces in higher education

Rationales for the introduction of market mechanisms have been linked to a variety of contemporary developments in higher education. The need to maintain and enhance quality in systems that have shifted from élite to mass ones has been cited as a critical factor. The marketization of higher education has also been linked to globalization and the emergence of the knowledge economy. Economic success in this context is perceived to rely on the production of higher value-added products and services, which are in turn dependent on knowledge, particularly scientific and technological knowledge and on innovation. Governments have therefore positioned universities as crucial sites for the production and transfer of economically productive knowledge (Carnoy 1994). A major force underlying the introduction of market measures is therefore the attempt by governments to harness public universities more directly than in previous decades to economic productivity (Orr 1997). Academics have been portrayed as resisting such changes and protecting their own interests against the interests of other stakeholders. The introduction of market forces may therefore also be seen as an attempt by governments to prise open higher education sectors and apply pressure on academics and universities to become more responsive to external demands.

In addition, there has been a global trend away from forms of funding and regulation which were based on Keynesian welfare-state principles and the 'social compact' that evolved between higher education, the state and society over the last century (Slaughter and Leslie 1997; Marginson and Considine 2000). Instead, new funding and regulatory frameworks based on neo-liberal market mechanisms and new managerialist principles (Dill 1997; Williams 1997; Deem 1998, 2001) have been applied. Such frameworks are based on the assumption that the contemporary higher education system has become too large and complex for the state to sustain its position as sole funder. There is also the belief that market competition within and between universities will create more efficient and effective institutions. In addition, management principles derived from the private sector which monitor, measure, compare and judge professional activities have been applied in the hope that the functioning of higher education will be enhanced. Such mechanisms are also expected to aid consumer choice so that consumers can be assured of what they are to receive at the outset of their studies.

The developments mentioned above have resulted in a decline in state funding for research and teaching. There has also been a tightening of external control over core elements of academic practice through quality assurance systems and market mechanisms including league tables and performance indicators.

The commodification of higher education

In order to understand how market forces lead to pressures to commodify teaching and research, it is useful to turn to the work of the French social theorist, Pierre Bourdieu, who has attempted to analyse the 'inner' life of universities. Although Bourdieu's work has been developed in the context of France, the application of his concepts to other national contexts (see, for example, Tomusk 2000 and Naidoo 2004) indicates the significant contribution his work can make to the study of higher education in general. Bourdieu (1988) has conceptualized universities as existing in a conceptual space, which he terms the 'field of higher education'. The field of higher education is relatively insulated from other fields in the social world such as the 'field of politics' and the 'field of economics'. The activities of individuals and institutions in a given field revolve around the acquisition of assets that are invested with value in the field. Bourdieu refers to these assets as 'capital' and distinguishes between 'economic', 'cultural' and 'social capital' (Bourdieu 1986). The 'capital' invested with value in the field of higher education is a type of cultural capital and consists of two types, namely 'academic capital' and 'scientific capital'. 'Academic capital' is linked to power over the instruments of reproduction of the university body such as attaining senior managerial and teaching positions, while 'scientific capital' is linked to the creation of knowledge and includes scientific authority or intellectual renown (Bourdieu 1988). There is a strong hierarchical difference between the two forms of capital. Academic capital is less valued and carries significantly less prestige than scientific capital. Bourdieu (1988: 99) suggests that, relative to scientific capital, academic capital 'tends to appear perhaps even in the eyes of its most confident possessors, as a substitute, or a consolation prize'. In both cases, however, the assets that are valued in the field of higher education revolve around academic forms of recognition and prestige rather than economic gain.

The argument of this chapter is that contemporary government policies have led to the erosion of the boundary between higher education and society with consequent implications for the nature of academic activities. In particular, economic forces are beginning to impact more powerfully on universities than in previous decades. In addition, changes in funding policy that require institutions to generate surplus income have led to the undermining of scientific and academic capital. The concept of 'commodification', which refers to the development of a product or process specifically for exchange on the market rather than for its intrinsic 'use' value, captures the shift from activities aimed at the acquisition of scientific and academic capital to activities intended for income generation. Forces for commodification, therefore, impact on universities by altering the nature of rewards and sanctions operating in higher education. Academic success shifts from being measured according to academic principles to being measured according to narrow financial criteria such as the number of student customers that are captured, the extent of involvement with commercial interests and the degree of financial surplus created.

Pressures for the commodification of higher education are thus likely to act in concert with other contemporary government policies to alter the shape and form of both teaching and research. The pedagogic relationship between student and lecturer is transformed into one that is dependent on the market transaction of the commodity. Education is likely to be reconceptualized as a commercial transaction, the lecturer as the 'commodity producer' and the student as the 'consumer'. In this way, previously integrated relationships between academics and students are likely to become disaggregated with each party invested with distinct, if not opposing, interests. The research function of universities is also likely to be repositioned to one of commodity production. The focus on advancing the frontiers of knowledge is likely to shift to an interest in the 'capitalization' of knowledge (Collins and Tillman 1988; Slaughter and Leslie 1997) and research is likely to be measured by its capacity to create market-value.

In addition, the reshaping of research and teaching to fit the requirements of the market place are also likely to tear apart the two activities. In the era of the global commodification of knowledge, therefore, the transition of research and teaching from 'a comfortable relationship' to one of 'mutual antagonism' (Barnett 2003: 157) may shift to a third phase where the necessity or even possibility of linking pedagogy and research simply withers away. In the next sections, I will discuss the various ways in which teaching, learning and research may be deformed by pressures for commodification.

Research as a commercial enterprise

One of the consequences of market forces on higher education is that the notion of research as a process of knowledge creation has been somewhat eclipsed by the potential for knowledge to generate financial returns (see, for example, Etzkowitz and Leydesdorff 1997; McSherry 2001). At the same time, the institutional conditions that have historically set academics apart from other knowledge workers, such as academic freedom, and occupational security and independence assured by tenure, have been eroded. In these circumstances, the status of what counts as valuable research has been challenged, particularly the belief that the real value of an intellectual product derives from its position outside the realm of political influence and the short-term interests of business. Knowledge ceases to be an end in itself, it loses its 'use' value and becomes valued primarily in the process of exchange and its capacity to generate income. In addition, how knowledge is packaged and presented in the market place of ideas has become, in some cases, more significant than the quality or robustness of knowledge itself. Research production has therefore been characterized by greater prioritization of research for commercial development, the more direct transfer of knowledge from the academic to the commercial sector and the intertwining of universities with large corporations.

Concerns have been raised that the developments cited above may alter the aims, values and processes of academic research. Critics have argued that a commercial focus may divert attention away from basic developmental research in favour of applied work that yields quick results for corporate sponsors. There is also the danger that the intense profit potential of information pushes economic interest to simply override research undertaken for the 'public good' (Moja and Cloete 2001). In more extreme cases, there may be pressure on researchers to 'manage' or falsify data in favour of sponsor interests. Commercial regulations such as patenting may also subvert academic practices such as the open dissemination of research findings and evaluation by peer review (McSherry 2001). Grey (2001) has cautioned that such developments indirectly compromise the distinctive contribution of academics as independent producers of knowledge. Pressures for commodification may therefore discourage critical engagement and stunt the long-term development of knowledge.

The distortion of teaching and learning

It can also be argued that the introduction of quasi-market levers has led to the commodification of teaching and learning. Various consumerist levers to enhance student choice and control over the education process have been introduced in numerous countries over the last ten years. The expectation is that students will utilize such mechanisms to demand high-quality provision. It is envisaged that consumer action will impact positively on the professional practices of academics as providers who respond to student pressure or lose out on 'customers'. While proponents present consumerist mechanisms as generic processes that can be applied to any organization to make it work more efficiently, various conceptual difficulties emerge when consumerism is applied to the higher education sector. Researchers have noted, for example, the difficulty of conceptualizing the relationship between students and staff as a simple transaction between service provider and consumer (see, for example, Hill 1995). They argue that students are not merely passive consumers of education with specific rights but are also active co-participants in learning with certain obligations. Rather than merely functioning as the 'drivers' of quality, students are a crucial component of the production and delivery of learning. In addition, universities are not merely service providers with responsibilities to students. They are also regulators of academic standards and are accountable to other stakeholders including parents, employers and the state (Baldwin and James 2000; Sharrock 2000).

One crucial consequence of the grafting of a framework derived from the commercial sector on to an institutional sector driven by a different set of values is that the pedagogic relationship between teacher and learner may be compromised. The findings arising from various national contexts has indicated that the reconceptualization of the complex relationship between students and teachers to that of 'service provider' and 'customer' is likely to distort the pedagogical relationship. Students who internalize a consumer identity are more likely to view the act of learning as a commercial transaction and to perceive of themselves as passive consumers of education (Sacks 1996). Education comes to be viewed as a 'product' that can be simply purchased and appropriated rather than a complex process that requires engagement and commitment on the part of the learner (Shumar 1997). Such changes in the cultures of learning are likely to lead to pressures for academic programmes to be developed in forms that can be consumed with little effort on the part of the student.

In addition, the adoption of commodified systems of learning in universities where income is derived via the economies of scale results in a high reliance on learning resources that are increasingly standardized. This can also represent an attempt to 'teacher-proof' delivery, particularly if institutions are planning to use 'cheaper' staff who are often less qualified and less experienced. In this standardized model of teaching, activities through which teachers adjust the curriculum and pedagogy to the needs of individual students, as well as peer-group learning, tend to be overlooked. The process of feedback to students may also be altered. Feedback may be rolled up into summative assessment, in the worst cases reducing it to the results of computerized multiple choice tests rather than the detailed qualitative feedback required for high-quality learning. In addition, the packaging and dissemination of programmes with the primary intent of generating market value, has the effect of 'sealing' programmes so that it is increasingly difficult to adjust, update or clarify course content in the light of research findings. The result is a model of learning which sees the task as simply one of providing students with more information rather than the skills and dispositions to acquire knowledge.

Under these conditions, learning is likely to be transformed into a process of selecting, consuming and reproducing an unconnected series of short, neatly packaged bytes of information. More importantly, the learning dispositions inculcated may encourage surface rather than deep processing (Ramsden 1998) and hinder the development of higher-order skills required for autonomous and lifelong learning.

The erosion of professional identities

As noted in previous sections, the commodification of higher education reduces the rewards and sanctions from one based on academic prestige to competitive activities intended to generate income. Thus pedagogic identities based on academic criteria may be displaced by a managerial and market ethic that re-conceptualizes students primarily as potential income generation units or as customers to be satisfied. The potential undercutting of professional knowledge by consumer demand and satisfaction could lead to the overshadowing of intellectual and disciplinary skills. Instead, competencies related to the administration and marketing of academic programmes are likely to be emphasized. In addition, the micro-auditing of professional activities in order to comply with the extensive monitoring procedures required by a consumerist framework may lead to what Power (1999) has termed a shift from 'first order' to 'second order' functions. The commitment to first order functions such as developing innovative, high-quality academic programmes may be transferred to second order functions such as documenting, measuring and accounting for academic activities in order to comply with consumerist frameworks.

There is also evidence that high-quality learning develops through the challenge of existing ideas and the introduction of 'measured' risk. The process of introducing risk to the pedagogic context is a time-consuming and skilled process. It is also a dialogical process and is therefore highly antipathetic to processes of commodification which tend to change the pedagogical relationship between teacher and student into one between producers and consumers of knowledge. In addition, the threat of student complaints and litigation is likely to encourage staff to opt for 'safe teaching' where pre-specified content can be transmitted to students and assessed in a conventional form.

The changing shape and form of academic programmes

There are currently trends in numerous countries to transform curricula from year-long sequential programmes to modular components within national qualification frameworks. Rationales for the modularization of the curriculum have come from many quarters. The equity argument, for example, was that 'non-traditional students' would have a greater chance of access to, and success in, higher education if it was undertaken in smaller, independent chunks in a system with multiple points of entry and exit. Other rationales included the importance of breaking down disciplinary barriers for new knowledge forms to emerge as well as the necessity for universities to make educational programmes more relevant to the world of work (Nowotny *et al.* 2001).

However, critics such as Muller (2001) have noted that there is strong evidence that close and sustained engagement with the content and internal structure of a discipline may be crucial in enabling students to master complex conceptual structures and modes of analysis for purposes of knowledge creation. There is evidence, for example, that learning and research is situated within distinct 'academic tribes' (Becher and Trowler 2001) or communities of practice (Wenger 1998) and that it is within disciplines that students engage in cognitive apprenticeships where they learn insights, conventions and procedures to define, address and solve problems. While it is important to avoid an uncritical endorsement of traditional disciplinary boundaries and to recognize the transformation of knowledge, there is a concern that pressures to develop and combine academic programmes through a system of unit standards within a national qualification framework can have both positive and negative consequences. On the one hand, the greater standardization of knowledge structures results in greater flexibility for students and universities so that 'educational products' from competing providers can be efficiently packaged, compared and transferred. On the other hand, there is a concern that the type of induction and support mechanisms offered by disciplinary structures may not be replicated in modular structures.

There is a particular danger with programmes that have been developed primarily in relation to market incentives. Problems in coherence, the lack of induction systems and the absence of analytical frameworks have been cited as placing students at a grave disadvantage (Muller 2001). In addition, numerous programmes have been hastily stitched together to capture particular market-niches by designing a curriculum to reflect in a simplistic manner students' everyday activities. There have been warnings that such approaches to curriculum development, which erode the distinction between the type of knowledge acquired in universities and the type of knowledge acquired in everyday life, may not have the capacity to enhance students' existing capabilities or induct students into complex intellectual work (see, for example, Young 2003).

The disruption of the relationship between research and teaching

The distortion of the research and teaching functions of universities as noted above is also likely to rupture the relationship between research and teaching. This is a crucial area of investigation, particularly since the Humboldtian ideal of the 'integration of teaching and research' remains deeply embedded in academic and institutional identity. Studies exploring the professional identity of academics (Colbeck 1998; Smeby 1998) have indicated that for many academics the integration of teaching and research creates an intellectual identity that represents to them what is distinctive and most valuable about higher education.

Researchers have also indicated that there is a strong conceptual link between high standards in the transmission of knowledge and high standards in the creation of knowledge. Many of the virtues associated with academic practice including originality, intrinsic interest and theoretical and empirical rigour, are directly related to high standards of research and publication. If academic research is taken as a paradigm of best practice for learning, then one of the key skills of autonomous learning is that of drawing on research theory and methodology the better to conceptualize and address ill-structured problems (Haig 1987).

Other researchers have also suggested that there is an underlying critical and process-related orientation in the way research-active staff experience research, subject matter and teaching. Rowland (1996), for example, has suggested that an approach to teaching that emphasizes its interactive nature and applies to it the critical orientation of research, can enhance the research by which it is informed. He argues that such an approach to teaching is likely to be highly effective, and the most effective teaching will in turn be supportive of research. The changing pattern of work which compartmentalizes teaching and research processes and increasingly fragments the role of academics is therefore likely to be as corrosive of research as it is of teaching.

Stratified and unequal higher education systems

It is also likely that pressures for commodification in concert with other contemporary developments in higher education are likely to exacerbate the development of a stratified and unequal higher education system. Bourdieu's work has indicated that institutions exist in the field of higher education at various levels of hierarchy and power according to the amount of academic and scientific capital held (Bourdieu 1996). In general, there is a correspondence between each university's position in the field of higher education and the social origins of the majority of students that are selected. Élite universities, which generally recruit students from privileged social groups, are more likely to possess both cultural and financial resources either to resist or to restructure forces for commodification in order to protect the value of the academic and scientific capital operating in the field, and hence their own status. Non-élite institutions with less capital and which generally admit students from disadvantaged groups are less likely to be able to resist the forces for commodification.

While the commodification and distortion of teaching and research are likely to occur across the higher education sector, the distortion is likely to be most severe in universities that are located at the lower end of the institutional hierarchy. If the concerns expressed about changes in knowledge content, structure and pedagogy are valid, then it is likely that commodification may result in differential learning outcomes for students from different social backgrounds. Rather than gaining skills of innovation and the ability to learn how to learn, the majority of students from disadvantaged social groups are likely to gain a narrow and instrumental higher education qualification.

In relation to research, current government policies that aim to concentrate research in a small number of élite institutions together with forces transforming research and teaching into commodities are likely to accelerate the separation of research and teaching. Academics and institutions are thus likely to become increasingly polarized between those classified as research active and those classified as non-research active with important consequences for the development of higher education systems. It was noted earlier that Bourdieu (1988) has argued that teaching and administration produces important forms of academic capital but that these forms of academic capital are seen as secondary to the scientific capital amassed by research activity. Bourdieu's work has been confirmed by numerous studies (see, for example, Hannan and Silver 2000; Lucas 2004), which indicate that research still holds prominence over teaching in terms of status within academic life.

Clearly, therefore, the level of participation in research and the quantity and quality of research produced enables academics and institutions to accumulate symbolic capital through which superior positions in the hierarchy of the field of university education are attained. In addition to the reputational capital gained and the importance of research in determining academic careers, current funding systems also result in significant financial rewards for institutions that undertake research. The exclusion of a significant number of academics and institutions from participation in research is thus likely to lead to a crisis in professional and institutional identity as well as a highly stratified, and perhaps dysfunctional, higher education system.

Conclusion

This chapter has not attempted to present a mythical golden age of teaching and research in higher education. There is abundant evidence that the quality of what has been offered in universities has varied enormously. In addition, throughout history and in a wide variety of countries, higher education has functioned in an élitist and exclusionary manner. It is also not inevitable that developments in higher education linked to market principles automatically lead to the adverse effects mentioned. My argument has rather been that the unreflective manner in which market forces are being currently applied to higher education is likely to set up certain pressures to force higher education down the commodification route, and that this pathway is, in general, inimical to high-quality learning and research. Rather than alleviating problems in equity and quality, forces for commodification are likely to distort teaching and research and exacerbate current difficulties faced by the higher education sector.

3

'Useful Knowledge': Redefining Research and Teaching in the Learning Economy

Michael A. Peters and Mark Olssen

We might have one university of medieval seekers after truth . . . as an adornment to our society. (Charles Clarke, Minister for Higher Education, UK, reported in *The Guardian*, Saturday 10 May, p. 3.)

Introduction

Ludwig Wittgenstein, one of the greatest philosophers of the twentieth century, published only one book during his lifetime, a small one by most standards, being less than 70 pages. He published the *Tractatus Logico-Philosophicus* with the help of his friends: Russell wrote the foreword, Ogden provided the translation, and Keynes helped with the publisher. Yet the *Tractatus* had a dramatic effect on twentieth-century philosophy as a source of inspiration for the Vienna school that established logical empiricism and dominated Anglo-American philosophy thereafter. Gradually the influence of the *Tractatus* filtered through to the other humanities and the rest of culture. Its full cultural effects would be difficult, if not impossible, to judge. The American liberal philosopher John Rawls, who died in 2003, reputedly took seven years to write *A Theory of Justice*, a book that spells out a set of liberal principles highly influential in law, politics and other humanities.

It may well be the case that these scholars, by today's publish-or-perish standards, would be excluded from the Research Assessment Exercise (RAE) that now dominates British universities. Certainly, the possibility that they might be raises interesting questions. Whether all traditional scholars of old would meet the criteria of the recent Roberts report, and the institution of a new assessment regime, which requires four pieces of work over a six-year cycle, is not clear-cut. And even if these two philosophers – leading thinkers of their generation – did meet criteria in terms of quantity of output, whether their research field could be adequately classified within the discipline unit in terms of which a particular university or department actually planned their submissions, or whether they might be asked to research in other areas, raises yet additional questions.

In recent years, there has been increasing attention given to the new synergies between universities and the business sector with a corresponding emphasis on the commercialization of research, new partnership arrangements, university start-up companies, technology transfer policies, and the tendering for researching funding in a competitive funding system. Now it appears that in the humanities, which are under-funded by comparison with science and engineering, the emphasis on scholarship has given way to returns through research contracts to the corporate university. In the realms of the humanities and social sciences, a crude pragmatic empiricism based on 'what works' has emerged to highlight a national research discourse of 'useful knowledge'.

The ideology of 'useful knowledge' with an emphasis on 'what works' is clearly evident in a range of related external forces and internal policy developments. First, a shift from national science systems to an international or global knowledge network which reflects the increasing speed, compression and digitalization of knowledge transactions in the global economy. Second, and largely as a consequence, a change in public service philosophy and mode of delivery towards a new 'consumer democracy' that proposes a more interlinked and diffuse set of interrelationships between the public and the private sector with accordingly greater stress on sources of private funding and new funding mixes. We may well refer to this as a marketization of the public sphere. Third, alongside these global transformations, changes in the mode of knowledge production with an emphasis on all forms of self-capitalization – human, social, symbolic – that impinge directly on knowledge and the more effective integration of academic labour into the post-industrial knowledge economy. Fourth, the associated automation or digitalization of tertiary services has encouraged the rapid growth of outsourcing and begun to reconfigure the global distribution of tertiary sector global labour. Fifth, and finally, a set of national science, technology, innovation and education policies that endorse or follow these tendencies focusing on the promotion of lifelong learning, work-based learning, professional learning – all elements of the so-called new learning economy.

The shift has been so marked that some have commented that we are witnessing the emergence of a new set of cognitive and social practices characterized by transdisciplinarity, heterogeneity, organizational diversity and enhanced social accountability (Gibbons *et al.* 1994). This speculative analysis also gels to some extent with a major reorientation away from the knowledge society, which emphasizes the centrality of theoretical knowledge, and towards the knowledge and learning economies that tend to stress, by contrast, practical knowledge, *practices* or competences (see Peters 2003; Peters and Besley 2005).

Philosophers such as Wittgenstein and Heidegger have long emphasized practical over theoretical knowledge, and others such as Michael Polanyi (1958) have considered the significance of tacit knowledge. These matters have become increasingly important in understanding a host of related developments, including the emphasis on social construction and postmodern theory and the central importance of cultures (e.g., learning and knowledge cultures, evidence-based cultures, organizational cultures). This tendency has been further reinforced by an emerging central focus on 'the practitioner' and practitioner knowledge, as it has been written into programmes of 'the reflective practitioner' dating from the work of Donald Schön (1987, 1995) and Chris Argyris (1974, 1996, 1999) and augmented by so-called 'communities of practice' (e.g., Wenger 1998) and notions of 'situated learning' (Lave and Wenger 1991). In general these developments – the cultural turn, the emphasis on the reflective practitioner and the turn to practice – means, among others things, that education activities are primarily viewed as engagements-with-others-in-the-world implying that learning and teaching are fundamentally social activities, 'doings', activities or performances without 'inner' processes.

Above all, what is required in pedagogical and learning theory and practice is an account of *practices* for it is possible to identify competing views of *practice* and the extent to which they are unified or dispersed, and integrated or disseminatory (see Peters 2003). The outline of these approaches sets up a rich set of connections between theories of practice and the ethico-political commitments they embody. The notion of practice is a contentious concept and it demands a coherent account of its *shared* nature, which also implies its transmittance. If current phenomenological accounts based on Heidegger, Wittgenstein and Foucault are accepted then professional practice and learning must be considered as *infrastructural*, that is, *non-cognitive, nonconceptual*, and *prelinguistic*, and if this is the case then it remains to be seen how practice can be learned or transmitted.

Clearly, there are competing views of knowledge as practice and competing views of learning that remain to be yet untangled and properly explored. The simple or crude economistic versions that trade on conceptions of 'useful knowledge' do not understand the cultural factors in learning (see Bruner 2000). Sometimes these trends and speculations have endorsed and legitimated the ideology of 'useful knowledge' where the emphasis is on 'the new', knowledge that is close to the product market cycle, and of clear and immediate benefit to the economy. The new pragmatics of knowledge has found its way into higher education policy.

The UK's Education Secretary, Charles Clarke, for example, reportedly told a gathering at University College, Worcester in 2003: 'I don't mind there being some medievalists around for ornamental purposes, but there is no reason for the state to pay for them' (*The Guardian*, Saturday, 10 May, p. 3). He urged universities to think more about how they benefit the economy and he threatened a cut in state funds for 'unproductive' forms of study. In other speeches, Clarke has asserted that the state should pay only for higher education that has 'clear usefulness' referring to 'the wider social and economic role of universities'. The Worcester speech was widely regarded both as an attack on the status of the humanities and a warning about further funding for humanities subjects during the new term of government. Clarke's comments, described as 'crudely utilitarian and materialist' by Jinty Nelson, Professor of Medieval History at King's College and President of the Royal Historical Society, should come as no surprise given the thrust of the White Paper *The Future of Universities*, that Clarke was responsible for issuing in January 2003.

The ideological discourse of 'useful knowledge' is based upon a set of policies for the commercialization of knowledge and the market exposure of universities without understanding either the significance of the distinctions between theoretical and practical knowledge, or knowledge and information, or the necessity of diversification of knowledge production. This ideology is reshaping the traditional relationships between research, teaching and scholarship with a greater accent on innovation in a learning economy where knowledge turnover is high and fast knowledge transfer is imperative. In this new policy environment, the state has a role to play in promoting both the means and access to learning and greater access to informal knowledge systems thus increasing competition and eroding the role of universities as privileged 'providers'.

This ideology of 'useful knowledge' with its emphasis on marketization of university knowledges risks an institutional levelling that turns the university into yet another corporation. The pressures of the learning economy increasingly force British universities to relinquish their comparative advantage especially in the under-funded humanities which traditionally combined both critical and creative functions – the basis of the so-called 'creative economy'. These functions, often seen as crucial to the university as a mainstay institution of democracy, now also take on a new and unexpected economic significance with the growth of communication and media studies, the diversification of cultural studies, and the 'culturalization' of the economy (Peters and Besley 2005). British universities also are losing their competitive edge regarding long-term basic research to focus on sunrise industries and the easily exploitable knowledge capital at one end of the market spectrum. Moreover, this instrumentalization of knowledge, which cannot be separated from the larger question of university control leads to the death of blue-skies research.

We explore the dimensions of these issues below, first, elaborating the role of the university in the learning economy focusing on an argument of Lundvall (2002) that as universities open themselves up to the market they must at the same time preserve the 'long-term, creative and critical aspects of academic research' if they are to survive. In the following section, we take up the question of changes in knowledge production and raise some criticisms of Gibbons' distinction between Mode 1 and Mode 2 knowledge, which has helped to legitimate the neo-liberal policy changes we describe. Finally, we argue that changes in knowledge production cannot easily be separated from questions of university governance under a neo-liberal policy regime and we investigate the effects of the funding of universities and specifically the Research Assessment Exercise (RAE) on blue-skies research.

The university in the learning economy

The notion of the 'learning economy' was first introduced into the discourses of the economics of higher education by Lundvall and his colleagues (Dalum, Johnson and Lundvall 1992, and Lundvall and Johnson 1994) in the early 1990s to indicate that the knowledge economy increasingly depended on new learning processes. Following this line of thinking, Gregersen and Johnson (1997), for instance, argue that the post-Fordist era of the fifth Kondratieff long wave has brought new learning processes based on ICT into being 'which have dramatically reduced the costs of storing, handling, moving and combining information, and have made different kinds of networking possible'. This has changed the process of innovation, shortening product cycles and making continual innovation necessary for firm survival.

They argue that in the modern learning economy,

> the rate of knowledge turnover is high; learning and forgetting are intense, the diffusion of knowledge is fast and a substantial part of the total knowledge stock is changed every year. Furthermore, learning has become increasingly endogenous. Learning processes have been institutionalized and feed-back loops for knowledge accumulation have been built in, so that the economy as a whole is learning by interacting in relation to both production and consumption. When economies learn how to learn, the process tends to accelerate. (Gregersen and Johnson 1997)

The knowledge infrastructure of universities and schools is seen as a major key to promoting innovation based on networking and interactive learning. There is also a much stronger institutional support of learning and innovation (dealing with intellectual property rights, technological service systems, tax rules and the like) leading to the development of 'a "learning culture" in which people regard long formal education, repeated re-education and retraining, and even life-long education, as necessary and normal aspects of economic life' (Gregersen and Johnson 1997). In this environment, the role of government policy has changed and the state has an important role to play in developing

> the means of learning (schools, training systems, etc.), the incentives to learn (intellectual property rights, taxes and subsidies, supporting learning networks, etc.), access to relevant knowledge (libraries, databases, technological service systems, telecommunication systems, etc.), decreasing the costs of forgetting (retraining, labour market mobility, social security, etc.), and, more generally, keeping options open by protecting technological and institutional diversity and promoting an openness to learning from abroad in different fields of knowledge. (Gregersen and Johnson 1997)

Lundvall himself has put the case of the university in the learning economy forcefully. He argues that, with increased internationalization and networking, universities have become 'more directly involved in market-driven processes and more exposed to competition from other producers of knowledge' (Lundvall 2002). Traditional modes of organization based on a sharp and rigid separation among disciplines and relative isolation from society are being replaced by strategies of alliances and networking. Yet 'as universities open themselves up, there is a need for changes in the institutional framework to ensure that the long-term, creative and critical aspects of academic research can survive' (Lundvall 2002). Market exposure of the university is not in itself a tenable policy aim and universities must consolidate their traditional ethical and social dimensions of knowledge in order to enhance the overall diversification and differentiation of knowledge production.

Much of Lundvall's case depends upon drawing a distinction between knowledge and information. He argues that the original argument for public financing of research given by economists (Nelson 1959; Arrow 1962) depended upon an account of knowledge production as 'information' as something easily copied and reproduced at marginal cost. On this basis the private sector would have no incentive to invest in the production of scientific knowledge to which competitors could gain free access.

Changes in knowledge production: Mode 2 versus Mode 1 knowledge

Merle Jacob and Tomas Hellström (2000) in their 'Introduction' to *The Future of Knowledge Production in the Academy* comment that three important developments have strongly impacted on the university research system: the shift from national science systems to global science networks; the capitalization of knowledge; and the integration of academic labour into the industrial economy, 'also known as the coming of the knowledge society' (p. 1). These developments, in large part, reflect the changing nature of capitalism within a more integrated world economy – in particular, the emergence of education considered as a form of knowledge capitalism (Peters 2004; Peters and Besley 2005) – and the force of the neo-liberal project of globalization (Olssen 2004; Olssen *et al.* 2004). As a consequence, it has become possible to talk of new forms of knowledge production. Lifelong learning and work-based learning are, in fact to a large extent, policy creations based upon the recognition of these developments. Of all the debate that has taken place around these changes, the distinction between Mode 1 and Mode 2 knowledge developed by Michael Gibbons and his colleagues (1994) has become a standard shorthand and dominant representation in policy discourses, which emphasizes a new pragmatics of knowledge based on practice.

As Jacob and Hellström (2000: 2) argue:

> In the *New Production of Knowledge*, Gibbons and his colleagues make two claims that have become symbolic representations in the debate about

the future of the academy. The first is that the nature of knowledge production is being transformed from Mode 1 (disciplinary, university-centred process) to Mode 2 (a transdisciplinary-based knowledge production in which academics operate with users and stakeholders to produce knowledge at the site of its application). The second is that this Mode 2 process is superior to Mode 1. From a sociological perspective, the symbolic significance of these two claims is easily explained. They serve as a convenient banner for collecting issues ranging from epistemology to labour politics in the university, and they may also be read as legitimizing the decline of the university as the central site of knowledge production.

Gibbons (1998: 5) in a paper to the UNESCO World Conference on Higher Education in 1998, clarifies his position, thus:

> It is my contention that there is now sufficient evidence to indicate that a new, distinct set of cognitive and social practices is beginning to emerge, and that they are different from those that govern Mode 1. These changes appear across the research spectrum and can be described in terms of a number of attributes which, when taken together, have sufficient coherence to suggest the emergence of a new mode of knowledge production. Analytically, these attributes can be used to allow the differences between Mode 1 and Mode 2 to be specified.

Gibbons (1998) argues that in contrast to Mode 1 where problems are generated and solved in terms of the interests of an academic community, in Mode 2 knowledge is produced in a context of application and problems arise out of that context. He goes on to indicate that where Mode 1 is disciplinary, Mode 2 is transdisciplinary. The former is 'characterised by a relative homogeneity of skills' whereas the latter is characterized by their heterogeneity. These changes in the production of knowledge have clear implications for organizational forms, for in Mode 1 the old hierarchical organizational model has maintained its form. In Mode 2, by contrast, 'the preference is for flatter hierarchies using organisational structures which are transient'. Thus, Mode 2 is 'more socially accountable and reflexive' because it 'involves a much expanded system of quality control' including 'a wider, more temporary and heterogeneous set of practitioners, collaborating on a problem defined in a specific and localised context'.

An important question concerns the *nature* of evidence that Gibbons presents, the economic perspective he adopts and the analytical framework he develops. First, we should remember that Gibbons presented the paper as part of the World Bank contribution to an international conference. Second, the underlying assumptions reflect a World Bank economic perspective which considers change in higher education as deriving from shifts in certain demand and supply factors. Third, the analytical framework of Mode 1 and 2 knowledge systems is developed to examine the history of massification in higher education and the nature of competitiveness in a global economy. He mentions the key empirical changes as being the diversification of higher education and 'the centrality of knowledge and intellectual capital in the innovation process brought about by globalising processes'. It should be clear that Gibbons adopts a neo-classical economic perspective on knowledge, even although he does not acknowledge its sources. His position is theoretically skewed and the nature of the evidence is both limited and debateable. He provides little in the way of empirical studies or analyses of data. The theory that is put forward is certainly underdetermined by the evidence and, it could be argued, functions more as an implicit neo-liberal World Bank policy prescription.[1]

The analytical framework itself is open to question on a number of fronts. Steve Fuller (2000: xii) summarizes a host of criticisms when he comments: 'The most pernicious feature of the "Myth of the Modes" is that the two modes are seen as not merely mutually exclusive, but also jointly, exhaustive – that is, not admitting of other possibilities.' The alleged exclusivity of the distinction tends to obscure wider questions concerning the interaction of the two kinds of knowledge, if indeed, they even exist in the forms Gibbons claims. Is this not simply a re-instantiation of the traditional theoretical/ practical knowledge distinction? And if so, it is clear that Gibbons fails to take account of arguments advanced by philosophers Wittgenstein, Heidegger and Polanyi that practical knowledge often contain a tacit dimension that depends upon the cultural background, which may not be able to be made fully explicit or can even be articulated in principle, and, therefore, easily converted into a publicly accessible and usable code. In other words, a new understanding of the production of knowledge demonstrates that significant parts of knowledge essential to economic growth take a practical and tacit form as 'know-how' that do not lend themselves easily to codification or to transfer from human beings to being embedded in knowledge processes.

Redefining scholarship and research: the death of blue-skies research?

Notwithstanding the shortcomings of Gibbons' distinction, the fact is that new pressures serve to constrain universities which militate against traditional forms of scholarship and research. Rather than classify a new mode or type of knowledge, a better strategy in our view, would be to identify the processes, mechanisms and strategies that produce the instrumentalization of knowledge. Changes in the type of knowledge cannot in our view be separated from the larger issues of control operating in universities. The production of knowledge, which has use-values, must be contextualized as a consequence of the new forces propelling global competition, which in turn

---

[1] Gibbons' view may be usefully contrasted with that of Lyotard (1984), Readings (1996) and Delanty (2001) and Olssen (2002).

serve to undermine the autonomy of universities as centres of disinterested and independent inquiry that characterize the liberal university within distinctive global-national arenas.

Neo-liberal forms of change exert structural pressures altering the relations between teaching, research and scholarship. The pressures exerted by 'top-up fees' will serve to increase the responsiveness of universities to the market order. 'Variable fees' are, in effect, a form of 'student loan', which must be paid back by students after education has been acquired. While in one sense they can be viewed as a form of targeted taxation, the effect on universities is likely to increase their responsiveness to market signals. Students will be reluctant to choose courses for which jobs are not easily obtainable, and which do not pay well in the market-place. In addition, universities will find it easy to devalue 'blue skies' research, and traditional discipline based subjects which do not have a easy translation to the occupational order (such as mathematics), will need to adapt in ingenious ways, by pairing up with new, high-demand subjects (such as music and sound recording). Courses in traditional subjects such as philosophy will decline in preference for courses that can attract students.

As it presently operates, the funding regime for universities also militates against blue-skies research and for certain programmatic forms of teaching and research. Adams and Bekhradnia (2004) describe how the UK's 'dual support system' of funding for higher education is changing to discriminate against blue-skies teaching and research. The dual support system has evolved primarily through 'custom, practice and policy convenience' (p. 3). As a system, it has provided for one stream of core support for general purposes (allocated by the UGC until 1989, more recently by HEFCE) together with a second competitive stream of project specific funds through the research councils, charities and industry. In the UK, funding council money is based on the Research Assessment Exercise (RAE), which assesses the quantity and quality of university research, while project grant funding is distributed in response to competitively tendered proposals. Funding council grants have effectively constituted block grants and core funding, which have permitted universities some discretion as to where research monies should be invested.

Adams and Bekhradnia point out that the nature of the system changed subtly in the mid-1960s when the research council system expanded. Although at that time universities had considerable discretion in the spending of the grant, confirmed in 1982 by the Merrison Report (ABRC/UGC 1982), which described the University Grants Committee grant as enabling universities to do research on their own account, by 1987, the extent of change can be seen evident in the ABRC Report (ABRC 1987):

University money for the support of research serves two purposes. On the one hand it provides for a basic level of research activity for all university academic staff. On the other hand, it provides the 'well-found' laboratory in which work supported by the Research Council and other funding agencies can be undertaken. (cited in Adams and Bekhrania 2004: 4)

New concerns arise in that while both research council and Funding Council sources have increased the overall amounts provided, the relative share from the funding council has decreased in value. The effects of this, as noted by May (2003), have been to introduce controls on the type of research carried out, as well as to increase the quantity of research obtained for the money spent. As such, research council spending constitutes a structural selectivity for increasing research output relative to cost. Increasing tendencies to fund only the direct costs of research leaving universities to fund infrastructure costs from core grants adds to this process and constitutes a way of lowering the cost of research output, thus indirectly also de-professionalizing academic labour in that control over variables such as time per job is taken out of the control of academics themselves.

Adams and Bekhradnia (2004: 2) state: 'The result has been that more and more project grants are being locked onto an inadequate research base, and the consequence is in part a decline in the ability of academics to conduct blue skies research, and in part a running down of the research infrastructure.' The general decline in the ratio between general research funds to project-specific grants provided by research councils 'has eroded the ability of universities to maintain the historical function of dual support' (p. 6). In relation to the overall structure of funding, Adams and Bekhradnia note how the two sides of the dual support system allocate funds in a remarkably consistent way.

There is also a very close alignment between what money is received by the universities from the funding councils and what they receive in grant and contract income from research councils, charities and other sources. Universities that receive more of one receive more of the other, and conversely, those that receive less of one receive less of the other.

Conclusion

Is there a space in this shifting web of forces for academic freedom to exist? It would be inaccurate to say that such spaces no longer exist just as it would be wrong to say they ever existed in anything like a pure and unconstrained form. Happy coincidences and chance alignments will invariably enable some academics to flourish in the new environment. Some will be able to redesign courses whereby their chosen areas of classical expertise and interest can be incorporated into a new programme with 'market-appeal'. Some will still do research as they have always done it, with little in the way of pressures exerted from higher up, and possibly highly valued by their institution and department. Yet, although these instances and spaces will invariably continue to exist, the general trend has been for a process of de-professionalization of academic labour, which negatively impacts on their authority as professionals – in relation to all areas of their role. While what they write may not be prescribed, the context and time-constraints in terms of which certain types of research must be balanced by the increased requirements of administration and teaching, and the externally directed necessities in line with the requirements of the RAE and other quality assurance processes, is likely to blunt its edge severely.

Pockets of freedom, or what seems like freedom, will continue. But what is undermined by the reform processes now underway is a shift in regulatory mode, an epistemic shift in Foucault's sense, whereby liberal norms and values, based on authority and expertise of the academic-professional is progressively giving way, slowly but imperceptibly, to a neo-liberal regulatory regime. This is one where the norms of professionalism are criticized as forms of 'rent-seeking' behaviour, and where line-management models, which see authority over research and knowledge are vested in managers, funding bodies, and governments, are taking their place. What is being witnessed is the end of the liberal modernist university.

Part 2

Reconceiving of Spaces

Overview

Before we can sensibly explore the possibilities for new relationships between research and teaching, and possibly for new spaces in the academy (the subject of Part 3), we first need to gain our bearings as to the current pattern of its dominant activities – and that is the concern of this section.

In short, the four chapters that constitute this section offer the following insights:

- While there are forces at work that are encouraging research and teaching to diverge from each other, there are both enduring and emerging considerations that point to convergence (Peter Scott). Accordingly, the contemporary set of relationships between teaching and research is far from clear; it offers threats, but it also presents opportunities.
- As is evident both in pedagogical and curricula practices (Mick Healey) and in tutors' perceptions and beliefs (Jane Robertson/Carol Bond), there are significant fine-grained differences across the disciplines. In part, these differences spring from the contrasting epistemological character of the disciplines.
- There is present in higher education a rival set of pedagogical dispositions that sees the educational process alternatively as a matter of critical inquiry and as a matter of persuasion (Stephen Rowland). Understanding higher education as a process of critical inquiry points on the one hand to the provision of pedagogical space – in which the student is accorded space for her/his own enquiries – but also, on the other hand, to intellectual love. The love of a tutor for her/his subject leads to the provision of intellectual space for the student for this love is not possessive in its character. This teaching is a generous teaching and is fuelled by the love that motivates the tutor's specialist research.

What is striking about these four chapters, especially when taken together, is that they indicate that the current situation itself contains spaces for creativity, for reconceiving of teaching and research *and* of their interrelationships. The messiness (as we may put it) of academic life – in its variations across and even within disciplines, in its pedagogical practices and its curricula models, in differing and legitimate conceptions of knowledge and its relationship to teaching and in the complex tacit exchanges between the academy and the wider society and community – contains spaces for doing things anew. And these spaces for positive creative endeavour in the academy may even be growing.

There is a paradox here, therefore. Precisely at the moment when extramural forces gain in strength and impose their will as pernicious ideologies on the academy and even when the academic 'community' itself buttresses those ideologies with myths and even ideologies of its own, opportunities arise for new ideas and practices that may take the academy forward in a positive way: on the one hand, imposition from without and within leading to a potential diminution of space; on the other hand, new spaces for new creative ideas and activities.

The skies darken and generate gloom, but the clouds also part, and light shines through. But how much light? And how much space between the clouds? These might be felt to be fair responses in this situation. Perhaps, though, those responses are too rational. We see through the gaps in the clouds partly because we are seeking to do so. Some just go forward with their heads down, muttering gloomily about the end of academic freedom, the university 'in ruins' or in 'crisis' and never seek possible signs of hopefulness. What matters, therefore, is less the objective reading of a situation than our dispositions. In part, the pessimists' response is understandable for to be optimistic imposes its own challenges: optimism is nothing unless it is put into action in some way. But these reflections are to jump ahead of ourselves. For now, in this section, the task is to try to understand the current pattern of the shapes that constitute the university.

4

Divergence or Convergence? The Links between Teaching and Research in Mass Higher Education

Peter Scott

Introduction

The relationship between teaching and research is among the most intellectually tangled, managerially complex and politically contentious issues in mass higher education systems. In intellectual terms, the boundary between 'teaching' and 'research' appears to be getting fuzzier rather than clearer. Not only is it increasingly difficult to establish categorical and conceptual demarcations between different forms of academic work, it is equally difficult to distinguish in practice between teaching programmes and research projects. Both 'teaching' and 'research' have become transgressive categories that overlap each other. The best example is the growth of deliberately hybrid activities, such as professional doctorates. However, this phenomenon is no longer confined to the boundary zone between taught and research postgraduate degrees, but extends 'backwards' into undergraduate courses and 'forwards' into mainstream research.

Yet in policy and political terms the opposite trend can be observed – towards a much clearer separation between teaching and research. This is happening at several levels – at the level of individual careers, because the ideal of the generic teaching-and-research academic is being superseded by more focused professional identities, of learning-and-teaching 'experts' on the one hand and research-only staff (and a growing army of contract researchers) on the other; at the level of funding streams, as 'block grants' and whole-institution budgets are replaced, in effect, by separate allocations for teaching and research calculated according to different criteria; and at the level of institutional missions as diversity (or hierarchy?) and differentiation are explicitly encouraged. The disarticulation of research and teaching within mass higher education systems is regarded by many policy-makers as inevitable (and even desirable), because the alternatives are to encourage inappropriate 'academic drift' and/or to produce a poorly focused (and attenuated?) university research system.

Caught in the middle are institutional leaders who have to confront two opposing 'realities' – on the one hand, the increasing 'fuzziness' of teaching and research domains; and, on the other, the imperative to focus on research strengths (which, inevitably, leads to the proliferation of 'research-light' departments and/or institutions). As a result, the tensions between the 'separate development' of both teaching and research, which has been encouraged by the professionalization of both functions within the modern university, and the interpenetration of teaching and research in intellectual terms (and their continuing interdependence in logistical terms) now present institutions with acute strategic challenges. They are caught on the horns of a dilemma – intellectual convergence but policy divergence. However, this dilemma does far more than create difficulties for institutional leaders in determining their strategies and priorities. The idea, and ideal, of the university and the purposes of higher education have also become embroiled in these research–teaching 'wars'.

All three perspectives – political, managerial and intellectual – will be explored in this chapter. All three intersect in contradictory – but also potentially creative – ways and all three contribute to a new articulation between research and teaching in mass higher education systems. None of these perspectives is straightforward. In the case of the first it is possible to draw a distinction between 'politics' and 'policy' – the former uncompromising (and naive?); the latter more nuanced. The managerial perspective is also complex: research strategies must address both the clear articulation of priorities and the effective mobilization of resources but also the management of institutional reputations (or 'brands'). The intellectual perspective, inevitably, is multiple and fractured – in some subjects (and contexts) more holistic accounts of 'knowledge work' (research, teaching and much else besides) are in the ascendant; in others (even) more differentiated accounts have become more persuasive. So it is far too simple to suggest that political forces are tearing research and teaching apart, while intellectual trends are pushing them together – with institutional managers caught in the middle.

The research–teaching relationship: two paradigms

In this section, the first of these perspectives – the political – will be explored. There are two contrasting paradigms of the links between teaching and research – the first emphasizes the inextricable, or indissoluble, nature of these things; the second their growing fragility, or tenuousness.

Inextricable links

According to the first, research and teaching are inextricably linked as different aspects of academic work. Effective university-level teachers must also be engaged in research and scholarship. Also a 'proper' university institution must not only provide higher education but also nurture a research culture. However, this first paradigm has never gone unchallenged. Cardinal Newman, for one, would not have subscribed to it. In his eyes – and in the eyes of many nineteenth-century university leaders – 'research' (to which they often attached the adjective 'useful') did not form part of the core mission of the university (Newman 1852/1966). Also until well into the twentieth century, there was little systematic state-sponsored and publicly funded support for research. Research councils are a comparatively recent invention. Finally, within many higher education systems, institutions with a limited stake in research have flourished – some of which have enjoyed great prestige (for example, *grandes écoles* in France or liberal arts colleges in the United States). On closer examination, this supposedly traditional paradigm appears less traditional than at first sight.

So it is probably misleading to imagine that in élite university systems the organic links between research and teaching were universally accepted, and that only since the emergence of mass higher education systems have these links been called into question. To the extent that the first of these statements is true the explanation was as much pragmatic as ideological. Because universities only educated a restricted élite of the future 'great and good' and research and scholarship were comparative inexpensive activities, it was feasible for undergraduates to be taught by those who were actively involved in research and scholarship (potentially at any rate – in practice many were not). In other words, the 'fit' between research and teaching in élite university systems was largely contingent. If this is true, the counter-argument (relied on by many contemporary policy-makers) must be treated with caution, namely, that because universities have become mass institutions and because research, at any rate in science and engineering, has become a very expensive and quasi-industrial enterprise, the 'fit' between research and teaching has become less good.

Separate development

According to the second paradigm, research and teaching are separate activities (worlds?). Several arguments are used to justify this separation:

1. The first argument is that, in a mass system, higher education (with the possible exception of a small number of élite universities) is not really different from further education or, even, secondary education – hence the popularity of the category 'tertiary education'. Consequently, most students do not need to be taught by active researchers. This argument, of course, ignores the key question of whether in a 'knowledge society' it is possible to divorce 'learning' from 'researching' – at any level of education.
2. The second argument is that too tight an association between research and teaching tends to devalue teaching because teaching cannot readily

escape from the shadow of research, success in which confers the bulk of academic prestige. It is certainly true that, in most higher education systems, promotion procedures (for individuals) and performance indicators (for department and institutions) are unhealthily dependent on research – although this is a more recent phenomenon than is commonly supposed. However, constructing alternative hierarchies of esteem, capable of quasi-independent validation, is not straightforward. Closely linked to this is the argument that students themselves perceive a tension between research and teaching (Lindsay, Breen and Jenkins 2002).

3. The third argument for separating research from teaching more clearly is the other side of the coin. Research is (or should be) a professional activity with its own career structures and resource patterns. Otherwise it is likely to be over-dependent on the imperatives of teaching and patterns of student choice. This argument was much employed in the 1980s when the first attempts were made to uncouple the development of research from the expansion of student numbers, which led – in the UK – to the introduction of the Research Assessment Exercise (RAE). Why, it was asked, should the nation's research capacity be increased in line (and in alignment) with the growing demand for student places?

4. The fourth, and final, argument is that, in order to produce world-class research, it is necessary to focus and concentrate research funding, establish critical masses of researchers, build stronger research infrastructures and, above all, nurture more productive and creative research cultures. The emergence of a 'knowledge society' and the processes of globalization, it is argued, have produced a cut-throat environment in which only the fittest, or cleverest, survive. In fact, this conclusion is by no means obvious. The idea of a 'knowledge society' implies that society is permeated by knowledgeable actions and actors, while globalization is far from being simply a neo-liberal and high-technology phenomenon.

A dual economy

There can be little doubt which view – for the present – is in the ascendant. The 2003 UK White Paper on the future of higher education explicitly questioned the existence of an organic relationship between research and teaching – reasonably so in terms of historical evidence that this relationship has been both a contested and a contingent one; less reasonably in terms of the policy conclusions that ministers then attempted to draw (DfES 2003). The most recent HEFCE strategic plan also asserts that higher education institutions will (or should) have highly differentiated stakes in the four core areas identified by the council – learning and teaching, research, reach-out (and, more broadly, community engagement); and widening participation (or social inclusion) (HEFCE 2003).

In effect, both political rhetoric and policy instruments are combining to encourage the emergence of a dual economy in higher education – for teaching and for research. Although higher education institutions continue to receive block grants from funding councils (and the wholesale transfer of research funding to the research councils has – so far – been avoided), the 'teaching' and 'research' elements in their grants are calculated in different ways – the former formulaically and the latter selectively. Because the bases of calculation are so different, and are also fully transparent, so-called 'T' and 'R' funding are now regarded as quasi-earmarked grants. However, this has happened through a process of policy accretion. When the RAE was first introduced, its ostensible objective was to match research funding with research outputs, because the former University Grants Committee's policy of 'informed prejudice' (in effect, the roll-forward of existing funding levels) could no longer be justified; and also to uncouple the strategic development of research from the dynamics of student expansion. But, in its early stages, the RAE was essentially a passive, or reactive, instrument, although from the start it had a profound effect on the behaviour of individuals, departments and institutions. Now, of course, the RAE has become an aggressive instrument, used not simply to concentrate research funding but to restructure the system by determining institutional missions (Sharp 2004).

A similar evolution has taken place with regard to teaching. Early attempts to strengthen the external examining system and to introduce academic audit were largely defensive – to reassure sceptical stake-holders. There was no explicit intention of encouraging the 'separate development' of teaching and research. More recently, of course, a formidable apparatus of quality assurance and enhancement has been developed through the establishment of the Quality Assurance Agency (QAA) (Brown 2004); institutions have also been required to develop learning and teaching strategies and large-scale investment in learning management systems has taken place. All this has had far-reaching effects – leading to the external regulation of academic standards but also, crucially, to the emergence of teaching as a professional domain in its own right, distinct from specific (and research-led?) disciplines. But, as with the RAE, these effects were the result of policy accretion rather than of any deliberate re-conceptualization of the relationship between teaching and research.

Because the development of a dual economy in teaching and in research in British higher education is best described in terms of the accretion of policy, and pragmatic responses to this accretion, it is difficult to draw categorical conclusions. The explicit repudiation of the organic links between research and teaching in the White Paper appears less significant in the light of the historical record which reveals that these links have always been essentially contingent (and often contested). Even the proposal to establish so-called 'teaching-only' universities – in effect, to designate as universities institutions that do not currently have the authority to award research degrees (but, of course, may have well-developed scholarly and research cultures) – appears less controversial when it is recognized that high-status teaching-oriented institutions have always been an important component of many higher education systems. The more the evidence of the complex articulations between research and teaching is assessed, the more it may be necessary to shift the emphasis from rupture, the recent, ruthless and unprecedented imposition of a dual economy (or 'separate development'), to continuity, the continuing evolution of research–teaching links; and this perspective held in the context of an essentially pragmatic framework of deeper structural changes within modern higher education systems and more ephemeral policy interventions.

Teaching and research: managerial perspectives

If the preceding analysis is accepted, the 'policy' messages to institutional managers on research and teaching are less clear-cut than is generally assumed – even if more crudely expressed 'political' messages appear to be unambiguous. If the real drivers of the relationship between research and teaching are pragmatic adjustments to the past – and future – evolution of higher education systems as much as high-profile but short-term political interventions, a much more open arena is created. Rather than being caught in the middle, institutions – and their leaders – are able to 'play' the dialectic between the top-down, and essentially political, forces of divergence and the bottom-up, and essentially intellectual, forces of convergence (or, if not convergence, complication).

So, although institutional leaders are obliged to adjust to policy interventions (for example, the ever more selective distribution of research funding in England following the 2001 RAE), they also need to pay attention to the *longue durée*, the underlying structure of higher education systems which is itself driven by fundamental changes in the scientific (and social) base. The present bundling together of research and teaching is no more 'natural' – and, therefore, inevitable – than their threatened unbundling. The modern university may have defined both as core missions but this is a comparatively recent phenomenon dating back at the earliest to the early nineteenth century – and effectively much later because the present configuration of research and teaching was really only established after 1945. So the possibility that the current bundling together of research and teaching in the university may have been contingent on the coincidence of two particular 'economies' of teaching and research (the former focused on the higher education of political and professional élites; and the latter on the extraordinary power of what Thomas Kuhn called 'normal science' (Kuhn 1962)) must at least be considered.

Mass higher education systems are no longer predominantly concerned with the formation of future élites – in part because they now enrol mass student populations many of whom will not pursue élite careers; but also in part because élites have themselves become more fluid, problematical and contested categories. At the same time, the research domain has also been transformed – becoming a quasi- (and sometimes an actual) industrial process, but also becoming much more open and distributed as the potential for intellectual (and even scientific) creativity spills out from the academy. Although the continued association of teaching and research within common structures cannot be ruled out because of these changes, it also cannot be taken for granted.

However, from a managerial perspective, there are three arguments for continuing to combine teaching and research missions even under these very different conditions:

1. The first argument concerns the basis of the university's academic authority – in two separate respects. The first is in relation to its capacity to maintain and enhance the quality of student learning and teaching, which has already been briefly discussed. This remains the responsibility of individual institutions, although the work of the QAA in developing subject benchmarks has been influential. Nor can this capacity simply be demonstrated exclusively through administrative processes. It is essentially an intellectual responsibility which can be subdivided into, first, sustaining academic rigour in subject-specific contexts, to which the quality of disciplinary research is clearly relevant, and, second, reflecting (and improving?) on academic practice, which requires systematic evaluation of that practice – presumably through effective pedagogical and institutional research.

The second relates to the university's right to police its own academic standards and to make its own awards, which are privileges enjoyed uniquely by universities (although not all higher education institutions). Clearly engagement in research is one component – and an important component – of the capacity of institutions to set standards, maintain quality and make academic awards. Research, of course, is not the only component of this capacity; administrative processes are also important. Indeed its contribution to legitimating standards and awards may be compromised by the unsettling, even subversive, effects that the best research and scholarship have on established knowledge and received wisdoms. But the best university education is also one that helps students to engage with the provisionality (and problematization) of existing knowledge. This connection between research and the university's authority is not merely a general principle; it also has more concrete manifestations. Here are two examples. The first is that many professional bodies insist on involvement in research as a prerequisite of accreditation; some, sadly, even insist on specified RAE grades as proxies for such involvement. The second concrete manifestation is that the QAA in discharging its core responsibilities has underlined the connection between good teaching and research. The new QAA Framework for Higher Education Qualifications makes the same assumption, which will be tested in institutional audits (QAA 2001).

2. The second 'managerial' argument is that that involvement in research enables universities to attract good teachers. Of course, it is wrong to insinuate that only active researchers make good teachers, although good teachers do need – in some way – to cultivate their disciplines. It is also wrong to

assert that research is the core responsibility of universities – and, therefore, that academics must be 'bribed' to teach by being allowing time to undertake research. The core responsibility of universities, even of the most research-intensive universities, is teaching. The issue, therefore, is how universities can continue to recruit a well qualified and highly motivated academic work-force – an issue that will become increasingly acute over the next decade as the 'bulge' of university teachers recruited during the 1960s and 1970s comes up to retirement. Higher education teachers want, and need, to be able to 'grow' in their own disciplines (which happens, largely but not exclusively through engagement in research); and they want to continue to be marketable, especially in the much more open and fluid markets for academic labour characteristic of the 'knowledge society' (which is difficult for teachers without research profiles). One of the strongest arguments against hyper-selectivity in research funding is that, far from strengthening teaching in less research-intensive universities (on the specious grounds that they will not be 'distracted' from their core, or teaching, mission by vainly pursuing unrealistic research ambitions), it may actually weaken teaching because of its impact on the constitution of the academic workforce.

3.   The third 'managerial' argument for linking research and teaching is the impact that research engagement has on institutional reputation, insti-tutional positioning and so on the overall shape of the higher education system. It is too simple to see this impact simply in terms of newspaper league tables, although in a higher education system increasingly characterized by market-like behaviour league tables cannot be lightly dismissed. Research performance, as measured by RAE grades, external research grants and PhD registrations and completions, is not only a major factor in the calculation of such league tables but is also used as a proxy for other measures of esteem (not entirely unfairly because there was a strong correlation between high RAE grades and high 'scores' in the QAA's teaching quality assessments/ subject reviews). Nor can it be denied that league tables have an important impact on institutional morale (as well as institutional fortunes) and that potential students are influenced by league tables – directly or, more prob-ably, indirectly through their parents, teachers, other advisers and friends.

It is also too simple to see the impact of research reputation on institutional fortunes in terms of 'academic drift', the desire of teaching (or access) oriented institutions to develop a stronger research profile largely for reasons of prestige. 'Academic drift' is a complex – and two-way – process with trad-itional universities taking on less traditional roles (for example, in knowledge transfer or widening participation) as well as less traditional institutions aspir-ing to more traditional roles (such as research). It is better explained in terms of the stretching of institutional missions within a mass higher education system – and especially within an increasingly 'market' system.

So neither the pressures exerted by league tables nor the aspirations (misleadingly?) labelled as 'academic drift' adequately explain the impact of research performance and reputation on institutional success. A more satisfactory explanation requires proper weight to be given not only to practical considerations – such as the difficulty of recruiting high-quality academic staff, which has already been discussed – but also to more general considerations such as the emergence of institutional 'brands', which are a novel and perhaps decisive development in modern higher education systems. These new-style 'brands' are not the same as older forms of institutional reputation. Although they contain traditional reputational elements, not least measures of research performance and teaching esteem, 'brands' also contain more subjective, volatile, ephemeral (and manipulable?) elements, particularly with regard to the life-experiences of students and graduates. Institutional leaders and higher education managers are likely increasingly to reach conclusions about the desirability of strengthening, weakening or modifying links between research and teaching within the context of the construction of 'brands'.

Research and teaching: intellectual convergences

The third, and most important, perspective on the evolving relationship between research and teaching is an intellectual one – which concerns both concrete changes in the practice of these activities (reconfiguration) and also more theoretical accounts of new modes of knowledge production (reconceptualization). The reconfiguration of research and teaching practice is easier to grasp than the reconceptualization of knowledge work as a whole, within which research and teaching are both embedded. Both 'teaching' and 'research' are, and always have been, labels covering a heterogeneous range of eclectic activities, although in policy debates they have often been collapsed into homogeneous, and unproblematic, categories. Moreover, these ranges of activities have tended to mingle – and even overlap.

Reconceptualizing teaching

Teaching has always been a diverse domain. This diversity has been expressed not simply in terms of scale, level, style, location and technology but also, crucially, in terms of different disciplinary cultures (Becher and Trowler 2001; Neumann 2001). Why such heterogeneous activities have been bundled together under a single label, 'teaching', is an interesting question. Part of the answer is organizational (because special-purpose institutions called universities have been created for this purpose, although there have been important differences – over time and space – in the range of teaching activities that have been seen as their special responsibility). Part is social (because all these different forms of 'teaching' have – had? – in common the socialization of young adults into various élite and expert cultures). Part is normative (because most forms of 'teaching' were grounded in ideas, and ideals, of improvement, emancipation, and enlightenment).

But all these answers are becoming less convincing. Universities, like many other institutions of modernity's high noon, are undergoing a process of deconstruction (which cannot be disguised by the shrill imposition of the so-called 'new public management'). They are no longer focused so strongly on the socialization of young adults into élite and expert cultures. Not only is the student population in mass higher education systems more diverse in terms of age, gender, class, ethnicity and culture; but élites have become eroded and fragmented and notions of expertise have become more ephemeral and more contested. Finally, in the wider intellectual domain the reach 'beyond modernity' (whichever label is preferred) has tended to break the ordered links between the university and science and enlightenment (Barnett 2000; Delanty 2001; Taylor, Barr and Steele 2002).

Perhaps because of this loosening of the rationales for integration, the diversity of 'teaching' appears to be accelerating (Northedge 2003). This is happening in four main ways:

1. Its structural variety is increased, most obviously in terms of the prolifer-ation of courses. New types of courses are being developed, such as foun-dation degrees with a much stronger work-based element and more open forms of lifelong learning and continuing professional development.
2. Course structures have become more flexible – partly as the result of modularization, which allows students to mix-and-match subjects with different economies of teaching and so exposes them to greater variety of teaching styles. Also new subjects, or interdisciplinary subject combin-ations, are being introduced, largely in response to market demands.
3. The development of computer-based learning management systems, and virtual learning environments, is introducing a whole repertoire of new forms of teaching. The most important effects of these new elements are a much enhanced capacity for interactivity and asynchronous learning – both of which extend the potential of, but also challenge, more traditional forms of pedagogy.
4. The emphasis is switching from 'teaching' to 'learning' – or, at any rate, to 'learning and teaching'. So teaching (as in 'teaching' as opposed to 'research') has undergone another extension. It now embraces all the activities and experiences that contribute to student learning – libraries, ICT, student services. As a result the definition of the 'teacher' has been problematized – in two senses. The first is the overlap between teachers and learners (encouraged, for example, by the development of peer-assisted learning), and the second is the extension of the 'teaching' community to embrace a wider range of professional staff.

Re-engineering research

'Research' is an equally diverse category (Brew 2001; Larédo 2003). The distinction sometimes between 'research' and 'scholarship' hints at that diversity. In the past this distinction typically referred to differences between the humanities, in which scholars were often regarded as academic 'sole practitioners', and the sciences, which research teams and specialized and dedicated resources were essential. More recently, the distinction has been used in a different (and more dubious) way – to distinguish between the people who really do the research and the rest who merely need to 'keep up' with it (Andresen 2000). But the eclecticism of research extends far beyond this distinction. Research undertaken in dedicated research setting such as universities or industrial and Government laboratories is now only one cluster within a much wider constellation of knowledge production. It is hardly surprising that, in a society in which knowledge has become a key resource, all kinds and types of institutions have had to become know-ledge organizations (just as they have always had to become learning organizations).

Some of this 'knowledge', of course, is really information that achieves its potency by being manipulated in massive data-sets – or volatile brands and images in our intensely visualized world. But it cannot be written off on that account. Nor is it correct to interpret the 'stretching' of research simply as a rebalancing of priorities, in favour of 'applied' research and at the expense of 'pure' research, or the rise of collaborative research (Smith 2001). It is a much more subtle and complex phenomenon which has been described in terms of the contrast between 'Mode 1' research and 'Mode 2' knowledge production, of 'contexts of application' (and 'contexts of implication'), of socially robust (and socially engaged?) research, and the inherent reflexivity of the research process (Gibbons *et al.* 1994). Two conclusions can be drawn. The first is that any discussion of the links between teaching and research must take into account the increasing instability, even volatility, of the two 'base' categories which overlap and interpenetrate each other in novel ways. The second is that, even if the overall demarcation between teaching and research remains valid, the links between them are not the same for all disciplines and at all times. They are highly context-dependent – and becoming more context-dependent.

Re-justifying the links between research and teaching

Against this background of the increasing interpenetration of research and teaching (which contains elements of divergence as well as of convergence), it is possible to identify three broad arguments for maintaining at least a close association between the two domains – even in mass higher education systems:

1.   The first is the argument that academics need to be engaged in their disciplines to be effective teachers, a traditional argument which needs to be carefully unpacked in the light of changing configurations of research and teaching. Good teachers must communicate to their students a sense of intellectual excitement, while contemporary research practice is not always (often?) intellectually engaging. 'Big ideas' have typically grown out of intellectual genres (essays, commentaries, lectures) very unlike modern research practice. Speculative essays still punch more intellectual weight than the empirical research reports. However, even if it is true that good teachers should be, in David Schön's overused phrase, 'reflective practitioners', the link between reflective practice and research is far from straightforward (Schön 1995). More than 70 years ago, the German critic Walter Benjamin in an intriguing fragment entitled 'we ought to re-examine the link between teaching and research' argued that, while in subjects 'that stand at the centre of modern life, there should be a strong link between the two', other more traditional subjects 'need to be emancipated from the forms in which [such] scholarly acquisition took place, if they are still to have any value and any defined character today' (Benjamin 1999).

It is also important to consider what kind of research is being compared and contrasted with teaching. If research is defined as a quasi-industrial process of systematic inquiry, the links with teaching may be more difficult to establish than if research is defined in more open and imaginative terms within the broader canvas or framework of academic work. In the latter case, the research-active (or, at any rate, intellectually engaged) teacher as a necessary role model for their students is perhaps more significant than a detailed mapping of the synergies between their research and their teaching. If one of the goals of mass higher education systems within a 'knowledge society' is to produce knowledge workers – who are 'more' than simply graduates with expert academic or professional skills and who have an active 'enquiry capacity', but are 'less' than professionalized researchers – the significance of the teacher-researcher (and even the teacher-researcher-practitioner) as a role model (and intellectual leader) is correspondingly enhanced.

2.   The second – intellectual – argument for maintaining a clear association between research and teaching has already been discussed, the growth of new practices that transgress the traditional boundaries between the two domains. There are many examples of this transgression (or, more accurately, interpenetration). One is the increasing weight attached to student assignments and projects that include a more explicit research element (Livingston and Lynch 2000). The idea of research teams has even been introduced through group projects. As a result, it is possible that today's students in mass higher education systems are more familiar with research, as a practice, than yesterday's students in more selective élite university system. A second example of transgression is the increasing emphasis placed in the research domain on evidence-based practice and policy and on the

dissemination of research results. Both encourage teaching-like behaviour on the part of researchers. Evidence-based practice requires more systematic interaction between 'evidence' (that is, research), and 'practice', which is powerfully shaped by professional formation and regulation (that is, teaching in a broad sense). Equally, active dissemination of research findings requires researchers to devise communication strategies that not only include conferences and seminars but other tools such as web-sites. Increased emphasis is now placed on communication strategies in determining which proposals to fund.

3. The third argument for continuing to associate research and teaching – even (or especially?) within mass higher education systems – is the impact of the 'knowledge society' (Stehr 1994; Scott 1999). In a 'knowledge society' everyone becomes, to some degree, a knowledge worker (or, at any rate, a knowledgeable actor). This has two consequences. The first is that knowledge is suffused through society. To be effective, it must be widely distributed because, to paraphrase Manuel Castells' idea of the Network Society, the uses (and the quality) of knowledge consists not simply in its own inherent worth, its primary production, but also in its nodes of communication, its secondary transmission (although it is probably misleading to characterize the former as a 'primary' and the latter as a 'secondary' activity) (Castells 1996–2000). As a result, the role of dedicated, specialized 'knowledge' institutions such as universities is changed, even challenged. All, or most, institutions now have to be 'knowledge' organizations, which may help to explain the dynamic behind the growth of corporate, virtual and for-profit 'universities'. The second consequence is that it is now more and more difficult to distinguish sensibly between primary producers of knowledge (researchers), those who disseminate or trade it (teachers and consultants) and end-users. The very terms may even have become an anachronism because they assume an out-of-date linear model of knowledge production – an 'old economy' of knowledge. Perhaps a 'new economy' is emerging in which segregated (and privileged?) domains labelled research or scholarship and teaching are becoming redundant (Nowotny, Scott and Gibbons 2001).

Conclusion

The challenge for mass higher education systems – managerial and intellectual, organizational and normative – is to be able to respond creatively to what may appear to be forces of confusion and fragmentation within this 'new economy' of knowledge work within an overarching 'knowledge society' ('divergence' in the title of this chapter), because these same forces can also be seen as forces of integration ('convergence'). The erosion of boundaries, categorical and institutional, is both a threat to the university but also an opportunity. The often difficult debates about the relationship between research and teaching in mass higher education systems, therefore, are simply one element (although a key one) within a wider and more fundamental debate about the future of the university in the 'knowledge society'.

There are two possible futures – the apotheosis of the university as the hegemonic knowledge institution *or* its redundancy as the need for dedicated knowledge institutions is dissolved by the pervasive action of the 'knowledge society'. Which of these starkly opposed paths will be followed may crucially depend on how various elements of academic work (including, of course, research and teaching) are reconstituted – either within normatively directed institutions (even if their value systems are different from those that prevailed in traditional universities) or within operationally driven organizations (whether orchestrated by the state or the market). No one can be confident about the answer. But a 'surface' drift of policy towards the enforced separation of research and teaching may make the latter (and surely less desirable?) outcome more likely: the deeper currents of intellectual and scientific change, which suggest more complex patterns of divergence-convergence, provide grounds for hope that the university can – once again – survive and continue to evolve.

5

Linking Research and Teaching: Exploring Disciplinary Spaces and the Role of Inquiry-based Learning

Mick Healey

Introduction

Much of the international debate about the relationship between research and teaching is characterized by difference. Individuals vary widely in their views about the nature of the linkage. Some believe that 'university research often detracts from the quality of teaching' (Pocklington and Tupper 2002: 7), while others argue that 'courses taught by those at the cutting edge of research will necessarily be of higher quality than those taught by those merely using the research results of others – whatever the apparent quality of their style of delivery' (Lee 2004: 9). These strong views in part reflect the importance of linking research and teaching in the identity of many academics (Henkel 2000). The research evidence also varies, at least in its interpretation. For example, Hattie and Marsh (1996) found no significant relationship between research productivity and teaching effectiveness; on the other hand, 'there is clear evidence from a range of studies in different types of institutions of students valuing learning in a research-based environment' (Jenkins 2004: 29). Given these differences, it is hardly surprising that a number of myths have developed about the nature of the research–teaching nexus (Hughes, see Chapter 1).

In this chapter, it is argued that some of the complexity and contested nature of the linkages between research and teaching reflect, first, differences in the way that the terms 'research' and 'teaching and learning' are conceptualized, and second, the nature of the disciplinary spaces in which the linkages occur, that is the environment associated with different disciplinary cultures in which research and teaching take place. In constructing links between research and teaching, the discipline is an important mediator (Healey and Jenkins 2003). This is because the conduct of research and the teaching approaches tend to differ between disciplines. This often leads disciplines to act as distinct 'academic tribes' (Becher and Trowler 2001) or 'communities of practice' (Wenger 1998). This chapter explores the disciplinary spaces in which the linkages between research and teaching are developed.

A further theme running through this chapter is that students are likely to gain most benefit from research, in terms of depth of learning and understanding, when they are also involved in research, for example, through various forms of active learning, such as inquiry-based learning (Healey and Roberts 2004). This presents challenges to university staff to reshape curricula and may lead to new ways for staff and students to work together in communities of inquiry, albeit ameliorated by the nature of different disciplinary spaces.

Disciplinary spaces and approaches

For most academic staff, their primary allegiance is to their subject or profession, and their sense of themselves as staff at a given institution is secondary (Diamond and Adam 1995; Healey 2003; Jenkins 1996). There is also a strong perception among staff that there are significant differences among disciplines in what academics do and how those activities are described and valued. There is much supporting evidence for these perceptions. Moses (1990), for example, has demonstrated in a study of four disciplines in an Australian university that attitudes to teaching and research tasks, as well as patterns of communication, vary between disciplines. For example, she found that a significantly higher proportion of staff in chemistry delivered conference papers and disagreed with the statement that 'When I revise a course I examine teaching and assessment matters to see whether they are appropriate'. The opposite findings characterized law. Donald (2002), moreover, has shown how different ways of learning occur in different academic disciplines. So, for example, interpretation is emphasized in English literature in which the meaning of texts is constructed through a hermeneutic process of tacking back and forth between our presumptions and the text. In contrast, in engineering high regard is given to the development of problem-solving skills in which procedures are followed to formulate a problem, do the necessary calculations and verify the logic used to see if the final answer makes sense.

Both Biglan (1973) and Kolb (1984) have distinguished different groups of disciplines. Whereas Biglan focused on how the actors within the disciplines see the characteristics of subject matter in different academic areas, Kolb attended to the predominant learning styles of students. Nevertheless, there is a remarkable consistency between the two classifications and both are used in Becher's work (Becher 1994; Becher and Trowler 2001; Neumann *et al.* 2002). Biglan's contrasts between hard pure (for example, physics), soft pure (for example, history), hard applied (for example, engineering), and soft applied (for example, education) disciplines are used here in preference to Kolb's rather more abstrusely named categories (abstract reflective, concrete reflective, abstract active and concrete active).

Given the importance of disciplines in the self-identity of academics and the learning styles of students, it might be expected that the nature of the research–teaching links varies between disciplines.

Nature of research–teaching links

Most staff, when asked about how their research impacts on teaching, point to the way in which their research findings are integrated into their lecture courses. However, there are many more ways of linking research and teaching than students learning about subject knowledge through lectures. Students may learn about research methods and techniques; they may undertake their own projects, whether individually or in teams; they may assist staff with their research; and they may gain experience of applied research and consultancy through work-based learning (Jenkins *et al.* 2003). Staff may model research-based approaches in the way they teach, through, for example, adopting an inquiry-based learning approach (Elton 2001a; Elton, see chapter 8). Staff may also exhibit the scholarship of teaching and learning and investigate the learning that takes place in their courses, so as to enhance their own teaching (Breslow *et al.* 2004; Cousin *et al.* 2003; Healey 2000). However, undertaking pedagogic research is not discussed further here; rather the focus is on how students may gain from subject-based research in the departments in which they are studying.

Departments and individuals vary in the way that they construct the linkage between research and teaching. It is possible to design curricula, which develop the research–teaching nexus, along three dimensions, according to whether:

- the emphasis is on research content or research processes and problems;
- the students are treated as the audience or participants;
- the teaching is teacher-focused or student-focused.

Inquiry-based learning, which benefits student learning through direct involvement in research, is towards the right-hand end of these three dimensions of curriculum design (Figure 5.1).

A range of terms is used in the literature, often interchangeably, to describe the research–teaching nexus. Griffiths (2004) suggests that a distinction might be made between teaching which is predominantly:

- *research-led*: where students learn about research findings, the curriculum content is dominated by staff research interests, and information transmission is the main teaching mode;

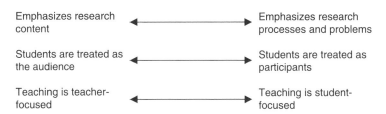

Figure 5.1 Three dimensions of curriculum design

- *research-oriented*: where students learn about research processes, the curriculum emphasizes as much the processes by which knowledge is produced as learning knowledge that has been achieved, and staff try to engender a research ethos through their teaching;
- *research-based*: where students learn as researchers, the curriculum is largely designed around inquiry-based activities, and the division of roles between teacher and student is minimized.

Figure 5.2 illustrates how curriculum design can be linked to the research–teaching nexus. The vertical axis runs from student-focused activities with students as participants to teacher-focused activities with students as the audience, and the horizontal axis stretches from an emphasis on research content to an emphasis on research processes and problems. Research-led teaching is in the bottom left-hand quadrant, while research-based teaching is in the top right. Research-oriented teaching occurs in the bottom right. This leaves the top left quadrant, which, although not recognized by Griffiths (2004), is student-focused and emphasizes research content. It is perhaps best illustrated by the Oxbridge tutorial system, where students engage in discussion with their tutors producing, in Oxford, an average of three papers or essays a fortnight (Ashwin 2003). 'Research-tutored', although slightly clumsy, might be an appropriate description to put alongside Griffiths' other categories. Interestingly at Oxford the term 'teaching' is not used when referring to tutorials (Gibbs 2004 personal communication). When tutorials

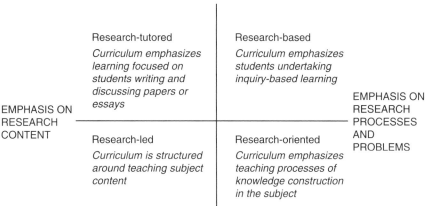

STUDENT-FOCUSED

STUDENTS AS PARTICIPANTS

Research-tutored	Research-based
Curriculum emphasizes learning focused on students writing and discussing papers or essays	Curriculum emphasizes students undertaking inquiry-based learning
Research-led	Research-oriented
Curriculum is structured around teaching subject content	Curriculum emphasizes teaching processes of knowledge construction in the subject

EMPHASIS ON RESEARCH CONTENT

EMPHASIS ON RESEARCH PROCESSES AND PROBLEMS

TEACHER-FOCUSED

STUDENTS AS AUDIENCE

Figure 5.2 Curriculum design and the research–teaching nexus

are used inappropriately in order to teach, they have a less positive impact on learning. Trigwell and Ashwin's (2003) research into the learning context at Oxford, shows that when students perceive that their tutorials or small-group classes are used for the purpose of teaching, explaining and checking on their knowledge, rather than for collaboratively discussing the subject matter, they are less likely to take a deep approach to their learning and more likely to take a surface approach.

Few curricula fit entirely in one quadrant. Although most traditional university teaching takes place in the bottom left quadrant, some disciplines have relatively more activity in the other quadrants. For example, some departments concerned with professional education, such as medicine, engineering and social work, focus their teaching on problem-based learning, a specialized form of inquiry-based learning, which falls predominantly in the top right quadrant of Figure 5.2. Many more departments engage students in aspects of inquiry-based learning for small parts of their curricula.

Each of the four types of research–teaching relationships can be subdivided further. For example, Barnett (2004 personal communication) distinguishes six types of research-led teaching according to whether individuals inject current or past research into their teaching and whether that research is, or was, carried out by themselves, others in their department or institution, or elsewhere. The extent to which it is necessary for effective learning that some of the research under discussion is undertaken by the specific teachers, or at least in the same department or university, is critical to the policy debate about the impact of research selectivity. There are similar arguments about the extent to which teachers facilitating research-based or research-tutored learning need to be active or experienced researchers. This, in turn, raises the question of how far the skills of facilitating learning and discovery research are co-located.

The different ways in which the terms 'research' and 'teaching' are used are also key elements in the contested discourse about their linkage (Healey 2005; Scott, see Chapter 4). Griffiths (2004), for example, distinguishes between empirical science, interpretative investigation, and applied inquiry with the first approach being associated particularly with the sciences, the second with the humanities and some of the social sciences, and the third with vocational fields. A decade-and-a-half ago Boyer (1990) argued for a broader definition of research to go beyond, what he called 'discovery scholarship' to include 'applied' and 'integrative' scholarships. According to Colbeck (1998) the broader and more inclusive the definition of what counts as research, the easier it is to integrate it with teaching.

To add to the confusion, the traditional distinctions between research and teaching are becoming blurred with the emergence of 'Mode 2' knowledge production, where the boundaries between discovery research and application are much more messy and integrated, alongside the usual 'Mode 1' disciplinary research generated in universities (Gibbons *et al.* 1994; Scott, see Chapter 4). Jenkins and Zetter (2003: 11) suggest that in a knowledge society:

research is context specific and multidisciplinary rather than pure and discipline based; it has social relevance rather than being hypothesis led; it uses fuzzy, rather than empirically based data; it is problem solving rather than deductive. In what might be termed the commodification of knowledge, how knowledge is managed, synthesised and adapted become as important as knowledge itself.

Teaching, as well as research, is also becoming more heterogeneous. Different approaches to teaching are reflected in different ways of linking with research. Teacher-focused approaches emphasize transmission of research knowledge to a student audience, whereas student-focused approaches emphasize students constructing their own knowledge through active participation in class. It has already been suggested that learning by doing is an effective way for students to benefit from staff research (Gibbs 1998). This is because active learning is more likely to encourage students to adopt a deep approach to learning, than is the transmission model which may encourage a surface approach (Biggs 2003; Brew and Boud 1995b; Prosser and Trigwell 1999). Further evidence comes from the work of Baxter Magolda (1999) and Blackmore and Cousin (2003), who show that students involved in research-based inquiries develop more sophisticated levels of intellectual development. Baxter Magolda sees such research as 'constructive development pedagogy . . . (in which) teachers model the process of constructing knowledge in their disciplines, teach that process to students, and give students opportunities to practice and become proficient at it' (p. 9). Student-focused approaches are possible in all disciplines, but their application varies between individuals and is affected by departmental and institutional cultures.

Discipline cultures also affect the nature of teaching and learning. Although Gibbs (2000) argues that many methods described as discipline-specific are applied widely across disciplines, he admits that generic principles of learning apply with different balances of emphasis in different disciplines. Neumann *et al.* (2002: 405) go further and suggest that there are many 'unremarked similarities and differences' in undergraduate teaching and learning between discipline groups. For example, in the hard pure disciplines they suggest that teaching and learning activities tend to be focused and the emphasis is typically upon the teacher informing the student. Moreover, decisions about teaching content are relatively straightforward and uncontentious and only a limited amount of time is required on course preparation; although where laboratory teaching is used, student contact time is high. In contrast, in the soft pure disciplines, they suggest that teaching and learning activities tend to be largely constructive and interpretive, and that time and care needs to be taken in course preparation. In turn, this preparation comprises a large component of their actual teaching time. Such tendencies in disciplinary differences affect the form of the research–teaching linkage.

Disciplinary spaces and the research–teaching nexus

Just as research can no longer be seen as simply discovering or creating knowledge, and teaching is more than simply transmission of what is already known, there are several different relationships between research and teaching and these vary between disciplinary groups (Colbeck 2004; Robertson and Bond, see Chapter 6). In terms of *subject content*, the linkages are more difficult to enact in the hard disciplines than in the soft ones particularly before the final year of the undergraduate course, because of the more hierarchical and cumulative construction of knowledge in the former. Hence it is more difficult to incorporate the latest research findings in the undergraduate curriculum in, for example, mathematics than it is in, say, history. In contrast, in terms of the *social process* it is more common in many of the hard disciplines for undergraduate students, particularly in their final year, to work with staff as part of a research team than it is in the soft disciplines. Hence undergraduate students are more likely to have opportunities to work as, for example, a research assistant on a research project in a biology laboratory, than to work alongside, say, an English professor interpreting a play. Teamwork also tends to be a more common feature of work in the applied disciplines than in many of the pure ones.

A further factor influencing the nature of research–teaching links is the role of disciplinary and professional associations. These bodies may influence the attitudes of staff and students towards research–teaching links, particularly where they accredit entry into the profession by controlling the curriculum. Webster (2002: 16), for example, refers to professional bodies encouraging 'curriculum creep' in response to the growing complexity of practice and the expansion of knowledge. This, he suggests, can lead to a 'distancing of teaching and research'.

The different disciplinary opportunities to engage in various forms of linking research and teaching may help to explain some of the disciplinary variations in the research–teaching linkage in terms of both staff and student experiences. In an interview study of staff opinions about the mutual influence of research and teaching at Norwegian universities, 67 per cent of academics in humanities, 59 per cent of social scientists, and 47 per cent of natural scientists felt their research had a meaningful impact on their teaching at the undergraduate level (Smeby 1998). This supports the differences between hard and soft disciplines, commented on earlier, in the ease of integrating the latest research findings into teaching. However, in contrast, a pilot workload survey of the time spent by faculty in one university in the United States on activities that integrated teaching and research, found the rank ordering of the discipline groups reversed (humanities 12.9 per cent, social scientists 16.8 per cent, and scientists 18.0 per cent) (Krahenbuhl 1998). These differences in findings need further exploration.

Although an under-researched area, there are indications that the attitudes and motivations of staff and students may vary between disciplines. For example, conflicts may occur in applied subjects between academic and vocational perspectives. In business studies in the UK, for example, Harrington and Booth (2003) report tensions over the role and relevance of research methods courses. They found fundamentally conflicting values, commitments and expectations both between academic staff, and between academic staff and students in 'new' universities, as to whether undergraduates should be developing an appreciation of research. Such conflicts are less likely in pure disciplines; although some students in all disciplines, who are primarily extrinsically motivated and uninterested in communication with staff, appear to be indifferent or have negative attitudes towards research (Breen and Lindsay 1999). Interestingly Breen (2002) found that discipline-specific motivation has a significant influence on student performance. She found from a study of 380 students across eight disciplines in one UK university that:

> student performance is better explained by looking at motivation within the disciplines than across the disciplines because some motivations conflict between the disciplines. For example, students who seek out 'social analytical thinking' activities are likely to perform well in history, but to under-perform in Computing, Geology and Food Science and Nutrition. (p. 40)

Variations in student experience of research are also apparent within the group of applied disciplines. One study found that whereas 43 per cent of students studying leisure, tourism, hospitality and sport in one university had experience of engaging in practical activities or fieldwork based on research and consultancy projects, only 9 per cent of students studying business had this experience (Healey *et al.* 2003). This brings us back to the argument about the benefits for students of active engagement with research.

Reshaping the university

This chapter began with recognizing that difference has characterized the debate about the relationship between research and teaching. Arguably in the twenty-first century, as student diversity increases and institutional missions diverge, a range of approaches to developing the research–teaching nexus, which are sensitive to disciplinary differences, are required. However, the evidence mentioned earlier supports the view that appropriately designed student-centred approaches foster deep learning. Elton (2001a: 43) recognized this when he argued that 'student-centred teaching and learning processes are intrinsically favourable towards a positive nexus, while more traditional teaching methods may at best lead to a positive nexus for the most able students'. This suggests that, although the balance and form might vary, a greater emphasis on engaging students actively with research would enhance research–teaching links and benefit student learning across *all* types of higher education institution. In other words, there is a case for reshaping universities to place greater emphasis on pedagogies which fall in the top half of Figure 5.2.

One type of active learning that focuses on student direct engagement with research is inquiry-based learning, which refers to forms of learning driven by a process of inquiry. Badley (2002: 451) argues for 'seeing both research and teaching as different forms of inquiry'. Recently several authors have called for developing research–teaching linkages in communities of inquiry in which staff and students are 'co-learners' (Le Heron *et al.* 2004) in the process of academic inquiry. Brew (2003: 16) argues that such communities are for all students and are not limited to high-flyers or élite institutions. She sees them as 'a key to the future for a mass higher education system'.

Robertson and Bond (see Chapter 6: pp. 79–91) suggest that higher education consists of 'multiple intersecting communities of inquiry'. Differences between communities are to be expected where they are organized around disciplines for the reasons discussed earlier. Academics also vary as to when they perceive it is an appropriate time for students to be engaged in their disciplinary community. Robertson and Bond found that in the hard disciplines many academics believe that students need to acquire a sufficient basic knowledge before they can contribute. This may restrict the opportunities for undergraduate students to take part in their communities until near the completion of their courses. In contrast, in the soft disciplines they found that academics anticipate that students will occupy a more participative role in their disciplinary community from the beginning.

The idea of inquiry-based learning is not a new one. For example, towards the end of the nineteenth century, Kropotkin (1885: 944) advocated replacing the rote learning method of teaching geography with independent inquiry and discovery-based problem solving. He noted from his own experience 'the rapidity of teaching on the "problems" method is something really astonishing'. Subsequently Stenhouse (1975) argued, in the context of the school curriculum, for an approach to learning and teaching that mimics as closely as possible the actual pattern of inquiry in the discipline being learnt. Much inquiry-based learning draws on ideas from experiential learning theory, which examines how 'knowledge is created through the transformation of experience' (Kolb 1984: 38). Inquiry-based learning provides opportunities for students to engage with a range of different learning experiences and styles, even though disciplines may have preferred learning styles (Healey and Jenkins 2000; Healey *et al.* 2005).

A few institutions are largely organized around inquiry-based learning. For example, at Hampshire College, Amherst, Massachusetts there is a whole institution focus on active inquiry, while at Roskilde University, Denmark, 50 per cent of the curriculum is based around group projects (Jenkins *et al.* 2003: 83–5). More commonly, elements of inquiry-based learning are integrated into programmes, such as through the undergraduate research movement in the United States (Kinkead 2003). Specific discipline examples include geography at Salford University, where the 'Project' took a third of contact hours in years 1 and 2 (Hindle 1993); and arts of citizenship at the University of Michigan, which develops courses in which students combine learning and research with practical projects that enhance community life (Arts of Citizenship 2004).

Although there is much theoretical support for inquiry-based learning, Colbeck (2004: 10) claims that of the various ways that research and teaching may be linked, inquiry-based learning, in the form of problem-based learning (PBL), is the only one

> for which there is systematic empirical evidence of student learning gains. Meta-analyses of the effects of PBL on medical students' learning found that PBL students gained less content knowledge (although they remember what they have learned longer), but gain more in skills and perform more effectively on clinical examinations than students receiving traditional lecture-style instruction.

Discussion and conclusion

This chapter has explored the disciplinary spaces within which the relationships between teaching and research occur. Three arguments have interweaved the chapter. First, it was suggested that some of the controversy about the research–teaching nexus is due to differences in the way the terms 'research' and 'teaching and learning' are used. Generally it is easier to develop the linkages the more acceptable it is to use the terms flexibly to include a wider range of forms. A fourfold typology of different kinds of relationship was suggested based on the extent to which learning is student- or teacher-focused and the extent to which emphasis is placed on research content or research processes and problems. Second, it was argued that disciplines are important for the way in which staff and students experience the research–teaching nexus. Although for some, the boundaries between disciplines are becoming less important, particularly with the growth of interdisciplinarity and Mode 2 knowledge production (Brew 2001), this chapter has indicated that, at least at the level of broad disciplinary groups, there are differences apparent in the way in which research and teaching tends to be conducted. These, in turn, influence the opportunities available for staff and students to link research and teaching (HEA, no date). Third, it was suggested that research-based learning structured around inquiry is one of the most effective ways for students to benefit from the research that occurs in departments. The nature of the inquiry is, in turn, influenced by the disciplinary space in which it is set.

Discipline is, of course, only one factor influencing variability in research–teaching links; others include national context, academic context (institutional type, and departmental practices), and individuals' characteristics (motivations, skills and dispositions). Each of these influences the disciplinary effects on teaching and research relationships (Colbeck 2004).

Most of the international research on linking research and teaching is generic; this chapter has reviewed those pieces that have a specific disciplinary focus. There are wide gaps in this literature. More systematic research is needed into the disciplinary differences (and similarities) in the way linkages are and can be constructed. Some of these studies should be comparative; others should involve detailed case studies within specific disciplines. Identifying the variation in practice *within* disciplines is just as important as analysing the differences *between* disciplines. Exploring and developing the disciplinary spaces in which research and teaching may be linked should be a priority.

Much current practice as to ways of linking research and teaching reflects tradition, but there is considerable variability in approaches *within* subjects. Inquiry-based learning, for example, may be infrequent in some disciplines, and occur at different stages of the curriculum in different disciplines. However, innovation is possible, as is shown by examples such as inquiry-based learning in English eighteenth-century poetry at the University of Manchester (Hutchings and O'Rourke 2001), and the use of research-based assignments in the introductory biosciences course taken by over 450 students at Rutgers, The State University of New Jersey (Devanas 2001).

The Boyer Commission on Educating Undergraduates in the Research University (1999) suggests that research-based learning should be standard and that it should begin with inquiry-based learning in year 1 and end with a 'capstone' experience based around a major project. For their recommendations to be implemented, significant changes in the ways of working and in the power relationships between staff and students would be necessary. More modest shifts in practice, through for example converting selected core modules at different levels in the curriculum, would be a sensible way for many departments to start to explore the benefits of inquiry-based learning and for staff and students to gain experience of working with this form of active learning. Staff and departments will need support in making these changes (Elton 2001a; Elton, see chapter 8). Accompanying these changes, it is essential that systematic research into the impacts of the introduction of inquiry-based learning is undertaken.

Badley (2002: 455) concluded that:

> Most I imagine will continue . . . to see teaching's role as the safer transmission of what is currently thought to be known. However, . . . for the purpose of academic *freedom*, of pedagogical *variety* and of student *growth* towards autonomy, a really useful (and much more stimulating) approach is to regard research and teaching as two different, but overlapping processes of inquiry.

There are many pressures that are pulling research and teaching apart. Barnett (2003: 157), for example, states that 'The twentieth century saw the university change from a site in which teaching and research stood in a reasonably comfortable relationship with each other to one in which they became mutually antagonistic'. Putting greater emphasis on actively engaging students with research, suitably adapted to recognize the variation and complexity of constructing knowledge in different disciplines, is one way of re-linking them in the twenty-first century.

6

Being in the University

Jane Robertson and Carol Bond

A unitary rhetoric

The University's mission [is]: the pursuit of excellence in learning through the advancement of research, scholarship and teaching (University of Manchester, 1997)

Our teaching and learning will be innovative, and invigorated by being informed by a culture of internationally recognised research (Victoria, University of Wellington)

The University will seek to: ... provide curricula that are informed by current research, scholarship, creative works and professional practice ... (University of Sydney, 1998)

These statements were selected randomly from university web-sites on the internet. Their rhetoric will be familiar to those working in higher education. Each statement appears to assume a similar relationship between research and teaching: research 'supports' or 'informs' teaching; teaching exists within an environment of research. Such generality implies something that is socially constructed and historically constituted, perhaps with its roots in Humboldt's notion of the unity of teaching and research. The extracts are institutional statements of intent that are sanctioned by those who count. They imply a given set of practices that are accepted and valued. As such they possess a particular form of power because they provide the lens by which research and teaching and their relation are talked about and judged. Moreover, the very blandness of the statements supports and perpetuates the illusion that research and teaching are related in a singular way.

The lens becomes more focused in New Zealand where the research/ teaching relation is enshrined in legislation. The New Zealand Education Act (1989) states that '[universities'] research and teaching are closely inter-dependent and most of their teaching is done by people who are active in advancing research'. This intention is monitored by the New Zealand Uni-versities Academic Audit Unit. The Unit investigates whether there are pol-icies to encourage a research–teaching link, and establishes whether such policies are effective in achieving the desired link. So most universities in New Zealand reflect the notion of interdependence in their administration and policy documents. For example, the University of Canterbury's[1] Charter (2003–2010: 6) states that 'the University of Canterbury is an institution in which scholarship is valued and where teaching and learning are strongly linked to research'. In response to the 1989 Act, Canterbury's 2000 Audit Portfolio states that 'for Canterbury, a strong relationship between teaching and research has always been a primary element of its culture' (University of Canterbury 2000: 1). The rhetoric is mirrored in other university communi-cations. For instance: 'research must be an essential component of the work of a member of the academic staff of a university and research and teaching are generally strongly coupled. It is well known that good researchers are generally good teachers, providing their time is appropriately proportioned' (Chair, Research Committee, e-mail).

A correlation between 'good research' and 'good teaching' is taken for granted. An extract from a faculty newsletter illustrates how 'interdepend-ence' is interpreted in practice and how the rhetoric is translated into prac-tice: 'the complex inter-relatedness of teaching and research in universities is obviously important in this debate – we must ensure that at every turn the research input to ALL teaching is highlighted and documented' (University of Canterbury 1998).

Not only must research and teaching be linked but the link must be close and visible. Such rhetoric pervades all levels of the university. It provides a set of discursive rules for institutional, departmental and individual academics' practices.

Yet, paradoxically, in most universities, claims of the inseparability of research and teaching are undermined by policies and structures that simul-taneously and perversely promote their fragmentation and position them as competing priorities (Robertson and Bond in press; Colbeck 2004). Given such a disjunction, it is unsurprising that the literature about the research/ teaching nexus is both contested and obscured. For instance, many studies

---

[1] The University of Canterbury is located in Christchurch in the South Island of New Zealand.

exploring the nexus at the level of the individual academic suggest that there is little or no relationship between research and teaching. Others indicate a strong belief in a symbiotic relationship. Variation in our understanding of the meanings attributed to the relation is evident, not only in an apparent contradiction between quantitative and qualitative accounts, but also *within* qualitative accounts (see for example, Jensen 1988; Colbeck 1998; Smeby 1998; Robertson and Bond 2001).

Debate about the relation between teaching and research – a feature of post-World War II higher education – can be traced back to the distinction between Humboldt's 'research' university and Newman's 'teaching-only' university in the nineteenth century. As a result of recent political impera-tives, deriving from assumptions about the relation between economic growth, knowledge economies, and research production, this debate has acquired new vigour and significance. The argument for 'research only' and 'teaching only' institutions is one such imperative. The separation of higher education funding based on research 'outputs' and teaching 'outputs' is another.

The way in which universities and academics understand research and teaching and act on the relation between them is key to their institutional and professional identities. Such understandings and actions comprise the ontological heartland of higher education. However, the research/teaching relation, and hence the accepted basis of that heartland, is under threat. For example, in New Zealand, studies that report 'no relation' or a 'negative relation' between research and teaching have been used to support a pro-posed weakening of the relation (Tertiary Education Advisory Commission 2001). We argue, as have others before us, that the outcomes of such studies are both illusionary and naive – illusionary because they are founded on assumptions of causal relations between variables that are ill defined, and naive in that they ignore the complexity of each of the phenomena involved. The complexity increases incrementally when research and teaching are placed in relation one with the other. Unless further light can be shed on the underlying conditions – the ontological meanings that constitute the field (Bond 2000) of academic experiences – on which this debate is based, further understanding will remain elusive.

Different ways of being

For the reasons outlined above, we sought, in a particular study, to under-stand the underlying conditions of the research–teaching relation – the kinds of knowledges that give meaning to this domain. We interviewed 24 male and female academics of varied experience across a range of discip-lines. We asked about their experiences, not only of research, teaching and the research–teaching relation, but also of learning and knowledge. We developed a picture of the interrelation of research, teaching, learning and knowledge (what we termed the 'experiential field') for each participant, focusing particularly on the metaphors they used. We then looked for similarities and differences across individuals.

The majority of our participants experienced a *close* link between their research and their teaching. What surprised us was the variation in the meaning attributed to this 'closeness' and the extent of cross-disciplinary differences in academics' experiences of the relation. The following descriptions trace this variation in relation to undergraduate teaching. Metaphorical expressions are indicated by the use of single inverted commas.

Teaching and research in weak relation

For participants who see research and teaching as weakly related, *knowledge* is a bounded commodity that is continually being 'added to' through research. Loose pieces of data are 'welded together', there is a need to see how the pieces 'fit' as in a jigsaw. *Research* is a process of 'exploration' and 'discovery' which occurs at the 'frontiers' of knowledge, while undergraduate teaching and learning deals in 'low-level' knowledge. Research, teaching and learning are linked hierarchically in a 'great chain of being'. *Learning* involves acquiring a 'body' of knowledge at one 'level' before 'advancing to the next level'. *Teaching* involves 'transmitting' that body of knowledge and ensuring that students have 'absorbed' it before they 'move on to' the next level. Research at the advanced reaches of the discipline and teaching/learning at undergraduate level are at opposite ends of the ladder or 'staircase' and are essentially unrelated activities. Metaphors emphasize the up/down, hierarchical nature of the *relation*.

Teaching and research as a transmissive relation

In this experience, *knowledge* continues to be viewed as a bounded commodity, constructed hierarchically. However, the process of discovering new knowledge (research) takes on an added dimension. *Research* involves not only 'exploration' and 'discovery' but also the 'construction of pieces into a whole' (the 'foundations' and 'roof' of a building) and, in a closely related metaphor, the solving of a puzzle or completion of a jigsaw by 'fitting together' the pieces. *Learning* continues to involve the acquisition of knowledge from an exterior source, but, in addition, it requires active involvement in solving the puzzle. To this end, *teaching* is not only 'transferring' (and even force-feeding) information/knowledge, but also 'propelling students up the staircase' to a point where they have acquired a sufficient number of pieces of the puzzle and can begin to fit these together with the aid of the teacher. The *relation* between engaging in research and teaching undergraduates is positive in that research involvement in the advanced reaches of knowledge, and teaching involvement at the basic levels of knowledge mutually inform and enrich each other. Teaching is also seen to be 'enlivened/enriched' by research. The relation is still hierarchical but closer than that described by participants who consider research and teaching to be in a weak relation.

Teaching and research as a hybrid relation

In the experience of a hybrid relation, *knowledge* continues to be something 'possessed' but, through this ownership, it can be shared and illuminated from different perspectives. Knowledge is less stable than previously. It can be 'knocked down and improved'. Participants conceptualize *research* in terms of a significant number of different but related metaphors. In addition to metaphors of exploration, construction, puzzle solving and perception, an explicitly affective dimension is introduced. Research has the capacity to 'ignite', 'propel' and generate strong passion. This passion is carried over into *teaching* that, while still involving the transfer of information, also involves engaging students in the excitement of 'finding out'. For the first time, students are invited to share in aspects of the research process and this *learning* involves a degree of risk-taking (making a 'leap of faith'). The up/down orientation of teaching and learning, the hierarchical nature of knowledge, ceases to be a focus. Instead, an important aspect of the *relation* involves inducting students into the research community. Research and teaching are mutually enriching.

Teaching and research in symbiotic relation

In this experience, the way in which *knowledge* is conceptualized undergoes a significant shift. The idea of knowledge as bounded, embodied and possessed disappears and is replaced with something less clearly defined, more permeable, resulting from interaction and 'engagement' with others. Rather than being constructed as a building, knowledge is constructed in a relationship with others. There is greater emphasis on the explorative process (journey) involved in research and less on the discovery (destination). *Research* involves 'making connections' but without the previous emphasis on linking all the pieces together to see the bigger picture. The metaphors constructing *teaching* and *learning* undergo similar changes. The notions of transferring information and 'spoon-feeding' students are contested. Teaching involves construction in the sense of providing a platform (bridge) for students to engage in shared learning. The notion of teacher as host (artist/conductor), someone who brings people and ideas together, who facilitates conversations, introduces strangers, and ensures appropriate conditions for social intercourse, is a new one. Given this environment, the learner is able to engage in an explorative process in the company of the teacher and other learners. The research/teaching *relation* is defined by the desire to involve students in the research community.

Teaching and research in an integrated relation

Although the notion of *knowledge* as a possession lingers in this experience, it is balanced by two powerful metaphors of knowledge as a journey (without a destination) and knowledge as birth/creation. Knowledge is ultimately 'unquantifiable and unknowable'. Engagement with knowledge(s) 'opens a space' for new knowledge to 'emerge', but not as the start of a new material construction. In *research*, the emphasis is on searching rather than finding. *Teaching* involves engaging students with knowledge(s) and preparing them to become independent learners. *Learning* is a transformative process with moments of illumination following complication and resistance. Research and teaching cease to be experienced as independent but related phenomena. Rather they are understood to be inseparable. The process of one is the process of the other. Teachers and students are all learners together.

These experiences and the disciplines in which they predominate are summarized in Table 6.1. What is evident in the table is the significant variation in the meanings that academics attribute to the link between research and teaching. Moreover, it is the meaning attributed to each of the parts that makes up their experience of the relation, that gives meaning to the whole, and vice versa. The parts are internally related in the context of a specific experience and as such cannot legitimately be described separately from that experience. An academic, who experiences the relation as *symbiotic*, reports experiences of knowledge, teaching, and learning that differ from those of one who experiences the link as a *weak* relation. Yet it is also evident that the meanings associated with 'weak' and 'symbiotic' are reflected in the particular notions of knowledge, teaching and learning. Each of the experiences of the relation described has a logical and coherent structure. They show depth and substance. They are also strongly associated with disciplinary knowledge interests.

Our conversations with David (*teaching and research as a transmissive relation*) and Astrid (*teaching and research in an integrated relation*) illustrate these characteristics. At the time of our study, David was a senior academic and prominent researcher in the sciences while Astrid was a mid-career academic positioned at the intersection of the social sciences and humanities. Both were passionate about the relationship between research and teaching in higher education and were prepared to articulate that conviction publicly. The relationship constituted an essential part of their way of being as academics. For example, David described it as a 'symbiotic relationship. There is a strong link between the two'. Astrid challenged the dichotomy of research and teaching, arguing that 'if they are not considered to be so distinct, the question of their "link" becomes less intelligible'. We might conclude, from this shared discourse of symbiosis, that David and Astrid's experiences of the relation were similar.

However, here are the same two voices (metaphors italicized):

Table 6.1 Variation in meanings attributed to aspects of the experiential field (at undergraduate level)

View by Discipline	View of Knowledge	View of Research	View of Teaching	View of Learning	View of the Relation
Weak relation Economics, mathematics	A bounded, constructed commodity added to through research	A process of exploration and discovery	Transmitting a body of knowledge; getting students to think like a '. . . . . ;'	Acquisition of skills and concepts; absorbing a body of facts	Distant (at undergraduate level); hierarchical; great chain of being
Transmissive rtn Chemistry, economics, linguistics, physics, zoology, engineering	An understanding of the world we live in; the sum of the pieces; the bigger picture	Exploration; discovery; the fitting of pieces to form a whole	Imparting knowledge and enthusiasm; distilling essentials; presenting information clearly; conveying how ideas are developed	Memorizing; acquiring skills; linking new information to current knowledge; positioning new knowledge in context of bigger picture	Transmission of research information & experience; engagement in research enlivens and informs teaching; teaching informs research
Hybrid relation Art history, geography, linguistics, plant and microbial sciences, maths	Shared system of concepts and beliefs; no longer absolute; can be contested	Framing questions, seeking answers, creating new knowledge	Passing on research knowledge and skills; modelling; encouraging students to become independent thinkers; induction into process of knowledge creation	Asking and answering questions; knowing more; understanding; interpreting; seeing something in a different way	Relation develops through undergraduate years; modelling a research approach to learning

Table 6.1 (Continued)

View by Discipline	View of Knowledge	View of Research	View of Teaching	View of Learning	View of the Relation
Symbiotic relation Classics, geography, Maori, philosophy	Understanding; constructed in relationship with others; contested; perspectival	Creating new knowledge; constructing alternative interpretations through dialogue; making connections	Working alongside, developing critical thinking and lifelong learning skills; bringing people and ideas together; bridging	A process of exploration in company of teacher & other learners; generating and 'owning' knowledge	Involving students in research community; engaging with students in a process of interpretation and inquiry
Integrated relation Feminist studies, French, history, Maori	A journey; a community construction; an act of engagement with the world: power	Understanding how the world is constructed; making connections; constructing new forms of understanding, new interpretations; learning	Engaging (with) students in research processes of interpretation, de/ constructive critique and inquiry; challenging ways of thinking & seeing the world	Understanding; engaging with the world; thinking differently; changing as a person; transformation	Inseparable— research & teaching are one and the same thing; teachers and students are all learners

What's at stake here is one's understanding of the *foundations* of the *well-laid framework*. You are looking at a *house that's built*, the *foundations of a house that's built* and you ask yourself how did the *builder tie that together*? But *up here* you want to put a *roof on the stables* or something and you realise hey, you could use that technique up there or the technique you see him use can be used back again . . . (David – talking of the research–teaching relation).

. . . knowledge . . . it's not a matter of building up knowledge to get some kind of *positive edifice* that results and we sort of get bigger libraries because we've got more knowledge. We're going to run out of space at the rate that books are produced . . . it's *building, building, building* more, more, more. Um, I see knowledge completely differently. So, it's an *act of engagement*, it's a . . . positive engagement with the world, not in the – positive in the sense of constructing something that becomes ontologically present and transferable (Astrid).

In these quotations, David and Astrid reveal the very different – almost oppositional – epistemological foundations of their academic belief and practice. David uses a construction metaphor (building a house) to illustrate the hierarchical nature of the relation between research and teaching. Research occurs at 'roof' level; undergraduate teaching focuses on the 'foundations'. For David, there is a strong and productive iterative relationship between the two. Astrid, on the other hand, explicitly challenges the construction metaphor – at least in the sense of a built edifice. She talks of seeing knowledge completely differently – as an act of engagement. Research and teaching merge.

David's understandings of teaching and learning are consistent with his belief that research occurs in an elevated space ('frontiers', 'up there') and that knowledge represents '. . . the process by which all the individual *loose pieces of data* are *welded together* into a *coherent view*'. His representations of teaching draw heavily on orientational (across and up/down) and conduit metaphors. For example, the teacher must 'put it across', 'get it through to', 'give them some illustrations', 'get it across to the level of the people involved' and this may involve the teacher 'taking a little bit out' or 'narrowing down' the material. In terms of introducing students to a research culture: 'probably the most efficient way of doing it is not to *give* them research right off, but to give them the *next step in the chain* because after all there's so many *steps in the chain* they have to *go through* before they can really appreciate *in depth* what the research is about.'

In David's discipline, knowledge is generally understood to be cumulative and hierarchical. This understanding shapes conceptions of research, teaching and learning. Metaphors position academic knowledge-making at a great distance from student learning, both spatially and temporally. The 'bringing together' of research and teaching is thus constrained at undergraduate level by the prevailing epistemologies and ontologies. Student engagement in the discipline is delayed.

In contrast, Astrid says of teaching (a term to which she takes exception): 'it's *got nothing to do with me transferring something to them.* It's a process of *challenge* and *engagement* . . . to *assist* a process of them learning to engage in this kind of work.' Learning involves students in knowing 'how to *critically engage* with the various discourses that are constructing that problem . . . and through that process *understand how the world is being constructed*'. For Astrid, knowledge involves a 'clearing away' so that one can 'open a space for action'. The emphasis in teaching and learning is to do with engagement. If we take the word 'engagement' in its broad sense, then we can say that teaching and learning are, metaphorically, about establishing close, positive relationships between student and teacher, student and student and between students and the discourse under scrutiny. Teaching (and learning) as relationship links to the metaphor of knowledge as creation (birth being one possible outcome of a relationship). Students ('who are learners as I am a learner') are invited to engage in the same research process as their teacher. The temporal and spatial dimensions are very different from those alluded to in David's interview. The sense of research taking place 'on high' and at a distance from student learning is no longer viable. Instead of transferring knowledge via a conduit, teacher and students engage in a joint process of knowledge interrogation and even deconstruction.

The architectures of knowledge fields

By perpetuating the 'myth' of a uniformly close relation between research and teaching, the modern university has failed to recognize and capitalize on the complexity and rich variation in experience of the relation. The postmodern university hosts a multiplicity of knowledges, and consequently many different spaces, shapes and chronologies around the research–teaching–learning nexus. In this section, we explore the implications of this plurality for student learning and for academic staff development. We also consider the interior space of the university and the relationship of the parts to the whole.

Table 6.1, and our conversations with Astrid and David show how experiences of research, teaching, learning and knowledge are integral one to the other. These experiences inform each other and make meaning each of the other. Such interrelation both creates and inhabits a coherent architectural space that houses the meaning of what it is to work and 'to be' in higher education. Each of these spaces or 'ways of being' has its own temporal and spatial dynamic. Nowhere is this more clearly revealed than in the process of bringing students into a relationship with a knowledge field.

For instance, one of the key roles of the university is to induct students into a disciplinary (or increasingly an interdisciplinary) community and to facilitate students' participation in that learning community. Lave and Wenger (1991) introduce the idea of learning as a situated activity which has as its central defining characteristic a process they call 'legitimate peripheral participation'. Rather than being seen as an individual act of internalization, learning involves participation – absorbing and being absorbed in a culture of practice. Participation is at first legitimately peripheral, increasing gradually in engagement and complexity. Because all members of the community are learners, all are transformed through their shared interactions.

If we look at the pedagogical concepts common to the experiences of *teaching and research in weak relation* and in a *transmissive relation* through the lens of Lave and Wenger's legitimate peripheral participation, then we can see that some academics *anticipate* a lengthy period of peripherality for students. The emphasis is on the acquisition of reified knowledge rather than on participation. Understanding is necessarily delayed until such time as a sufficient number of 'pieces' have been acquired to put it all together and see 'the bigger picture'. Academics assume a temporal, as well as a spatial, dimension to the act of learning. Some students experience a similar temporal dimension (Thomas 1990; Bond 2000).

In contrast, for academics who experience the relation as *symbiotic* or *integrated*, knowledge does not exist 'out there' waiting to be discovered. Rather, it is socially de/constructed in a dialogic relationship with a scholarly community to which students belong. Students occupy a less peripheral, more participative role in the disciplinary community right from the beginning. There is little or no emphasis on the *structure* of knowledge, much on the *engagement* of students in disciplinary conversations. The experience suggests a context in which knowledge and expertise are less 'authorized', more distributed.

Academics who experience *research and teaching in a hybrid relation* both 'transmit' knowledge and 'engage' students in its construction. However the significant emphasis for 'hybrid relation' participants is on the *modelling* of a research approach to learning. Modelling, it seems, may play a 'transitional' role between 'telling about' (*weak or transmissive relation*) and having students 'participate in' (*symbiotic* or *integrated relation*). Such modelling offers students a glimpse of the research culture of the community prior to their own engagement in disciplinary inquiry. In terms of legitimate peripheral participation, it provides students with an 'observational lookout post' (Lave and Wenger 1991: 95).

We have argued that the interrelation of research, teaching, learning and knowledge is not homogeneous across the campus. The dynamic is shaped differently for different academics and appears to be contingent on understandings of knowledge. This has implications for the practice of 'academic staff development'. As researchers and 'academic developers', our initial response to these findings was to privilege the symbiotic and integrated experiences of the research–teaching relation. We were advocates of an inquiry approach to learning and we favoured teaching that enabled students to engage in an inquiry process from the very beginnings of their university careers. We continually questioned the appropriateness, in this age of supercomplexity (Barnett 2000), of graduating students who may have no understanding of the fluid and of the perspectival nature of knowledge

(Bernstein 1971, 1996). Initially, we were unduly drawn towards dichotomizing and labelling experiences of the research–teaching relation as 'good' or 'bad' in terms of their perceived effect on student learning. We were advocates for a unitary 'space'.

Gradually as we engaged in and reflected on the academics' experiences we came to accept that, in a postmodern world, variation might not only be acceptable but desirable and necessary – that there is a rhythm and pace to learning that is an integral part of the architecture of a discipline; that different disciplinary fields of action possess their own structures and chronologies which largely determine the nature of engagement. The notion of academic experience as an *experiential field* challenges approaches to academic development that focus on – and attempt to change – 'conceptions' of teaching, or learning or of the research–teaching relation. The logical coherence underpinning an academic's work suggests that efforts to influence one component of the experience in isolation from the others are unlikely to be successful in any meaningful way. Instead, the research points to a need for professional development that is embedded in an awareness and understanding of the broader experiential field.

Attempts to homogenize experiences of research and teaching and the research–teaching relation are likely to undermine the integrity of disciplinary epistemologies, and the ways in which students are brought into a relation with particular knowledges. However, there is also evidence that disciplinary boundaries are becoming more blurred (Brew 2003). This growth in interdisciplinarity may well act as a catalyst for interdisciplinary conversations and hence for a heightened awareness of the different ways in which research and teaching can be related. If higher education pedagogy is understood to be grounded in multiple, intersecting communities of inquiry, then the structures of knowledge that determine the nature of those inquiries need to be worked with, explored and challenged. We need to analyse critically what we understand knowledge to be in the different knowledge fields and to engage students in such an analysis. We need to understand the 'what is' in order to apprehend a *possibility of being* (Ricoeur and Thompson 1981). Such a possibility of being can emerge when the significant meanings behind metaphors, symbols and codes are brought to the surface and made available for conscious consideration (Herda 1999).

As a result of this interpretive interaction and consequent 'apprehension', we are in a position to redescribe and refigure our existing world – to begin to change ourselves, and our conditions. This can be achieved not only through an extended process of intradisciplinary reflection and dialogue, but also through ongoing, vigorous interdisciplinary debate. Kögler (1996) recommends that we do not attempt to reconcile difference but that we use the 'other' as a point of departure for critical insight into the self. Through the views of others we can perceive more clearly our own taken-for-granted background of symbolic assumptions and practices. Thus the very existence of and attention to difference has the potential to act as a catalyst for change.

We suggest that academic staff development can and should play a significant role in facilitating such critical reflection and action.

Conclusion: spaces for 'being' – attending to diversity

Austrian architect Adolf Loos conceived of interior space as a cascaded arrangement of individual spaces[2]. Horizontal divisions between individual stories disappeared, rooms led almost imperceptibly to one another, depending on their function and the rhythm of household living. We can think of the university similarly. Each knowledge area has its own function, rhythm and shape – a rationale for the space it defines and inhabits. But such knowledge areas are not and must not be hermetically sealed. Access across knowledge boundaries is critical – both to enable the creation of new knowledges, and to keep open channels of communication that might facilitate greater understanding in an insecure world.

Our aim, in this chapter, has been to engage with the discourses of academics across an institution. Close attention to the voices of individual academics reveals a complex variation in epistemological and ontological belief. This variation, which is ordinarily masked by discourses of 'sameness' has significant pedagogical implications. Moreover such variation and complexity reinforces the notion that the university can no longer be read as a unitary 'community' but must, at the very least, be understood as a heterogeneous and frequently dissensual (Readings 1996) collection of communities.

There is a need to recognize and acknowledge the variation and complexity in experience of the research–teaching relation. There is also need to understand that while, for some academics, there is little experience of a relation at undergraduate level, for many others the relation sits at the heart of their scholarly 'being' and shapes their academic practice in a variety of ways. Attempts to 'legislate for' a closer relation or to sever the relation are likely to cause an ontological crisis for the very people who embody the higher education enterprise. In any discussion about the future of higher education, the issue of what it is 'to be' and 'to know' must take centre stage.

Finally there is a need to find new ways of conceptualizing and talking about the 'research–teaching relation', about the inner character of universities and the relation between the parts and the whole. For example, the notion of interior space and the ways in which the routes between spaces are navigated might be reconceived. We would argue for recognition of the integrity of the parts with their particular spatial and temporal configurations. But we also make a plea, not for unity, but for dialogue that enables the productive co-existence of different ways of being.

---

[2] An example of this cascaded arrangement, accessible to the public, is the Müller Villa in Prague.

7

Intellectual Love and the Link between Teaching and Research

Stephen Rowland

Introduction

'When I recall the teachers that most influenced me, what I remember is their love of the subject, their desire to engage me in their enthusiasm and their sense of the excitement of discovery.' Something along these lines has been said to me many times. So the question – is there a close relationship between teaching and research? – seems to be almost rhetorical when applied to the higher branches of learning. How could one enjoy teaching without being fascinated by the subject and wanting to find out more about it?

Yet when we consider the ways teaching and research are dominated by relationships of power, vested interests and purposes apart from the search for understanding, the question ceases to be rhetorical. It challenges institutions to create and protect spaces for genuinely open enquiry where research or teaching can be mutually enhancing.

That is the conclusion I would like to arrive at. But there is also an opposing perspective: that teaching and research are fundamentally different activities. Research consists in the discovery or creation of new knowledge whereas teaching is the passing on of established understanding. From this point of view, teaching and research may require different kinds of spaces and they may not serve to enhance each other.

The difference between these two perspectives has much to do with how we understand the role of discovery in learning. If discovery is an important aspect of learning, as it is of research, then it could serve to link teaching and research: the space for discovery could be a requirement of each. This is a question of pedagogy. It concerns the relationship between knowledge, the knower and coming-to-know. It is also perhaps the most ancient of unresolved pedagogical problems: does one learn best by discovering or by instruction?

I therefore want to start this exploration by considering this pedagogical problem concerning the roles of discovery and instruction in learning. To do this, I shall give a historical sketch from a few of the many writers who have struggled with this problem since the times of ancient Greece. My references will not be scholarly, or accompanied by critique, but will simply be to inform a conception of enquiry that might provide a link between instruction and discovery, and between teaching and research.

A historical sketch

Plato is perhaps the most well known and earliest exponent of what might be called discovery methods of teaching adults. Writing through the voice of his teacher, Socrates, Plato constructs a number of dialogues between Socrates and an interlocutor, often in the role of student. The Socratic method, as it came to be known, was based upon the teacher posing only critical questions, rather than solutions, and in this fashion leading the student towards a better understanding of the subject in question. Of course, much of Socrates' questioning led his interlocutors to realize the falsity of their assumptions. But realizing the falsity of one's idea – acknowledging one's ignorance – is often a precondition for entertaining a new one. It creates the space for new knowledge. Thus, for Plato, it was through Socratic questioning, rather than through instruction, that new understandings emerge in the adult learner.

This Socratic method (see especially Plato's *Meno*) was based upon Plato's belief that life has a pre-bodily form in which the individual is fully acquainted with knowledge (or the Forms as Plato would have said). It follows that learning – certainly concerning mathematical and moral knowledge, which were the most important aspects of education for Plato – is not so much a matter of teaching as of being reminded, or brought to an awareness, of this innate knowledge. The teacher's task is then to prompt this reminiscence: the learner rediscovers the truth; the truth is, as it were, reborn. The term 'maieutic' (from the Greek *maievtikos*, meaning midwifery) is sometimes used to describe this Socratic method, or 'dialectic', in which innate wisdom is elicited through critical questioning (Levin 1999).

While Plato's ideas about pre-bodily life and innate knowledge seem out of place today, even this brief account has some interesting parallels with modern thinking about learning. Chomsky's idea that the brain is genetically programmed with the ability to learn languages (Chomsky 1983) contains this Platonic idea of innateness which has implications for teaching. Carl Rogers's emphasis upon facilitation and student centredness, as opposed to instruction (Rogers 1969), owes much to the maieutic method of Socrates. And the importance that reflection is currently held to play in learning relates to the Platonic idea that knowledge and understanding are to be gained by questioning and thinking in depth about what we know, rather than by being presented with new facts.

We can thus see Plato's Socratic method as being aimed at discovering, or perhaps more accurately uncovering, the truth, through critical dialogue. This process was essential for learning, according to Plato, whether we conceive of this in terms of students learning from their Socratic teacher, or in terms of the dialectical processes of researcher or thinker at the forefront of knowledge. What we might now think of as pedagogy (as applied to adults) and research methodology would not then have been distinct.

At the same time in Athens there were others, such as Isocrates, who was also a pupil of Socrates, who held a very different view about knowledge and learning. Isocrates was interested not so much in encouraging the learner to discover the truth for themselves as in persuasion or rhetoric. *Rhetoric*, in its original meaning, is a persuasive argument designed to bring an audience over to the speaker's point of view.

The ancient Greek rhetoricians were not so much scholars or academics as lawyers, diplomats and other powerful functionaries. Their 'learners' were often those in positions of political power whom they advised and persuaded through their smooth talk. While their rhetoric might be dialogical (as in a court of law in which different viewpoints compete), its purpose was primarily practical rather than theoretical, and its form competitive rather than reflective or contemplative. The rhetorical approach thus indicates a pedagogy that is quite opposed to Plato's in closing down, rather than opening up, processes of discovery and theoretical understanding. Indeed, Plato's ideas are thought to have developed in reaction to the prominence of rhetoric at the time and in favour of a more dialectical approach.

Again, the present-day context is very different, but we can see how rhetoric also plays an important role in teaching today. Indeed, the university lecture might be seen primarily as a rhetorical device, or a form of instructional method, in which the lecturer persuades the students concerning the subject matter being presented. Taking this further, one might even see the idea of a discipline as being a structure of thinking formulated through rhetorical argument.

There was thus a conflict of views in ancient Greece between those who would emphasize discovery through critical dialogue and those for whom practical needs are best served by instruction through rhetoric. This dispute has many parallels with the more contemporary debates about the value of involving students in discussion rather than lectures.

If we go forward nearly two thousand years to the sixteenth century, we can see a similar debate at the very beginnings of what has come to be termed the Enlightenment, following the break up of Christian unity in Europe. The French writer Montaigne (1533–92) came from a wealthy family where he naturally took on such responsibilities as becoming the mayor of his town at a relatively early age. But in his mid-thirties, Montaigne decided to devote his life to independent study, scholarship and writing. At that time in Europe, formal education was highly structured by scholastic and doctrinaire approaches. Students were expected to learn passages from Roman and ancient Greek texts, translation from Latin and Greek was important in the curriculum, and subjects such as grammar and logic were learnt formally through rules and procedures committed to memory. The Classics had become the subject of drill and conformity rather than enjoyment and enlightenment.

Montaigne reacted against this climate (rather as Plato reacted against the sophists and rhetoricians). In his essay *Of The Education of Young Boys* (Montaigne 1935: 142–78), he puts forward a radically different view in which the curriculum is based upon activity arising from the learner's interests, rather like what are sometimes called 'active learning' and 'problem-based learning' today. His view was that the scholastic forms of education prominent at the time produced students who knew a lot but did not know how to use their knowledge wisely. In sympathy, perhaps, with modern students who have suffered too many lectures, Montaigne says: 'I am not prepared to bash my brains for anything' (de Botton 2001: 157). Learning should be a pleasure for students, he argued. Students should not tolerate boredom and undue prominence should not be given to the difficult texts of dead authors. Montaigne himself quoted widely from classical texts which he loved. He even adorned his library by carving 54 quotations from ancient Roman and Greek writers into its wooden beams (Robertson 1935: xxviii). But he was appalled by the way teaching had become little more than drill and not a way to instil a love of Classics or any other subject.

The theme is taken up in the early eighteenth century, when Jean Jacques Rousseau (1679–1778) argued that education should take place in an environment in which students learn to think for themselves rather than have their teachers do their thinking for them. Teachers should not just hand inherited orthodoxies down to their students. Again, this sounds very much like the kind of criticism that has been made of so-called 'traditional' methods of instruction.

At the turn of the twentieth century, John Dewey (1859–1952) developed the point further, arguing that education should not be the cramped study of other people's learning. He would have been familiar with the caricature of Mr Gradgrind from Charles Dickens' *Hard Times*, a satire of Victorian education a generation earlier, in which the discipline of knowledge was intimately related to the brutal discipline of a rigidly hierarchical society. In contrast, he claimed that education had a democratic purpose.

In this sketch, it is important to acknowledge the philosophical differences between these thinkers: the idealism of Plato, the romanticism of Rousseau, the pragmatism of Dewey. Such differences would be difficult to explain *only* in terms of the place and time of their writing. But underneath – or alongside – these differences is a shared concern to create an environment in which learners have the space to discover knowledge as a result of their own autonomous and critical participation, rather than by being cramped by orthodoxy and didactic instruction. Of course, few would argue that instruction should not play *some* part in learning. Plato, in particular, believed that instruction played an important role in the education of young children. But each of these writers presents the view that the space for discovery needs to be emphasized in the face of a system, or culture, of education that collapses teaching into mere instruction and seems more concerned to discipline thought than to emancipate it.

The relationship between discovery and instruction still presents problems.

It needs to be understood if we are to create kinds of spaces in which teaching and research might productively relate to each other.

Intellectual love and the nature of enquiry

The concept of discovery is too narrow to encompass the richness of the kind of experiences, relationships, attitudes and values that underlie teaching and research in the university. For that, I want to develop a concept of *enquiry* that encompasses and extends beyond discovery and suggest that intellectual love is a key component of the kind of enquiry that forms a basis for both teaching and research.

Enquiry (Latin *quaere verum*, to seek the truth) involves seeking. Pedagogically, perhaps the most important task of the teacher is to develop, among students, an atmosphere or an attitude in which they seek. Jerome Bruner (1966: 142) describes how the teacher, in order to develop such questioning, attempts to 'become part of the student's internal dialogue'. With adults specifically in mind, Radley (1980: 42) describes how this is a symmetrical process in which 'both student and tutor are engaged in a two way process of expressing what they are trying to formulate and grasping those things which the other person is indicating'. Like the Socratic dialogue referred to above, such a reflective dialogical stance leads learners to generate questions and become aware of what they don't know, but need to know. This might lead to an awareness of the need for instruction from a textbook, lecture, demonstration or whatever. Or it may lead to discovery from experimentation or data gathering. Or it may simply lead to further open questioning and enquiry. The important issue here is not so much about whether instruction or discovery best promotes learning, but that *either* should emerge from genuine seeking on the part of the learner, that is, from enquiry.

In this way, the learner's enquiry provides the basis or ground for discovery and the motivation for learning from instruction. Without the questioning arising from the learner's enquiry, discovery is unlikely to emerge and instruction unlikely to be successful.

Similarly, for the researcher, enquiry provides the ground for discovering new knowledge and the motivation for its scholarly dissemination. Such a description of research coincides with Stenhouse's definition: 'systematic enquiry made public' (Stenhouse 1980: 5).

Enquiry is thus a link between teaching and research. Teaching consists of instruction *in the context of enquiry*. Research publication (and other research outcomes) consists of scholarly dissemination *in the context of enquiry*. But what sustains enquiry? Why do researchers, teachers or learners enquire?

A colleague of mine who taught dentistry explained to me how his teaching of dentistry was based upon one aim: to inspire in his students a love of dentistry (Carrotte 1994). As someone who experiences dentistry as little more than a necessary evil, his love of the subject was intriguing. But it was soon clear to me that this was similar to the love that historians, physicists and other academics have expressed and with which I find it easier to identify. This love of the subject characterizes their enquiry, whether that enquiry be directed at discovering new knowledge (research) or becoming more acquainted with what is already known (often referred to as scholarship) or imparting that knowledge to students (teaching).

It is difficult to speak of love. Definitions seem oddly out of place. Sometimes the word seems to mean nothing more than a positive feeling towards its object. At other times, its use appears to be merely an expression of sentiment. Yet it also represents the most significant form of human commitment possible. The significance of the term is highly context dependent. The readiness and passion with which many academics claim that they love their subject, however, demands that we should at least be able to say something about the nature of this love which appears to be central to academic enquiry, rather than to dismiss it as mere sentiment or sloppy use of language. Such love may be an ideal which is often unrealized in practice. But it is helpful to consider the nature of this ideal before exploring its application in practice.

For the rationalist philosopher Spinoza (1632–77), the love of knowledge of God the Creator (*natura naturans*) and God as his creation, Nature (*natura naturata*), was the ultimate human characteristic. It is what brings man closer to God, in Spinoza's terms. This 'intellectual love' might therefore suggest an ideal basis for academic pursuit. As a pantheist, Spinoza believed that everything was an aspect of God: He (as the Creator) cannot be separated from that which He created (Nature). Spinoza's intellectual love combines what modern-day psychologists would call the cognitive and the affective. It is for him the highest form of human happiness (Elwes 1955: xxviii–xxix). Unlike the Puritans at the time, who scorned the passions as being the source of human evil, Spinoza's intellectual love involved both intellectual thought and emotion, or self-motivated passion. Spinoza often distinguishes between those passions in relation to which we are passive (such as lust) from those in relation to which we are active (such as compassion). In fact, the etymology of the terms 'passion' (suggesting passivity and suffering in the face of forces we are unable to control) and 'emotion' (suggesting a motivating force) indicates the distinction being made.

My colleague's love of dentistry was of the latter, active, sort. Indeed, it would have seemed very peculiar if he had said 'I just can't *help* loving dentistry', as one might say 'I just can't help loving cream buns'! Academics may say they are 'passionate' about their subject, but in this context the word no longer carries its earlier association with passivity as implied by Spinoza's distinction. It is, indeed, an active love rather than a passive lust.

For Spinoza, intellectual love is the desire for knowledge of God, understood to be co-extensive with all existence. Thus, the desire to know more about dentistry or physics is, from Spinoza's point of view, a desire to know more about God. Since God is infinite, this search for knowledge is never complete. The more we know, however, the closer we come to Him. And the closer we come to God, the more we become identified with Him and take on His characteristics, in particular, the characteristic of intellectual love. Intellectual love therefore gives rise, in principle, to a virtuous cycle of increasing knowledge of God leading to increasing intellectual love or desire to know more of God.

This ideal conception of intellectual love is useful in the more secular context of this discussion of enquiry and what it is to love one's subject. The object of intellectual love's desire – the subject matter – is never fully known. We may come to know better, but we can never come to know completely; we can find out what we wanted, but this leaves further questions for enquiry, further knowledge desired. Like the love of the lover who always desires greater intimacy with the loved one, so intellectual love always wants a more intimate acquaintance with the subject matter. Intellectual love, like personal love, is thus strengthened, rather than exhausted, by being expressed.

Intellectual love therefore provides an excellent basis for academic enquiry. Unlike other forms of enquiry (such as criminal investigation), it suggests a continuing and developing interest rather than one which becomes exhausted once the initial question has been answered. It might lead to an awareness of what is not known but needs to be known in order to answer one's question, or it may lead to changes of direction and focus of the enquiry as one becomes aware of new aspects of one's ignorance.

An awareness of one's own ignorance, like the realization of one's own error, is perhaps the most crucial moment of learning (as Plato had indicated through his Socratic dialogues). It creates the intellectual space for new knowledge. Whether this is provided by a teacher, a text, or by a colleague, such contributions to understanding are purposeful because they arise to meet the needs identified in the enquiry. Arising from a context of enquiry such contributions to knowledge serve the further development of enquiry.

Those involved in such enquiry (be they teachers with students or collaborating researchers) acknowledge the subject matter's, or discipline's, existence beyond the sphere of their intimacy. The subject therefore always remains open to further interpretation, further questioning and new ways of knowing. Familiarity does not breed contempt but invites new avenues of exploration. Karl Popper's Searchlight Theory of Science adopts this view of the progress of science research as the asking of ever more significant questions. He contrasts this with his Bucket Theory of Science which views research as the cumulative addition of truths (Popper 1979). In relation to teaching, a parallel distinction is made by Paolo Freire (1972), who contrasts a critical or questioning approach to learning with the more traditional 'banking theory of learning'.

In the context of Spinoza's theology, intellectual love is an attribute of God. To the extent that it exists in humans, it is directed towards increasing knowledge of God. It is therefore an open rather than a secretive and jealous love. Translating this into a secular context, intellectual love is inclusive rather than exclusive, it seeks to share rather than hoard. The idea of academics loving their subject but not wanting to share what they know with others would be incongruous. It would not be an instance of intellectual love. It may be an example of what Freud called 'epistemophilia' or Derrida has described as 'archive fever' (Newman 2003): an obsessive-compulsive disorder more akin to lust than love. Of course, many well-known scientists have, like Isaac Newton, been shy people (Gleick 2004) and many do not like talking about their work to large lecture halls of listeners. But it is inconceivable to imagine that, in circumstances and by means of their choosing, they would not want to share their knowledge with others.

I have begun to present a picture of enquiry – motivated by a love of the subject matter – as being at the centre of academic practice. In an academic environment, enquiry is a necessary condition for effective teaching and research. In that way, it suggests a link between them. The more intellectual love is expressed through research, the more it is strengthened. And the more it is strengthened, the greater can be its contribution to teaching. Thus, for our academic dentist, the more his love of dentistry is enhanced by his own enquiries into dentistry, the greater will be the intellectual love which inspires his teaching. This is not to suggest that teachers should teach students their particular specialism, but that their teaching is fuelled by the love that motivates their specialist research.

It does not follow from this that, even under ideal conditions, those who are best able to disseminate the products of their enquiry through publication would necessarily be the same individuals as those who are best able to engage their students in enquiry. Other abilities are involved. Intellectual love is a necessary, but not sufficient, condition for effectiveness in research and teaching. The more it is enhanced, the greater will be the impact upon both.

Reformulating the link between teaching and research

The ideal I have so far presented does not necessarily portray what actually happens in practice. It does, however, provide a framework for interpreting observations and conclusions concerning research and policy into the matter of how teaching and research relate. A much quoted (and often misquoted) conclusion of a meta-review of research into this relationship (Hattie and Marsh 1996) was that there was little correlation between those who are good teachers and those who are good researchers, and that this lack of relationship indicated a problem to be addressed. This research was quoted out of context in the UK government White Paper *The Future of Higher Education* (DfES 2003) which claimed that the lack of correlation *justified* a policy of further separating teaching and research. In fact, as the authors make clear, the finding can equally be used to justify bringing them closer together. Our discussion suggests that research enhances intellectual love to the benefit of teaching.

The lack of correlation between effective teaching and effective research is more likely to be the result of the weakness of a culture of enquiry (in both teaching and research) in higher education. The conclusion of many writers, such as Elton (2001a), Brew (2001) and Boyer (1990), that teaching and research are more closely related when teaching follows an enquiry-based approach, would be consistent with the framework offered here. So also would be the view that the common feature of both research and teaching is that they are both acts of learning (Brew and Boud 1995b), inasmuch as learning can be a form of enquiry.

The strengthening of enquiry in higher education may do something to address the common complaints that many academic staff make that their students are no longer motivated by a love of their subject, and that research output is now driven by the demand to meet assessment. But this presents problems as long as discussions of higher education policy, relating to both teaching and research, are invariably predicated upon the assumption that the purpose of higher education is primarily to increase individual and social economic advantage. Under such extrinsic pressures, the intrinsic value of a love of knowledge, essential to enquiry, inevitably takes second place. Were there to be greater public recognition that 'the primary purpose of education should not be the living that students will earn but the life they will lead' (Halsey *et al.* 1961), then enquiry based on intellectual love might be assured a prominent place.

But intellectual love requires space. Such a relationship with the world is not easily managed. It does not readily submit to technical control and cannot so easily give an account of itself in terms of the kinds of measures that readily translate into the 'league tables' of a competitive market environment. Its value being intrinsic rather than instrumental, intellectual love is a way of being in the world rather than a means of producing outcomes. It is therefore vulnerable to an educational ethos that is increasingly driven by indicators of performance. For that is inclined to misconstrue a love of the subject matter as being inappropriate for a state funded mass, rather than élite, system of higher education.

Charles Clarke MP, the UK Education Secretary, wrote: 'the medieval concept of a community of scholars seeking truth . . . is not (in my view) the most powerful argument for seeking state financial support' (Clarke 2003). The implication of such a statement is that the seeking of truth, and social value, are alternatives between which we have to choose rather than mutually enhancing values. Such a point of view is problematic, especially when the identification of what in fact *is* of social value is not at all clear and appears to be largely led by markets outside democratic control. But for the purpose of our argument, this disparaging of truth-seeking by identifying it with medieval monasticism is a significant indication of the anti-intellectual climate in which spaces for enquiry founded upon intellectual love are difficult to maintain.

If, as I have argued, a culture of enquiry provides a link between teaching and research, then the weakening of enquiry would have a negative impact upon research as well as upon teaching. Has it?

A very strong argument concerning this question was presented to the

Association of University Teachers in UK in 2002. Drawing upon observations of a range of prominent senior academics, this document identified ways in which the audit culture associated with research 'perverts research' and 'obstructs innovation' (Tagg 2002). A central part of its argument was based upon a sociological idea that parallels Heisenberg's uncertainty principle in physics, that is, that the attempt to measure something inevitably changes the value of that which is to be measured. Often referred to as 'Goodhart's Law' – after Charles Goodhart who was, for several years, Chief Adviser to the Bank of England – this states that in business organizations, as soon as the government attempts to regulate any particular set of financial assets, these become unreliable as indicators of economic trends because financial institutions can easily identify new types of financial assets (Goodhart 1984).

According to McIntyre (2001), this same principle applies to the measurement of higher education's 'assets' of teaching and research. In this case, the identification of certain indicators of research value (such as academic publications, research contract income) inevitably leads institutions and individuals to maximize their 'score' on these items, regardless of the consequences elsewhere. Such an approach to audit is likely to show increased measures – be they of research publications and income or factors related to teaching – merely because the actors have become adept at playing the game of maximizing their scores. The real purpose and value of new knowledge created by research is not always readily measurable and so an emphasis on maximizing scores takes attention away from the more important intellectual purposes of research. Thus, they argue, audit 'perverts' research (and teaching).

Such forms of audit characteristically lead to unintended outcomes, as has often been observed. One of these is the elimination of risk that comes about as human action is transformed into technical production (Grundy 1992). A preparedness to take risks is as fundamental a part of the dynamic of intellectual love as it is of personal love. It is through taking risks that greater intimacy can arise, new territories encountered and trust built. In this way, accepted knowledge, understanding and methods can be challenged and disciplinary rigour enhanced. Furthermore, if higher education is to fulfil its economic and social purposes, it must be prepared to take the kinds of risk that necessarily accompany innovation. The risk-averse culture associated with audit stifles innovation and undermines professional trust.

In the context of our discussion of intellectual love, Tagg's use of the term 'perversion' to describe the impact of the culture of audit upon research is apposite. For the perversion of intellectual love implies the prostitution of intellectual endeavour. The love of knowledge is then replaced by a lust for power in the competitive knowledge game. Enhancing the relationships between teaching and research may require us to resist the forms of perversion that infect both.

Conclusion

Our initial problem of exploring the relationships between teaching and research and resolving the tensions between them has transformed into one of attempting to preserve, create, or re-create, the space for enquiry based upon intellectual love. The qualities of such space are an increased acknowledgement of the values of risk, ignorance and trust and a reduced requirement for outcomes measurement, competition and predictability. Such a value position has immediate implications for how we work with colleagues. It will not ensure that good teachers become good researchers, or vice versa, but it will contribute to a culture in which research, teaching and learning can be mutually enhancing.

Part 3

Possibilities for Spaces

Overview

There may be many forces acting on and in the academy that both threaten to drive its central activities – research, scholarship and teaching – apart from each other and are presaging a closing of the spaces that the academy enjoys. Neo-liberalism, the marketization of the functions of the academy, the shift to performativity both in research and its teaching, policy developments (such as research 'selectivity'), competing forms of knowledge production *and* learning opportunities in the wider society, separate and contrasting national evaluation systems for teaching and for research, and the academic community's own conservatism and defensiveness: these are just some of the forces at work that are heralding a closing and a diminution in the spaces that are the university's. Under such circumstances, it is easy to become pessimistic about the possibilities available to the university.

The previous section of this volume, however, has already begun to show that the *present* conditions of the academy are such that there are currently spaces for thinking things anew and doing things afresh. And this is in part the outcome of the new situation in which universities find themselves. The very calling in of the university by the wider society, and its opening itself to new relationships both in its internal disciplines and its external audiences, pulls the university apart. One downside, as we have seen (for instance, in the chapters by Naidoo and Scott), is a splitting apart of research and teaching. The pessimists might say that the university is 'fragmenting'. A more neutral way of depicting the situation, however, might be to say that the university is experiencing a loosening; what has been characteristically a 'loosely-coupled' organization (Clark 1983) is now becoming even looser. This more benign view in turn opens the possibility that, in this greater looseness between its constituent parts, new spaces open up.

This, then, is the task – and, I believe, the achievement – of this last section: to offer some creative ideas, and point to some contemporary practices, that might herald the reshaping of a new university that is educationally and academically fulfilling its possibilities in the twenty-first century.

Injurious as it is crudely to summarize complex stories and arguments, the following are among the ideas and practical possibilities mooted in this section:

• Pedagogic scholarship can build a bridge between research and teaching. A necessary condition for such an aim being brought off, however, is that 'scholarship' be understood and practised as 'learning in a research mode'. Such a view of learning is, by definition, inherent in research itself but it can – and, in some places, is already coming to – characterize teaching as well. (Lewis Elton)

• Doctoral dissertations offer another space where conventions may be challenged and where learning in a research mode can be demonstrated. But to do that seriously implies a challenge to research, not least in its modes of communication; for, as they are currently constituted, theses may not fairly represent the processes of research, which are much less linear and coherent than is typically implied in the format of research-based writings. (Kathleen Nolan)

• Doctoral dissertations are but one part of a complex of activities that help to 'make an academic'; and doctoral work offers another activity that does not have to be bound in by regulatory or performative regimes. 'Faithful love', as a constituent of the pedagogical relationship, can engender new energies, new relationships, new identities and new communities of a positive kind. 'Faithful spaces' can be forged, of an enduring character, even amid the fragmenting nature of the university. (Alison Phipps)

• We may conceive of the university as a theatre and then try to live out the challenges and the possibilities that that idea offers. This stance would be to turn the university into a space in which questions are asked, questions often without sure or single answers, and in which students would accordingly be cast into forging their own resolutions of difficulties. Those offerings might, in turn, come to constitute part of the discursive space (as we might call it) of the university; in short, students could themselves be part of the research community. (Jan Parker)

• The idea of performance has come in for a battering of late: 'performativity' has become a term of abuse, in its implication that educational activities might be structured by considerations of impact and return (especially in the economic sphere). But the ideas of 'performance' and even 'performative' and 'performing' can have more positive connotations: such ideas can point to and urge practices that invite involvement, commitment and energy on the part of the student. (Nolan, Parker, and Phipps)

• Love, of a proper kind, has its place on campus and can energize those who experience it; it can help to create new spaces. (Rowland, Elton, Phipps)

• Research, scholarship and teaching – even if interpreted generously to include consultancy activities – do not exhaust the activities of the university. Space exists for universities to take on a significant 'service' role and that space may even be growing. Or, at least, it is possible that imaginative universities could develop their service role such that the latter came to constitute a vibrant place in the spaces of the university. (Bruce Macfarlane) Such a role, we might additionally observe, would help to develop the university as a provider of public goods (as distinct from the more private goods that 'academic capitalism' (Slaughter and Leslie 1997) is fostering).

- While the creation of new kinds of purposive activity that uphold the traditional values of the academy is, in the first place, a matter for individuals, the academic community also has a collective responsibility in the matter. The level of such collective responsibility tends to be especially low so far as teaching is concerned. Regulation of the academy's activities are characteristically seen as injurious to the academy's interests; but academics, in acting collectively to support and develop the regulatory framework, can help to take the academy forward and supply a measure of independence, even in the context of the large forces now exerting their claims on the academy. (David Dill)
- Community is not given in university life; it has to be worked at; and there are spaces for it to be realized. (Macfarlane, Dill) In particular, the students themselves can form different kinds of community, and can be strengthened in that endeavour where they are supported and encouraged by their tutors. (Parker, Phipps) Furthermore, the more communication there is between tutors, the more likelihood is there of creative things happening in relation to student learning. (Dill)
- In the end, however, creative energies are unlikely to be released unless the value system of the academy is collectively nourished. An academic ethic is not a matter of rules and regulations but has to be lived, and lived collectively. In turn, where the academic community, qua community, is nurtured, there is more likelihood that the really worthwhile and positive innovations will be better known and taken up by others. Once opened, effort has to be put in to support spaces newly opened by initiatives. (Dill) Implications arise, therefore, for management and leadership within universities.

As the chapters in this section testify, there are many examples that can be identified that are testimony to the efforts of individuals, often brave and indomitable efforts and not infrequently of younger or less experienced members of staff, working to effect change. And these may be not just peripheral changes but changes in the way in which the key activities of the university are understood and practised. Through such personal courage, new ways of going on may be forged and new spaces inserted into the university.

8

Scholarship and the Research and Teaching Nexus

Lewis Elton

The findings from the study reported here, illustrate considerable confusion in some academics' thinking concerning the concept of scholarship. This confusion was hitherto absent from the literature and is rarely
taken into account in policy documents. It does not seem unreasonable
to suppose that attempts to redefine the concept noted earlier and/or
to claim the concept for political purposes are a cause of that confusion.
Yet the confusion conception is a strong element of the outcome space
of the data in this study.

(Brew 1999b)

Overview

The starting point of this chapter is the idea that pedagogic scholarship can –
through learning – build a bridge ('nexus') between research and teaching.
However, this idea needs exploring in the light of the different meanings
that have become attached to the concept of 'scholarship' in general. My
concept of it, which is close to the German concept of *Wissenschaft*, is that of
learning in a 'research mode', that is, it should always be questioning and
exploring and never just routine. The potential nexus between research and
teaching is therefore primarily in the common associated processes rather
than their outcomes. However, while researching in a 'research mode' may
be the norm, the same cannot be said about traditional teaching, where – in
order to teach in a 'research mode' – there is a great need to innovate,
including putting students at the centre of the curriculum. Thus, this definition of scholarship itself helps to heighten the potential links between
research and teaching; and it leads to the concept of 'pedagogic love' which
in due course may re-energize universities.

Translating concepts

Brew's observation as to the degree of confusion surrounding the concept of scholarship – at the head of this chapter – forms a suitable starting point for my attempt to clarify the relationship between research, teaching and scholarship. 'Scholarship' does not have a well defined meaning, but it is at the same time crucially important as concept, belief and practice. Scholarship in a discipline constitutes a deep and critical understanding of that discipline and an extensive knowledge of the wider field in which the discipline is embedded. To swear that an academic should do nothing that conflicts with such a conception of scholarship ought to be the academic equivalent of the Hippocratic oath of doctors, although at present there is no professionalism in academic life to parallel the training and education of medical practitioners.

A good starting point for an understanding of scholarship (see also Naidoo here, Chapter 2) is von Humboldt's paper on the future University of Berlin (Humboldt 1810, transl. 1970). While I do not intend to engage in an exegesis of that paper (see for instance Hartwig 2004), it is important to analyse what Humboldt proposed and what later happened in his name. Furthermore, this really ought to be done in German, as Humboldt's dense prose translates only with difficulty. Inevitably, something is 'lost in translation' (Hoffman 1989).

The two Germanic concepts that are most important for an understanding of the Humboldt paper are *Wissenschaft* and *Akademische Freiheit*. The first – *Wissenschaft* – is usually translated as 'scholarship' or 'learning' (and sometimes, quite incorrectly as 'science') in the sense that a scholar is a learned person, but neither is adequate (see e.g. Pritchard 1990), as we are dealing here with the translation of a concept that is deeply embedded in German, but not in British culture. While the English word 'scholarship' is predominantly seen as applying to individual disciplines – an interesting Dutch critique of C. P. Snow's two cultures (Casimir 1973) is relevant – the German *Wissenschaft* is supra-discipline. Also, while the German concept of *Wissenschaft* has acquired over centuries, to some extent, an intuitively agreed meaning within German culture, the opposite is true for the word 'scholarship', which over the past 20 years has acquired a number of current meanings, as was demonstrated by Brew (1999) and will become apparent below.

More generally, it may be observed that English as a language remains Aristotelian, with the law of the excluded middle between thesis and antithesis, while German has moved to Hegelian synthesis. This point can be illustrated in a different – but still educational – context through another German word *Ausbildung* (in French, *formation*) which unites education and training, while in English these two concepts are often treated as opposites. (Exceptions in particular disciplines are medical and legal training.) Later in this chapter, I will use the phrase 'professional development' to correspond to *Ausbildung*.

The second concept, *Akademische Freiheit*, usually translated as 'academic freedom', differs quite basically from the English concept, since the relationship between universities and the State in Germany and the position of students in German universities, both dating back to the Middle Ages (see Cobban, 1990), are radically different from their English counterparts (Pritchard 1998). Thus in Germany, within each university, the concept of academic freedom has always applied as much to students learning (*Lernfreiheit*) as to teachers teaching (*Lehrfreiheit*), while in their relationship to the state, the universities have been represented through their professoriate and not as corporate bodies. In turn, until recently and to some extent still, professors individually were able to exercise – and often abuse – a considerable amount of academic freedom. In parallel, the state developed a mode of support to universities, enshrined now in the Constitution (*Grundgesetz*) (Elton and Lucas 2004), according to which the state is obliged to support universities in their general academic and cultural work.

All this is very different from the situation in the English-speaking world where academic freedom is largely unprotected from financial pressures. Also, the concept of *Lernfreiheit*, including the freedoms for students to switch courses and to fail, is totally foreign in the UK university system which is increasingly tightly controlled, both from within and without. Even the concept of scholarship, that is, *Wissenschaft*, as an essential element of a university was introduced only quite recently, possibly first by Elton (1986a) – although claims regarding priority are dangerous – and extended by Boyer (1990). The latter introduced the idea of scholarships although his (four) scholarships were not disciplinary, but those of discovery, practice, integration and teaching. It is not easy to find a convincing rationale for this list which, in any case, is divisive and, indeed, other additional forms of scholarship have been suggested by others (including Brew (1999) and Elton (2003)). Additional scholarships might include those of judgement (evaluation and assessment) and of management and administration, both of which tend to unify rather than divide. Indeed, this line of thinking could go further and reach the assertion that in a university, all activities should be influenced by scholarship. Here, the word would have regained its German all embracing meaning of *Wissenschaft*.

Finally, I readily concede that I am comparing here the British system as it is with the German system as it might like to be. The realities in the German system fall as far short of its ideals as is the case in Britain, though not in the same way (see e.g. Hunt 2004). But in pursuing Humboldt's ideas we are dealing with ideals and it is from these ideals that we can learn.

Humboldt's central idea

Humboldt's central idea (Humboldt 1970) was that, in both teaching and research, 'universities should treat learning always as consisting of not yet wholly solved problems and hence always in a research mode'. This applies to *both* research and teaching: neither routine research nor school-like *(verschult)* teaching is appropriate in a university context. This idea led to a huge blossoming of research over the next 150 years, but it had less influence on teaching, which continued to consist largely of lectures, teacher-led tutorials and, where appropriate, laboratory classes (respectively *Vorlesung, Seminar* and *Praktikum* in German). However, at its best (Paulsen 1908) the *Seminar*, although teacher led, was significantly different and more adult than the English tutorial.

A real change in the attitude towards teaching has come about only in the past 30 years, and largely in the Anglo-Saxon world, as ideas of scholarship have influenced teaching – Boyer's fourth scholarship – and have led to a scholarship of teaching, learning and assessment. This has resulted increasingly in learning, rather than teaching, becoming central, a shift from teacher-centred to student-centred learning in general (see e.g. Biggs 1999) and such curriculum innovations as problem-based learning in particular (see e.g. Savin-Baden 2000). This last is probably nearest today to Humboldt's ideal of *forschendes Lernen* – or 'learning in a research mode' – and the very different manifestations of it in widely different disciplines illustrate well the importance of the disciplinary component of this and other innovative modes of teaching, noted by Healey in Chapter 5.

What is involved in 'learning in a research mode'?

An essence of research is that it is initiated in the minds of researchers, and in a similar way, learning in a research mode must be initiated in the minds of learners. Such learning is active and questioning in a way that traditional learning, in which learners react in the main to inputs from teachers, rarely is. The vital role of teachers, therefore, consists of a pedagogic understanding of how such questioning learning can be facilitated by them. This is the scholarship of teaching and learning.

I therefore see learning in a research mode as creating in the learner's mind a connection between teaching and research. In parallel, the scholarship of teaching and learning – which consists of a deep and research influenced understanding by the teacher of the student's learning processes – may be seen as the way to bring about that inquiry-led learning by the student. Together, these two parallel processes constitute the essence of the teaching–research nexus.

Other forms of the research–teaching nexus

It must be conceded that Humboldt's prescription of 'learning in a research mode' is not the only one that is generally identified as providing a research–teaching nexus, although it is almost certainly the only one that is internal to the learner and penetrates a whole curriculum. Others are learning about the outcomes of research; and learning to do research.

The first of these latter is of long standing and can be very motivating to students, particularly if the research was carried out by the students' teachers (see Hodgson 1984 on 'vicarious experience'); but it provides the nexus in only the most limited manner. The origin of the second almost certainly lies in the Undergraduate Research Opportunities Program (UROP) at MIT in the USA in the late 1960s, from where it has been imported into Britain, for example, at Imperial College London. At MIT, it was quickly noticed that UROP was inappropriate for most undergraduates in their early years, and in Britain it is confined essentially to project work in the final year. Both these two modes can enhance the teaching–research nexus, but by themselves they cannot create it in the first place. Only 'learning in a research mode' can do that.

Why *forschendes Lernen*?

While Humboldt established *forschendes Lernen* (that is, learning in a research mode) as a principle, he did not give any fundamental justification for it. At school level, such justifications have appeared at intervals throughout the ages, for example by Comenius (Murphy 1995) and Dewey (1917) and it is worth quoting the former (Comenius 1910):

> That the education given shall not be false but real, not superficial but thorough; that is to say, that the rational animal, man, shall be guided, not by the intellects of other men, but his own, shall not merely read the opinion of others and grasp their meaning or commit them to memory and repeat them, but shall himself penetrate to the root of things and acquire the habit of genuinely understanding and making use of what he learns.

It is intriguing to note that in the Slavonic languages – Comenius was Czech – to learn literally means 'to teach oneself', e.g. the Czech for 'to teach' is *uciti* and 'to learn' is *uciti se*. I have to thank Jane Robertson (2004 personal communication) for pointing out to me that in Maori too, the same word, *ako*, covers both.

At university level, Ogborn (1977), in asking 'whether science should not more often be shown as something human beings do, by more active contact with those who do it', may have been the first in Britain to argue for 'learning in a research mode'. What unites all those who aim to find the nexus between teaching and research is an emphasis on experiential learning, starting from where the student is (most teachers claim that they do this but how many really do?) and the centrality of the student in the learning process. In excess, this approach leads to one in which students are expected to rediscover knowledge by themselves, as at times seemed to be attempted in the Nuffield Science approach.

An important aspect of 'starting from where the student is' in the pursuit of 'learning in a research mode' is the recognition that students are normally less sophisticated in their approach to a discipline than their teachers; all good teaching is an act of translation – in this case from the level of the teacher to that of the learner. And as in all translating – in this case not between languages but between levels of sophistication – there is inevitably some loss and some distortion (Elton 2001a). This point needs stressing in the light of much experience that academics, once they are persuaded of the importance of student-centred learning, are liable to conduct it at their own level of learning and not at that of their students. This fault also exists in wholly traditional teaching (see the discussion of Mendeleyev's teaching below), and in general results from teaching that is wholly discipline oriented and lacks a pedagogic understanding.

The need to innovate

The fact that most current university teaching does not start from where the student is, or – at best – only from where the best students are, raises the issue of how far a study of best current practice can provide the evidence to support the existence of a research–teaching nexus. Thus, the experience of problem-based learning and other similar experiences may indicate that in order to turn the hope of the research–teaching nexus in traditional teaching into a reality it is necessary to innovate, that is, not just to use existing methods better, but to use better methods (Elton 2000a).

Both research and common sense indicate that learning in a research mode will take different forms for different disciplines; what can provide a link between them is a concept of 'intellectual love' (see Chapter 7) that underlies the academic's claim to love their subject. Teaching is, however, one of the few verbs in the English language that has two objects – one teaches students a subject. There is therefore a second academic love – of students. Both, I believe, are equally legitimate and the good teacher loves both, in different ways – disciplinary and pedagogic love (Elton 2000b). Although I cannot accept the critique of this view by Rowland (1998), that 'pedagogues become like experts of love who have no lover; or professors who have nothing to profess', his dictum must be a standing warning to all academics who take pedagogy seriously.

Academic traditionalism

That academics, whether in Britain or Germany until very recently and even now, do not take pedagogy seriously is easy to argue but difficult to demonstrate, since research was not possible in a climate in which it has always been accepted as part of academic freedom that nobody observed – let alone intervened in – a colleague's teaching. But although I do not know of any evidence from research into traditional teaching, the fact that it can be very uneven – from marvellous to appalling – has always been known to students, although apparently not to the Quality Assurance Agency. Occasionally it surfaces, for example Tobin (1996), and there is also the supporting testimonial of Lord Ashby (1985), in old age:

> For many years I taught in universities. Like most academics I assumed that the only qualification I needed was expertise in the discipline I taught (which was biology). It did cross my mind that *how to teach* might be a discipline in its own right, but I never gave it much thought. I marked thousands of examination scripts without examining what the scripts could teach me about my capacity as a teacher and examiner.

Professional development

Could this apparent lack of professionalism in the many activities of an academic be a result until recently of the total absence of professional development in any academic activity except research? Even now, academic staff development in the teaching area is largely confined to an initial training at what might be described as craft level, although recent research (Gibbs and Coffey 2004) has shown even this to be significantly better than no training at all, and Alison Phipps (Chapter 10) shows what can be achieved with graduate students. As regards management, the UK's Leadership Foundation for Higher Education, recently established, is unlikely to produce substantial development courses. And yet, universities are prepared to provide professional development for all other professions, as I discovered from an internal circular of University College London headed 'Continuing Professional Development – College Policy': the circular covered the provision of CPD for all professions except the academic one, and not of course for college's own staff.

The absence of self-consciousness among traditional academics regarding their own professional development may also – at least in part – account for the 'myth' of the automatic relationship between research and teaching (which Hughes in Chapter 1 explores as one of several myths). A possible explanation lies in the perception of students who sat at the feet of eminent academic researchers. One such was Mendeleyev, whose apparent teaching excellence was described (*Encyclopedia Britannica* 1929) as follows:

> Mendeleyev was one of the greatest teachers of his time. His lecture room was always thronged with students, 'Many of them', writes one of these, 'I am afraid, could not follow Mendeleyev, but for the few of us who could it was a stimulant to the intellect and a lesson in scientific thinking which must have left deep traces in their development'.

What is apparent from this account is that Mendeleyev, like many 'excellent' university teachers, was successful only with his best students – the future professors. Could the result of this apostolic succession be the dominant feature in the myths that Hughes discusses in Chapter 1, that is, that the mutually beneficial nature of the relationship is effectively automatic? In the last century, one of the outstanding 'excellent' teachers of this kind was Richard Feynman, but he was honest enough to realize and accept that such excellence was in fact a failure (Feynman 1963), quoting Gibbon's dictum that 'the power of instruction is seldom of much efficacy except in those happy dispositions where it is almost superfluous'.

The inescapable conclusion appears to be that the majority of academics consider the presentation of and research in their discipline as the only activities to be treated professionally and it is those activities that constitute their professionalism, while every other activity in which they engage in their university work does not require a professional approach, appropriate to the activity. This does not mean that they do not treat such an activity seriously, but they treat it as amateurs – often in the best sense of that word – and this in turn creates resistances to any suggestion that professional development is appropriate and desirable for any academic activity, except research, in which they engage. This view, which is still prevalent, was probably best expressed in the earlier passage by Ashby (1985).

Continuing professional development (CPD)

Over the past few years, the UK's Institute for Learning and Teaching in Higher Education – now the Higher Education Academy – has convinced both government and universities that academics require an initial training in teaching and this is now a compulsory part of the probationary period for new lecturers in most British universities. Furthermore, although Gibbs and Coffey (2004) have established that it is useful, it must be doubtful as to whether it would be judged to be at university level in comparison with – say – one year of a first degree course, let alone an MA, in either level or length (Elton 2001b). Also, it implicitly assumes that more established academics do not need it. In fact, most of them probably do, as it is rare for academics seriously to reflect on their teaching practice or to have it evaluated. (The statement 'I have taught for twenty years' may be little more than 'I have taught for one year, repeated twenty times'.)

An ongoing problem in academic staff development is the tension between the generic and the discipline-specific in both initial and continuing professional development. Most training courses are predominantly generic, while most resulting practice is discipline-specific. There are, however, ways to overcome this problem. Thus, the current voluntary course at Oxford University follows an action research model, with each course participant linking a generic input to disciplinary practice, including reflective thinking and improvement. This model can be extended to MA level (see e.g. Stefani and Elton 2002) for those who want to be teachers of their fellow academics. An alternative model, first proposed by Elton (1987) and used in the Enterprise in Higher Education Initiative (Wright 1992), is based on the existence of discipline specific and educationally committed staff in Departments working jointly with a central generic unit in the training and development of other academic staff. While in the first model the integration of the generic and discipline-specific is in the mind of individual academics, in the second it results from appropriate organizational arrangements.

Whatever model is used, the development of a scholarly attitude towards teaching and learning leading to a scholarship of teaching and learning must be an essential component of academic staff development. What this should mean is discussed in the final section of this chapter.

Professional excellence and *arête*

Excellence is difficult to define, as Pirsig (1974) found long ago. However, in the end, he discovered it in what the Greeks called *arête*, the outcome of duty towards oneself (see Vassallo 2004). For a profession (Elton 1986b), *arête* is the duty to maintain professional standards and for academia these are in the first place standards of scholarship. However, it also includes standards of duty to those whom it serves, the duty to assess the work of its members and, if necessary, discipline those whose work falls significantly below these standards (matters that the academic profession tends to neglect). None of this would, however, appear strange to the General Medical Council, which has also now recognized that the trust implied by such reliance on professionalism cannot be absolute. However, to replace it by accountability, as is becoming increasingly common in all professions is a counsel of despair (O'Neill 2002): what is needed is what Yorke (1994) has called a 'guarded' trust, which replaces total trust by the guarded kind, in which an audit trail is there for individual instances in which trust appears to fail.

In discussing the concepts of profession and professionalism, it is worth noting here too that they have no simple translation into German. The word *Beruf* applies to both a profession and a trade, and German lacks the class distinction between 'profession' and 'occupation'.

Interpersonal relationships

A consequence of the majority of academics putting love of subject before love of student may indeed result in a more general atrophying in interpersonal relationships. Perhaps there is a limit to a person's ability about what they can be passionate about, but it is significant that most academics at least confine their lack of 'love of student' to undergraduates. They mostly act quite differently in the area of their work where teaching and research integrate most obviously, that is in the supervision of research students, where the relationships are often quite personal.

Sheer numbers may of course make it difficult to extend this interpersonal relationship to undergraduates, but it is worth noting that the balance is different in all other areas of education, where teaching is dominant, that is in school or in adult education. While these areas do not commonly relate directly to research, they do recognize a nexus between the *how* and *what* of teaching and the beneficial influence of keeping the two in balance.

The role of innovation in establishing the teaching–research nexus

Inevitably, research into the possible existence of the relationship of teaching and research had to be based on the improvement of existing practices. However, increasingly it would appear possible that a relationship of the kind characterized by Humboldt's principle of 'learning in a research mode' may at best be tenuous in present practices and that conditions for a strong nexus between them may have to be created. In that case, improvements in existing systems may not produce the nexus. What is then necessary is to innovate, before research into the innovative practice can produce improvement (Elton 2000a).

This is the lesson behind the development of innovative practices, such as enquiry-based learning (Kahn and O'Rourke (eds.) 2003), of which problem-based learning is a special case. These are forms of learning driven by a process of enquiry and not of the accumulation of knowledge. They consequently put Humboldt's principle of learning in a research mode into practice, in a way that had been rarely if ever practised before. What can be learned from this experience is that not all improvements can be made to depend on the evaluation of existing practice; they may require an imaginative leap of the kind inherent in putting a radically new idea into practice in the first place.

The differences between such innovative practices and traditional teaching practices are concerned with all aspects of the curriculum, with the preparation of both teachers and students for such a curriculum and indeed with fundamental epistemological and also ethical differences. This makes it difficult to make direct comparisons between the two. To make this point is important in the current climate of 'evidence-based practice', which compares the relative efficacy of different 'treatments' – in this case of fundamentally different approaches to a curriculum – as if the latter were no more complicated than the replacement of a medicine by a placebo. The jury is therefore likely to be out for a long time.

It must also be conceded that the current improvements have been made largely in order to make teaching more like research, and little if anything has been done to make research more like teaching. We are still at the beginning of a change which makes both into aspects of learning (Brew and Boud 1995a).

Reshaping the university?

Universities on the whole are traditional and yet they can be persuaded to change as circumstances change. However, changes in the past have been in the main structural; changes in academic practices have been much rarer. The change with which this chapter has been concerned has been in learning and in the practice of teaching, through a nexus between teaching and research, based on pedagogic scholarship. The same nexus should influence research (Elton 1986a), but this point has not been discussed. The origin of the change lies in the concept of *Wissenschaft*, as advocated in very different circumstances nearly 200 years ago. Does this concept still have any strength and if so, is it the right concept on which to base the university of the twenty-first century? And is German tradition and experience still relevant? In 1810, universities were for the élite and *Wissenschaft* was an élitist concept. Does it even have relevance to the mass university of today, where students exceed 50 per cent of the population, teaching appears to be largely a matter of preparing students for the job market and research is so specialized that even within a single discipline, researchers may have little to say to each other? Could the same or perhaps a different scholarly basis to both teaching and research provide the enthusiasm that seems to have so much drained away from academia? This latter possibility is perhaps the only feature in universities today on which traditionalists and innovators seem to agree.

I look for scholarship in teaching, in research, and particularly in the nexus of teaching and research to revive the coherence without which universities may die. But what is this 'scholarship'? Does it lie in the concept of 'learning'? It is significant that the question is not at the top of the agenda where *Wissenschaft* has been accepted as fundamental for a long time. Where it is new, as in the Anglo-Saxon countries, let us not kill it by trying to define it; let us instead practise it. The best things in life are beyond detailed definition; after all, who has ever succeeded in defining 'love'?

Acknowledgements

My thanks are due to Lydia Hartwig and Jane Robertson who have stimulated my thinking and to the firm guidance of the Editor who at times seems to have known better what I wanted to say than I did.

9

Publish or Cherish? Performing a Dissertation in/between Research Spaces

Kathleen Nolan

Introduction

At a recent seminar, a colleague returned a copy of my doctoral dissertation exclaiming: 'There's something in it for everyone . . . even my parents enjoyed it!' This colleague had unconsciously placed my dissertation on the coffee table as she took occasional breaks from reading it. During this time, many members of her family picked it up out of curiosity and were initially enticed to read further by colour, photographs, poems, and interesting textual layouts. As they began to read parts of the text, they soon became intrigued by the personal stories of participants, the focus-group newsletters, the visual forms of the text, and several other (re)presentation approaches. While a goal of my dissertation writing was not to produce a coffee table book, I was certainly conscious throughout the research process of my likely audience and my preferred audience. From my perspective, a text speaking in some way to everyone was a far more desirable outcome than a text sitting on a library shelf.

An intention of this chapter is to explore the links between research, learning and knowledge; indeed, to argue for research *as* knowing *as* learning. In doing so, questions relating to the overall purposes of academic educational research are asked and explored. Is there a space for academic research that speaks to everyone? To what extent are research and teaching (and learning) separate but parallel worlds? And, alternatively, to what extent can research reflect the processes of learning?

In addressing these questions, this chapter is written within the context of a recent research project, that is, my doctoral dissertation in education (Nolan 2001). In the research, elementary preservice teachers' experiences of learning mathematics and science were explored in order to understand more about how those experiences have shaped their images of knowing, including what counts as knowledge and what it means to know (in) mathematics and science. My research text introduced and explored several different stories of exclusion from the cultures of mathematics and science, and it does so through a re-presentation of the participants' lived experience narratives as a 'kaleidoscopic text' (Nolan 2001). A kaleidoscopic text can be thought of as a form of 'performative' text, a term frequently employed in arts-based qualitative research (Barone and Eisner 1997).

One of the goals of my dissertation, in exploring how the research participants experienced learning in these subject areas, was to use the kaleidoscopic text to imag(in)e other possibilities for mathematics and science education. My desire was to not only write the research text *about* different ways of learning and knowing (in) mathematics and science but actually to write the research text *through* different ways of learning and knowing. The meaning behind the prepositional choice of 'through' over 'about' highlights the intimate connections between research, learning, and knowledge, proposing a paradigm shift for understanding and realizing the possibilities of a performative text.

---

kaleidoscope

n. [Gr. ? beautiful + ? form + -scope.]
An instrument invented by Sir David Brewster, which contains loose fragments of colored glass, etc., and reflecting surfaces so arranged that changes of position exhibit its contents in an endless variety of beautiful colors and symmetrical forms. It has been much employed in arts of design. (*Webster's Revised Unabridged Dictionary*, 1998)

kaleidoscopic text

... loose fragments of text, images, poems, etc. and reflective pieces so arranged that changes of position (lived experience and perspectives) exhibit its contents in an endless variety of beautiful ways of knowing and understandings. It has been much employed in Nolan (2001).

Learning is a personal journey of change, proceeding in so many directions I cannot be its narrator.

I am instead immersed in an atmosphere of motion, my own thoughts changing even as I write.

In this chapter, I will discuss how my dissertation is performed and how such a performance opens space for rethinking the connections between research and learning. In the discussion that follows, I will move within the themes in the title of this chapter, namely, what it means to *perform a dissertation*, the tensions inherent in performing it *in/between research spaces*, and then finally how the familiar academic expression of 'publish or perish' is more aptly expressed in the context of a performative research text as '*publish or cherish*'.

Performing a dissertation

In the brief story introducing this chapter, the surprise was evident in my colleague's expression that an academic research text could have 'something in it for everyone'. A comment such as this, however, shows that the research can be accessible and meaningful on a personal level. Teaching and learning are common lived experiences. Research on teaching and learning, however, generally remains predominantly in academic circles, where theory and practice struggle to inform each other in meaningful ways.

'Given such an articulation of postmodern textual practice, this text that I have created feels more traditional than not, no radical departure from the tradition it interrogates.'
(Lather, 1991, p. 10)

Research, teaching, and learning are messy and complex processes, yet when one glances through academic journals and books there are few remnants of messiness. If the *processes* are messy and complex, why are the *products* of research almost always in the form of a neat and tidy (often linear) text? Perhaps Code (1991) best responds to this query by claiming that '[c]lean, uncluttered analyses are valued more highly than rich, multifaceted, but messy and ambiguous, narratives' (p. 169).

By deconstructing the legitimacy associated with such neat and tidy presentations, I hope to illuminate the legitimacy of performative text. In doing so, the connections (and disconnections) between research, teaching, and learning will be made explicit through a focus on existing disparities and contradictions. Code's (1991) reference to rich, multi-faceted, messy, and ambiguous narratives provides a good introduction to a purpose for a performative text. I have already alluded to several visual characteristics of a performative text in the introduction – photographs, poems, colour, and layered textual forms. But beyond the visual, what the eye can see at a glance, a performative text also means:

> To personalize
> To act/live/speak in authentic ways
> To attempt to reside in the present in a research text,
> Not to privilege product over process
> To imagine life both inside and outside of the box

Denzin (1997) defines a performance as 'a public act, a way of knowing, a form of embodied interpretation' (p. 185). With regard to the possibilities for performing a research text, Denzin states: 'If performance is interpretation, then performance texts have the ability to criticize and deconstruct taken-for-granted understandings concerning how lived experience is to be represented' (pp. 182–3).

Limited *perFORMance*

Before discussing particular aspects of my dissertation itself, it is critical to look at a few of the issues that presently limit form and performance in research texts. In defining the *art of interpretation*, Denzin (1998: 313) identifies two phases involved in the act of making sense of what has been learned in qualitative inquiry: 1) field to text and *then*, 2) text to reader. Even though Denzin indicates that writing and fieldwork cannot be separated, the division into phases is *not* representative of a complex and reflexive process: 'As a series of written representations, the field-worker's texts flow from the field experience, through intermediate works, to later work, and finally to the research text, which is the public presentation of the ethnographic and narrative experience' (Denzin and Lincoln 2000: 17). This quote is problematic in that it portrays a neat and tidy process. In turn, this process is portrayed as culminating in a final research text that, if constructed successfully, erases all signs of the process itself. The research process (field to text to reader), however, is a performance that should be re-presented in/through the research text. In moving from field to text to reader, the traditional ways of erasing the performance obstruct one's view of the relationships between research and teaching and learning. The movement from *field* to *text* to *reader* in reality blurs boundaries and is not actually *a* movement at all but a space of doubling (Aoki 2000; Nolan 2001). In a doubling space, one does not feel compelled to distinguish *either* field *or* text but, instead, is willing to reside in the ambiguous space of *both* field *and* text. Richardson (1998) describes writing as a way of knowing:

> Although we usually think about writing as a mode of 'telling' about the social world, writing is not just a mopping-up activity at the end of a research project. Writing is also a way of 'knowing' – a method of discovery and analysis. By writing in different ways, we discover new aspects of our topic and our relationship to it. Form and content are inseparable. (p. 345)

In a performance of field to text to reader, there is a critical awareness that meaning cannot be made for someone other than self. A narrative text should provide the reader with opportunities to experience her/his own tensions, instead of the researcher usurping her/his position clearly to delineate the tensions and themes of the research text. 'Narrative accounts are valuable in their insistence that knowledge is a human construct, hence that it is possible to evaluate it better when one understands the construction process' (Code 1991: 172). A brief discussion on constructivism may help to clarify the complex relationship being highlighted between a research text and its interpretation, between the researcher and the reader.

Research and learning as constructivist spaces

Constructivism is 'an epistemological view of knowledge acquisition emphasizing knowledge construction rather than knowledge transmission and the recording of information conveyed by others' (Applefield, Huber, Moallem 2001: 37). In highlighting the connections between constructivist theories of learning and the relationships between research, teaching, and learning, a case can be made to demonstrate that research knowledge is a construction in much the same way as student learning is a construction.

Turn for a moment to the teacher and students within a traditional classroom setting. In this traditional classroom, Bruner (1986) describes 'the process of education as a *transmission* of knowledge and values *by* those who knew more *to* those who knew less and knew it less expertly' (p. 123). Angela Brew (1999) also criticizes such a transmission approach, writing:

> [A] basic assumption of a lecture-based approach is that the one who knows hands over knowledge to those who do not know. The learner is viewed as acquiring a body of knowledge, concepts or information which are assumed to exist externally to them and the lecturer's task is to present such knowledge in as 'objective' a manner as possible. It assumes that by and large the knowledge that is presented (or transmitted) is what the learners acquire. (p. 294)

This traditional model describes learning as a finished product *acquired* by the learner, not as a process; it does not focus on teacher as learner or on students as active participants in the learning process. Is this not analogous to the predominant view of research? In traditional research writing, an effort is made during the transition from *field to text to reader*, to eliminate all the fits and starts, trials and tribulations, thoughts and re-thoughts – in other words, the researcher's own learning. 'The idea that research is the creation or discovery of a body of knowledge which is detached or separated from the people who developed it is . . . still widely assumed' (Brew 1999: 292–3).

We can begin to see, therefore, parallels between constructivism as an epistemological issue in the context of learning in *teaching* and constructivism as an epistemological issue in the context of learning in *research*. Windschitl (2002) describes a constructivist classroom as a place where '[t]eachers make their own thinking processes explicit to learners and encourage students to do the same through dialogue, writing, drawings, or other representations' (p. 137). If, in this description of a constructivist classroom, 'student' is replaced by learner or reader and 'teacher' by researcher, what implications would it have for understanding research as a constructivist space? What would it mean to encourage the reader's construction of knowledge in the text by, for example, offering the researcher's thinking processes by making them explicit in the text? What would it mean for the reader to experience multiple representations throughout the text in the form of dialogue, drawings, poems, reflections? What is amiss with a research text that does not focus solely on transmitting the results, the interpretations, the answers, the knowledge?

From my experience, a researcher constructing a research text (in)formed by such constructivist principles receives criticism that does not differ discernibly from the criticisms that constructivist teachers often endure. As Windschitl (2002) states: 'The very features that make constructivist classrooms so effective also create tensions that complicate the lives of teachers, students, administrators, and parents' (p. 164).

In the public eye, the idea of constructivism suffers the same handicap as previous progressive philosophies because it is often framed as a questionable alternative to what already exists. The status quo is privileged by descriptors such as 'basic', 'fundamental', even 'real'; by contrast, constructivist orientations are marginalized by terms such as 'alternative' or 'experimental'. (Windschitl 2002: 157)

> The very features that make a constructivist research text so effective also create tensions that complicate the lives of researchers, teachers, learners, and positivistic readers.

Brew (1999) connects research and teaching and knowledge by highlighting the link between the 'objectivist assumptions of a traditional lecture-based approach to teaching through transmission and the rational empiricist assumptions of traditional research methodologies' (p. 298). Constructivist connections need not be limited to how the researcher constructs his/her own learning; it is important to acknowledge that the learner is not only the researcher, but also the reader of the research text. In other words:

IF a constructivist view of a learner requires the teacher to view teaching as contextual, learner-centred, negotiated, discursive, and reflexive,
THEN a constructivist view of the *reader as learner* requires the researcher to view researching as contextual, learner-centred, negotiated, discursive, and reflexive.

Brew expresses the relationship between research and learning in a way that aptly corresponds to this constructivist relationship by pointing out that 'learning and research are both conceptualized as processes of constructing knowledge' and researchers should 'recognize the ways in which their activities parallel those of students' (p. 298). In other words, if in fact constructivism takes the emphasis off the teacher and transmission of knowledge and places it on the learner, then a constructivist approach to academic research should take the focus off the researcher and transmission of knowledge and place it on the learner, or reader of the texts arising from that research.

> Turning the text into a display and interaction among perspectives and presenting material rich enough to bear re-analysis in different ways bring the reader into the analysis via a dispersive impulse which fragments univocal authority. Such writing works against the tendency to become the locus of authority; it is writing that probes the blind spots of the interpreters' own conceptualizations and attends to its own constitutive elements. (Lather 1991: 91)

This discourse on performative and constructivist research is closely related to how Barone and Eisner (1997) define arts-based research. According to these authors, arts-based research 'is defined by the presence of aesthetic qualities or design elements that infuse the inquiry and its writing' (Barone and Eisner 1997: 73). They describe arts-based research in terms of seven characteristic features, summarized as follows (pp. 73–83):

- the creation of a virtual reality
- the presence of ambiguity
- the use of expressive language
- the use of contextualized and vernacular language
- the promotion of empathetic understanding
- the use of the personal signature of the author
- the presence of aesthetic form.

As Butler-Kisber (2002) indicates, the heart of arts-based research is in the belief that form mediates understanding and that 'different forms can qualitatively change how we understand phenomena' (p. 231). Polkinghorne (1997) supports this by suggesting that 'researchers need to use a format that can communicate the depth, complexity, and contextuality of their knowledge generation' (p. 13). In addition, Butler-Kisber (2002) indicates that the non-traditional forms of arts-based research 'help disrupt the hegemony inherent in traditional texts and evoke emotional responses that bring the reader/ viewer closer to the work, permitting otherwise silenced voices to be heard' (p. 231). I would also add to this that arts-based, or performative, research highlights how the message is (in) the medium. A performative text has the potential to contribute in meaningful ways to questions relating to ways of knowing, highlighting connections between *what* we know and *how* we know it. In my own dissertation research, I presented the research text *through* (not merely *about*) different ways of knowing (in) mathematics and science. In such a format, the message is not only in the medium, the message IS the medium.

Performative writing, however, is still viewed with a skeptical eye. It is often equated with process writing – writing that many researchers believe should only be part of an author's journal, or at least only in a first draft of a research paper, since the writing has not yet been carefully crafted into a focused, linear text.

Sometimes our field texts are so compelling that as researchers we want to stop and let them speak for themselves. Field texts may consist of inviting, captivating family stories, conversations, and even dream texts. But researchers cannot stop there, because the task is to discover and construct meaning in those texts. Field texts need to be reconstructed as research texts. (Clandinin and Connelly 1998: 170)

Implied in the above quote is the idea that a *field* text is not a *research* text because it is not 'finished'. Disrupting the hegemony associated with traditional texts means that we question the conventions of academic discourse; that we question the legitimacy associated with a linear, typewriter text by opening spaces for a creative (re)presentation of ideas which is more likely to provoke the reader into careful and critical thought.

. . . in/between research spaces

Traditional norms for what it means to construct dissertation (academic research) knowledge are familiar to most and entrenched in academic ideology, with the scientific method still underlying expectations for journal manuscript submissions and academic conference proposals and papers. It is quite possible that we are not ready to embrace the features of arts-based qualitative research (for

> **A *familiar* construction of knowledge?**
>
> Abstract
> Acknowledgements
> Table of Contents
> 1. Introduction & Significance of Study
> 2. A Review of the Literature
> 3. The Research Process
> 4. Discussion of Data
> 5. Conclusions and Recommendations
> References
> Appendices

example, the use of contextualized and vernacular language, the personal signature of the author, and others as cited in Barone and Eisner 1997) when required actually to live them out in the text; in other words, most researchers still write *about* these features rather than *through* them.

Several issues became a major focus in (the defence of) my performative dissertation text and those issues echo Barone and Eisner's (1997) delineated features of arts-based research. The issues can be broadly described as language, linearity, ways of knowing, representation, and legitimation. The problematic nature of each of these issues, as they are lived out through the dissertation research text, elicited many responses from committee members and other readers. These responses are most aptly recalled through a one-word summary question posed by committee members and other readers:

One word sums it up?	
🦗 Language ...	'**colloquial?**'
🦗 Linearity ...	'**dizzy?**'
🦗 Ways of knowing ...	'**answers?**'
🦗 Representation ...	'**colour?**'
🦗 Legitimation ...	'**anything goes?**'

Language . . . colloquial?

Conversations are personal and contextualized.
So is knowledge.
The research text reflects this.

Since the research involved conversations with participants that were personal, contextualized, informal, and accessible, I felt that a representation of the conversations needed to reflect this. Clandinin and Connelly (1998) observe how life and method are inextricably intertwined; that

> **col·lo·qui·al**
> *adj.*
> 1.Characteristic of or appropriate to the spoken language or to writing that seeks the effect of speech; informal.
> 2.Relating to conversation; conversational.
> (*The American Heritage® Dictionary of the English Language*, Fourth Edition)

ways of making sense are always personal and based in experience. Seldom does a researcher deny this, yet it is also seldom that the language and (re)presentation of the text reflects this. The perceived requirement of forcing colloquial language through an academic filter has the effect of erasing important aspects of the conversations. Butler-Kisber (2002) suggests that 'Through accessible language, and a product that promotes empathy and vicarious participation, the potential for positive change in education becomes possible' (p. 229).

the use of contextualized and vernacular language
(Barone & Eisner 1997)

Linearity . . . dizzy?

Thinking and learning are not linear processes.
The research text reflects this.

Engaging a research text is not a linear process; a reader's thoughts continually connect to other thoughts and experiences such that it cannot be mapped on to a flow chart. A comment from one of my committee members about her experience of reading my dissertation (in its kaleidoscopic form) made me aware of how uncomfortable learning could be: 'I'm twisting in circles, dizzy, in fact! This is all very postmodern but how do you connect it with your question – young women and science?!' (Nolan 2001: 64) When I received this feedback, I grappled with the contradictions apparent in how this committee member claimed to be open to different styles of research presentation but, at the same time, conveyed how she wanted a focused and linear text that provided answers. I interpreted her comments to mean that she wanted these answers presented through a more comfortable text, one that did not challenge her to engage with the text at so many different levels that she might get lost. Lather (1997) helps me to articulate hopes for my own research text when she expresses how she wanted to work against such a comfort text and require the reader to work her/his way through the layers of information, occasionally becoming lost across the layers, but eventually finding meaning for themselves (p. 288). She writes about her 'efforts to construct a book where the reader comes to know through discontinuous bits and multiples of the women's stories' (p. 296) but that such a method of 'textual dispersal' became a source of confusion and even frustration for many readers.

We have been well trained, as readers, to expect a linear, tidy narrative that may not fully challenge us to make our own connections within multiple layers of meaning or to risk getting lost in thought and understanding. It is crucial to remember, however, that research is often messy, ambiguous and even twisted at times. In my research, the stories of the participants' experiences of learning mathematics and science convey much discomfort. The stories convey back and forth movements between anger, frustration, hope, and uncertainty. They have jagged and unfinished edges that cannot be smoothed over. They consist of dynamic designs and relationships such that with each turn of the conversation new designs and relationships emerge. My hope for a 'dizzy' text (or, in Lather's (1997) words, a kind of 'rigorous confusion' (p. 301)) is to enable the reader to experience *the kaleidoscope that is learning*, in all its complexity and uncertainty.

Ways of knowing . . . answers?

Education is filled with unanswerable questions.
The research text reflects this.

Many important questions in education are deeply personal, unavoidably political, and frequently without resolution. A research text should reflect the ambiguity inherent in such questions. It is clear from the traditional structures for writing dissertations that a final chapter with conclusions and recommendations – in other

To **know** is *poiesis*, a world in process, a text in the making. (Nolan 2001)

words, 'answers' – is expected. Improving
mathematics and science education is a
complex and problematic issue and, despite

the creation of a virtual reality
(Barone & Eisner 1997)

solutions being proposed throughout educational research literature for
many years, little has changed. Experiences of learning mathematics and
science still appear to leave the learner with the impression that knowing in
mathematics and science means knowing 'answers'.

To legitimize diverse ways of knowing, that we do indeed have knowledge
without answers, I could not maintain the integrity of the research text by
providing 'answers' to the problems facing mathematics and science education (as if there are such answers). The need expressed by my committee
members for purposeful closure (in the form of clear solutions and recommendations) made me ponder how it might be possible to divert attention
from such a familiar expectation for closure and, instead, create spaces for
openings. In an attempt to draw readers out of this expectation and to draw
attention to their perceived need for it, I constructed (colluded?) a final
chapter entitled *Conc(ol)lusions*. In this chapter, I reviewed and reiterated
participant voices as they grappled with some of the critical questions in
mathematics and science education.

While I still feel shadowed by a perceived need for answers, I believe that
writing *through* knowledge-without-answers speaks louder than writing *about*
knowledge-without-answers. The pressure to provide answers in a research
text perpetuates several dangerous assumptions. First of all, it assumes there
are simple answers to complex problems. There is a need to acknowledge
that, instead of simple answers, multiple understandings provide greater
opportunity for change. The expectation of simple answers ignores the
complexity and ambiguity in the to-and-fro movement between text and
reader in the creation of meaning.

A second assumption perpetuated in the search for definitive answers is
that the researcher *knows* the answers and, simultaneously, the reader *does
not*. Hence, the reader needs to be *told* them. In terms of the text-reader
interaction, to assume that the text transmits meaning, rather than guides
and facilitates the construction of meaning, is naive. It removes personal
agency from the reader and assumes that the researcher's construction of
meaning is most meaningful for all. My goal is to construct 'a text whose
significance will not be exhausted by the meaning attributed to it by any one
person' but one that 'elicits differing capacities for understanding, hailing
an audience with ears to hear' (Lather 1996).

From a constructivist perspective, 'the learning environment should represent the natural
complexity of the real world and avoid over-
simplification' (Applefield *et al.* 2001: 49). The

the presence of ambiguity
(Barone & Eisner 1997)

real world of teaching and learning mathematics and science, along with
the real world of understanding and re-presenting *the experiences of* teaching
and learning mathematics and science, is complex and replete with
ambiguity.

Representation . . . colour?

Knowledge is not black or white, right or wrong.
The research text reflects this.

The kaleidoscopic style of performative text used throughout my dissertation requires the reader to step out of the comfort zone of black and white text and into the realm of colour text, images, and pages. The colourful kaleidoscopic pieces are dispersed throughout the text in unpredictable and non-linear ways to jolt the reader into imag(in)ing other ways of knowing (in) mathematics and science. The rationale for colour in the kaleidoscopic research text is, however, more significant than an aesthetic break from black and white text.

WHAT IS THE COLOUR OF THE SKY IN YOUR WORLD? I have always liked this (sarcastic and rhetorical) question as it sends a clear message that what a person is saying or how she/he is acting seems so *out of the ordinary* that she/he must **G**enerally **B**e from a **V**ery different world.

the presence aesthetic form (Barone & Eisner 1997)

Colour is a light metaphor for non-dichotomous thinking, embracing the potential for residing in slash spaces of black / white, right / wrong (answers), knowing / not knowing (Nolan, in press). A constructivist research text enables and encourages the reader to move back and forth between knowing / not knowing, the to-and-fro movement in the slash space that is learning. The to-and-fro movement in the slash space of the black / white metaphor, between total absorption and total reflection of light, is an experience of colour. The light metaphor of colour focuses attention on the spaces between black and white as spaces of partiality, where there is ambiguity and possibility. Thus, the metaphor of colour is full of possibility, and peril, for academic research. On the one hand, the metaphor of a kaleidoscope highlights the possibilities for acknowledging different ways of knowing. As the reader turns things over in her/his mind, the colourful bits and pieces slide about and (re)arrange themselves into new imaginings, for both the topic of the research and the research methodologies. On the other hand, the perils associated with colourful academic research are evident when one encounters the desire of monochromatic researchers to defend their textual traditions.

Legitimation . . . *anything goes?*

There is lived experience.
There is research about lived experience.
A text legitimates itself through its connections between these.
The research text reflects this.

Postmodernity marks the birth of a new aesthetics; one devoid of absolutistic, positivistic, essentialistic notions of justice, peace, community, society, culture and such. The postmodern historical period is much more attune to the incommensurable complexity of life in a social order and being human; that is, the non-linear dimensions of existence, e.g., its ironies, absurdities, inconsistencies, contradictions. (*Dictionary of Critical Sociology*)

To encounter and engage with a text that does not attempt to legitimate itself through the traditional criteria of reliability, validity, and generalizability can be uncomfortable and unfamiliar. But to characterize the text as 'an escape to relativism' is, in my mind, an excuse, emerging out of fear and loss of comfort and familiarity.

One of my committee members, faced with such a loss, made the comment that if this dissertation is successfully defended, then perhaps it means that in a postmodern world, 'anything goes'. Such a comment, coming from a self-proclaimed 'post' researcher, calls to mind an appealing optical metaphor. Sporting glasses with a positivist lens in postmodern frames begs the query: you look good but are you *seeing* differently?

Education in a world so postmodern in nature demands that we clean our lens, if not examine the basis of its appropriateness. What, then, is appropriate? Perhaps the most appropriate lens is that which affords us the richest, most eclectic vision imbued with possibilities and meaning, signifying not only the denseness of context and diversity but also questions, problems, and perhaps even solutions that speak from these very contexts. (Ninnes and Metha 2000: 206)

the promotion of empathetic understanding
(Barone & Eisner 1997)

The reference to context and diversity by Ninnes and Metha, as well as the feature of empathetic understanding proposed by Barone and Eisner, brings me full circle to the comment shared at the opening of this paper, that there is *something in it for everyone*. As Butler-Kisber (2002) reminds us: 'in-depth, context-specific work . . . allows others to take away from the particular what resonates with their experiences and use these understandings to enhance educational practices in other settings' (p. 231). The concept of resonance is central to the notion of *something in it for everyone* because it highlights the possibilities for a narrative research text to resonate in different ways with different reader experiences. It seems both naive and egotistical to believe that an author could possibly predict when and how resonance will take place through the lived experience narratives of the text.

When a researcher constructs and performs text in 'alternative' ways, that is, outside of the box for what is traditional (and perhaps hegemonic) in that field, considerable energy can be expended defending and doubting oneself. Is it (legitimate) knowledge? Is it (academic enough) research? Perhaps this defensive self-questioning of writing practices should take an offensive turn and ask '*why not*'? What legitimacy is associated with the academy holding on to tradition in academic discourse? In holding on to traditional forms of research and representation, what creative possibilities for highlighting connections between *what* we know and *how* we know it are not being explored? In creating research spaces for the presence of arts-based qualities such as ambiguity, aesthetic form and expressive language, the world of published academic research could speak to and for different people. Such spaces could challenge the disconnections between the space to *publish* and the space to *cherish* research text.

Publish or cherish?

In deconstructing the boundaries of language, linearity, ways of knowing, representation, and legitimation in scholarly writing, I have attempted in this chapter to highlight the problematic nature of academic discourse in its rigid compliance with certain norms and traditions for what counts as research and as knowledge. In doing so, I have directed attention toward the connections between the construction of academic research knowledge and the construction of knowledge in, for example, mathematics and science education. The issues discussed in this chapter strive to illuminate the struggles involved in bringing about a shift in thinking about academic research and its (re)presentation – a shift that requires one to acknowledge a different textual performance of research as more than an unfinished field journal filled with 'raw' data and musings of the author. As McWilliam (1997) puts it, 'the issue of whether to embark on a very different sort of textual performance . . . can be a tricky and demanding one' (p. 223).

The choice to create a different textual performance is a tricky and demanding one indeed, given the proverbial academic expression of 'publish or perish'. As a new academic, it is tempting to learn the acceptable traditions and persevere within these expectations rather than embark on a unique journey. Choosing the space to *publish* one's research is, after all, viewed as more rewarding than the space to merely *cherish* one's research.

Publish

v. t. [imp. & p. p. *Published*; p. pr. & vb. n. *Publishing*.] [F. publier, L. publicare, publicatum.

See **Public**, and **-ish**.]

1. To **make public**; to make known to mankind, or to people in general; to divulge, as a private transaction; to promulgate or proclaim, as a law or an edict. (*Webster's Dictionary*, 1998, author's emphasis)

Cherish is the word I use to describe
All the feeling that I have hiding here for you inside
You don't know how many times I've wished that ...

Cherish

Function: verb

Definition: care

Synonyms:

Perish is the word that more than applies
To the hope in my heart each time I realize
That I am not gonna be the one to ...

Cherish, by Nina Simone

admire, adore, appreciate, **clasp**, cling to, coddle, comfort, **defend**, dote on, embrace, **enshrine**, guard, hold dear, hug, idolize, **imagine**, like, love, nourish, nurture, pet, **preserve**, prize, revere, safeguard, shelter, treasure, value, venerate, ... (*Roget's Thesaurus*, 2003, author's emphasis)

Challenging the disconnections between publishing and cherishing scholarly work is not an easy task for a new academic. In terms of my own dissertation, several committee members expressed concern about my future publishing possibilities given the 'alternative' form of my research text. After discussing the merits and possibilities of my dissertation text with my committee, one committee member asked 'What of Kathy's future?' My response was: 'Oh, there are now *some* journals that accept performative educational research text.' Not long after this discussion, I submitted a manuscript to a journal for publication. While there were many comments on the review (relating to both the *message* and the *medium* of the text), I found myself more intrigued by the monochromatic perspectives on the *medium* of textual practices. The text box on p. 135 relays the story as described in Nolan (2001).

Concluding words

To reiterate the initial questions presented in the opening of this chapter: is there a space for academic research that speaks to everyone? How does current educational research *on* teaching and learning reflect the messiness and ambiguities inherent *in* teaching and learning? To what extent are research and teaching (and learning) separate but parallel worlds? And,

PUBLISH		CHERISH
Clearly, you are wise to pursue topics that energize you. Yet **if you hope to publish what you write**, you must **balance** your passion with the passions of the audience. (Moxley 1992: 21)	Do I hope to write what I (can) publish or publish what I write?	Researchers should be sensitive to both the poetics and the politics of knowledge, as well as to the institutionalized gate-keeping arrangements that **preserve traditions** of belief and practice. (Paul and Marfo 2001: 544)
You can be a pro, publish successfully, avoid perishing, and maybe even get some money and satisfaction from your efforts. Many of our fellow academics have done all three. This book will give you information that will help you **stiffen your spine** when you approach publishers, even under tenure-track conditions, and help you get the most you can … (Benjaminson 1992: 18)	If I stiffen my spine when I approach publishers, will I snap under the pressure of stifling pleasure?	It is not more timid or paralyzed performances we need but more adventurous ones. We need adventures that allow us to perform knowing in ways that are **pleasurable** to ourselves and a larger audience of others. (McWilliam 1997: 230)
	Avoid perishing Perish the thought Preserve or transform? Enshrine or challenge? Public or publish? Publish or cherish?	Even as **transformation** in general thinking and attitudes develops more support and adherents, there continue to be resistance to the **challenge** to the existing order, the **comfortable**, existing ways of viewing the world. (Applefield *et al.* 2001: 35–6)
The referencing system in the social sciences discourages the use of footnotes, a place for secondary arguments, novel conjectures, and related ideas … Knowledge is constituted as **focused**, problem (i.e., hypothesis) centered, **linear, straightforward**. Other thoughts are **extraneous**. Inductively reported research is to be reported deductively. (Richardson 1990: 16–17)	My mind wanders, questioning why **focused, linear, and straightforward** text is desirable in research/learning when the topic is **ambiguous, nonlinear, and complex**	Increasingly, educational research suggests that the more **traditional**, textual descriptions of qualitative findings do not adequately reflect the **complexity** of studying human behavior. (Butler-Kisber 2002: 230)

alternatively, to what extent can research reflect and embody the processes of learning? The question of 'publish or cherish?' is a question of both possibility and peril in academic research. I have suggested in this chapter that if learning is highlighted as being the ultimate desire for both research and teaching, then the creative and constructive ways to link research and teaching are obvious. The potential of performative and constructivist research-writing

Inside Research

Two of my colleagues and I recently submitted a paper to a particular journal on women and 'other' minorities, relating to science and engineering fields. I was actually fairly conventional in how I wrote my part of the paper—I left out my poems, my text word art, and most of my other favourite features that I enjoy play/writing with. I included a few minor textual inter-ruptions, as I thought a journal devoted to writing/reading women's voices might be supportive of difference. The reviewer's comments, however, did not *really* surprise me.

A participant quote, written with intentional <Enter>s for poetic effect, rather than one long extended line of words with lifeless voice ...

received the written comment: 'write like all other APA formatted quotes'.

A sentence using parentheses to denote either and/or both as with 'knowing (in) science' ...

was circled as if to suggest that I must have forgotten to carry out the proper spelling and grammar check on this page.

A participant quote inside a lightly shaded text box, to set it apart from those other theoretically validating quotes from people out of context that I don't even know ...

attracted the reviewer's attention as s/he wrote (but did not think) outside the box: 'remove shading'.

So
there I was
writing inside the box of shade
thinking outside the box of their shadows

... and their shadows prevailed.

lies in its ability to highlight the complex nature of knowledge in process. While most would agree that knowledge is always and only in process, there is strong resistance to acknowledging this through performative research-writing – writing that portrays researching and learning as contextual, learner-centred, negotiated, discursive, and reflexive. If 'publish or perish' rests solely on a researcher's ability to produce simple, straightforward solutions to complex questions, presented through neat and tidy packages of research text, then inquiry ceases to be (or, in fact, never had a chance of being) about negotiated meaning or meaningful learning.

Post/Script: The lure (or lore?) of colour

While I live and write and think in colour, I find myself confined, yet again, to the black and white publishing wor(l)d. I shall continue to dream of a kaleidoscopic textual perFORMance.

10

Making Academics: Work in Progress

Alison Phipps

Is there a scholarship that grows as naturally as the lichen?

R. S. Thomas

Lemons and Make-Believe

They have transformed the room. For a moment I think I must be entirely mistaken. This is Room 5. Usually the benches are fixed and raked, sounds echo round a dead space, and the centre passageway is all there is for creating an atmosphere when teaching students. But these students have taken this dead, empty space and all is fairy lights and laughter. Black drapes cover the dusty old blackboard and stars twinkle. Candles burn in jam jars, there are smiling faces welcoming me into the room, pressing me with wine, food, greeting me with mischievous pride. I join colleagues in anticipation and then we take our seats, a little nervous, uncertain as to what to expect. They have managed, through some judicious sweet-talking with the janitors, to move the benches into a semi-circle and make a stage.

And then the stories begin. They have written them themselves. We are taken from saints buried alive on holy islands to the Californian world of a woman called Seldom Sweet. 'I picked up one of the lemons and took a long, slow sniff. The lemon's colour enveloped me. I became yellow, yellow as the sunlight fingering my mother's face. I became tart then sweet then tart again. I was that juicy lemon. It felt so good to *be* something.' We exchange glances, childlike delight replacing our critical habits, relaxation following the bedtime stories. We are all being made and unmade.

How *do* we make academics? This is the question that this chapter sets out to answer. It does so not by dealing with the psychoanalytic dimensions of academic personality, the influences of childhood or the inward identification of the academic pathway. The question here is one posed for ourselves: how do *we* make academics? Of course the answer is quite simple in many ways: *we* do not. The process of making academics is precisely that: a process. And it is one that articulates with numerous, complex factors, interplaying with dreams and desire, ambition and agency, structure, possibility and challenge.

This chapter presents work undertaken with graduate students (in one faculty of a university) in the service of their development as researchers, teachers and scholars. Graduate students are chosen, to this end, as together they represent an aspect of the university in formation. The ways in which they relate, affectively, to the task of being scholars, researchers and teachers enables us to see an aspect of the university in action, one in which future directions for research, teaching and scholarship are tested out. In this respect, graduate students, as well as representing the actuality of the university, also represent and embody our hope for the university of the future.

It is in the starting point of this book that universities are becoming fluid institutions, having differing missions and internal characteristics. Universities are ultimately spaces in which love and the human creative drive may be fostered. Consequently, this chapter takes the ideas of promiscuous love and of faithful love in order to show some of ways in which these spaces for love and creativity may be used. It is also the argument of this book that new, open, less rule-bound spaces may need to be fostered for contemporary universities to continue creating themselves. Their histories, their disciplinary arrangements, the subjects they offer, the research they undertake, the ideologies that underpin their teaching, the patterns of power they institute and the spaces in which their activities and the bodies of their subjects unfold – staff and students alike – all have their bearing on the shaping of the university.

In this regard, we may approach the idea of making academics more generously than an understanding of this enterprise as a career-track, gatekeeping exercise for lecturers might allow. Graduate students do not enter a programme of study devoid of academic being and leave it replete. The making of academics is a more subtle process, one that is uneven and hardly amenable to understandings that may equate 'making' with 'manufacturing'. Academics are not only to be found or made in the institutions of the university. They also people and influence life outwith the university precincts, embodying the fluidity of knowledge that characterizes today's world. Their making, we may also argue, is never done, but is a continuous, creative process.

The dominant discursive space

The Graduate School for Arts and Humanities (GSAH) at the University of Glasgow attracts a large number of students to its taught and research degree courses. As Director of the School for the last eighteen months, I have had the opportunity to engage in the complex processes of helping to create the spaces in which research students also grow as academics. This work takes place in the context of the prevailing conditions of audit, quality assurance and quality enhancement. Under these conditions, we find the external bodies driving graduate education currently placing their faith in the new twin shibboleths of training and skills. The *Set for Success* Review of higher education in the UK, conducted by Sir Gareth Roberts, and the shift to funding council status of the Arts and Humanities Research Council (AHRC) are part of a context in which the way that we go about encouraging and forming academic dispositions in graduate students is placed under a spot-light. Money is pouring in with the aim of improving the quality of the bureaucratizing of training initiatives in higher education, that is to say, in systematizing their audit and assessment. GSAH is, therefore, a space, mod-estly funded (currently an overall operating budget of £5,000), in which some of this work of training 600 graduate students, masters and doctoral candidates, can take place.

The official line taken by the funding bodies, according to their joint state-ment on postgraduate skills (www.ahrc.ac.uk), is that we make academics by attending to the following domains of activity: research skills and techniques, research environment, research management, personal effectiveness, com-munication skills, networking and team working and career management. This list of domains has led to a plethora of courses run within and outwith universities for postgraduate students that seek to train them in each of these skills and with varying degrees of success. Sometimes, as in the UKGRAD 'courses' for students who are funded by the research councils, an intensive week bonding with others while learning to abseil off the side of Great Gable in the Lake District provides a useful pause from the tough worlds of data collection and its analysis. Staff development courses are being opened out to graduate students so that the delights of 'gant charts', tools for training in project management, can be available to all and not just to engineers. Library 'skills courses', 'advanced IT courses', 'equipment handling', and qualitative and quantitative methodology seminars followed up by a session with the Careers Service are now *de rigueur* for graduate students.

The problem with all of these approaches is that they fail to question the dominant discourses of training and skills, and to entertain alternative approaches, in their often anxious rush to implement the latest thing. In other words, the work of making academics, devolved now to trainers, becomes work carried out in the space of an abstracted language of skills and of management. This is what we might term the default discourse – a techni-cist and managerialist view of research that plays to the auditors as audience and 'does training' to the students. 'Discourses' are, as we may note in the words of James Gee 'seeing-doing-being-valuing-believing-combinations': 'Discourses are ways of being in the world; they are forms of life which integrate words, acts, values, beliefs, attitudes, and social identities as well as gestures, glances, body positions, and clothes' (Gee 1989).

In many ways, astoundingly, but also unsurprisingly in a marketized system of higher education, this dominant discourse relies on a banking model of education. Such approaches to education have been the subject of much of critical ink, but despite this we continue to operate *as if* it is indeed the case that learners are empty vessels into which we pour knowledge and which take on particular capabilities. If we *see* student A is struggling to write up his thesis then what we must *do to* student A is send him to *be* on a two-hour workshop on time management. Lo and behold, when we *value* training and skills, we *believe* a fully formed thesis will rapidly appear. It will not.

When subject to the skills discourse, the hard collegial task of making academics is taken out of the domains of teaching, research or scholarship and put into the hands of the management's trainers. These are well intentioned, relatively richly resourced, university people. We know this the minute we set foot in their facilities. They are not academics – or not any longer – and their training sessions will never replace the *scholarly* work of making academics. Graduate students know this, as do academics. This is not to say there are not tasks to be accomplished through training, but it is to say that education and training mix like oil and water. When given the opportunity, graduate students learn much by doing the impossible, retrospectively separating the two.

On the other side of Babel

We are in a hotel board room. The Funding Council has chosen to hold its information and training day on the new criteria for research training and preparation in a four-star hotel. The environment is rather alien to us. We are more used to cramming into offices, the student union and the bars down on Byres Road.

I am particularly nervous. It seemed like a good idea to involve graduate students in this workshop at the time, but to let them run with it completely still feels rather risky. Luckily they don't actually know who they have in here. The name badges may speak to me, but they don't yet mean much to these two high-octane PhD students.

At present these students have professors of French and architecture working alongside creative practitioners and some folk from the Funding Council on an ice-breaker. Three different groups of academics have been given the task of building the highest possible tower out of paper, scissors and sellotape. At varying intervals different groups are being systematically deprived of various resources. One group has to ask quite specifically for every piece of sellotape they require. At the first sign of complaint, the students inform the academics that there are moves afoot to introduce a 30-page form, detailing the applicants 'readiness' for 'tower-building' and their prior experience of such tasks.

I'm sitting on the side lines where I belong and letting them get on with it. It's a game, of course, and, contrary to my worst fears, the academics have entered into the spirit of things and are playing along. And the students are loving it. They are on fire, taking gentle, playful revenge in a world they have just deftly upended, holding the power they have been given responsibly, lightly and with mischief in their eyes.

The towers are built, hung from chandlers and they transform the stilted, plush room. The students begin to draw reflections from the academic staff. They are confident in their task. Their bodies move, question, laugh, nod, encourage, their faces flush with nerves and concentration, their pupils are dilated, they are in full flow. They are good at this, teaching, reflecting, instructing, encouraging, repeating, criticizing, pushing, suggesting, pulling out links to their fields, their own beloved PhD projects, and to the literary worlds they inhabit; 'The best charms are just words. They are easy to carry about and on the whole you don't lose them', they say, quoting Margaret Elphinstone.

The point is well made. The actual connections do not need spelling out, not here, not to this audience, not now. Skills training? *This is the real thing.* This takes the skills discourse and transforms it. This is skilful work done by students who are demonstrating that they are more than capable 'researchers', 'university teachers', 'scholars'. They are academics, made.

At this juncture we might ask ourselves how it is that we have ended up with spaces dominated by the skills discourse and surrendering the work of making academics to trainers? In other words, what is it about university education that means the skills discourse can take root so effortlessly and that resource can be poured into service units and leave scholarship depleted? Whose interests are served by a discourse of transferable skills?

Promiscuous spaces

Once upon a time, undergraduate students came to university with a clear idea of what they were to study, with a limited selection of options for study. They entered into a relationship with a subject – law, divinity, classics, medicine, physics, philosophy – learning to think in the service of the professions, responsibly pursuing knowledge for the sake of society. The range of subjects now on offer to undergraduate students is considerable and the marketization and ideology of choice in the university has led to a decline in some traditional areas of study – chemistry, mathematics and modern languages – as newcomers such as business studies, psychology and media studies have prospered alongside history and English. Within the new spread of subjects is a further level of optionality through stand-alone modules and a system of calculating the total value of a course through the accumulation of credit over the course of a degree. In short, undergraduates learn to move promiscuously between modules, taking up what they fancy for a semester and then moving on, though with certain restrictions.

The metaphor of love may be one which can illuminate something of the changing nature of the spaces and relationships within the university. We may argue, in fact, that the university encourages spaces and relations of 'promiscuous' scholarship. That is to say it promotes the accumulation of learning experiences and sees learning itself as improved as much by the quantity of experiences as by their quality. It does so out of a need to be accountable for its student retention figures and student demographics. Against this, we may ask whether it is possible to create spaces where these are not the only choices of relation and where different modes of loving may take shape.

In his elegiac discussion of the changing nature of the experience of love, Bauman maintains that: 'This sudden abundance and apparent availability of "love experiences" may (and does) feed the conviction that love . . . is a skill to be learned, and that the mastery of the skill grows with the number of experiments and assiduity of exercise' (Bauman 2003: 5). Undergraduate programmes are now largely modelled on this principle. The modularized, semester-length relationships between student and university teacher, module topic, time of day, rooms, buildings and assessments are constantly changing. An undergraduate may study a wide range of different subjects, with a wide variety of tutors, accumulating numbers of experiences that are 'shot through by the a priori awareness of brittleness and brevity' (Bauman 2003: 5). Under such conditions, relations between students as a coherent year-group or class are tenuous and are forged out of assessment necessity or task-oriented group work or problem-based learning, rather than out of a common experience of a subject.

In such environments, the relations of love are superseded by assessable skills and experience, and are of a 'trained incapacity' for loving (Bauman 2003: 5). Universities begin to foster not love as unlearnable radical creativity, growing out of a rare but sustained commitment to discipline, nurture, humility, risk and courage, but rather they market promiscuous love and creative practice, as learnable. Faithfulness to a subject, a department, a teacher, a student body, and even to an institution may ensue but it is not required. Indeed, for successful outcomes to be reached, the seeds of learning are widely sown, often randomly from a whole variety of sources of knowledge, both material and virtual, within the domain of the university and outwith it. The outcome becomes a transaction. The commodity promises wealth, security, employability, skills:

> The promise to learn the art of loving is a (false, deceitful, yet keenly wished to be true) promise to make 'love experience' in the likeness of other commodities, that allure and seduce by brandishing all such features and promise to take the waiting out of wanting, sweat out of effort and effort out of results. (Bauman 2003: 7)

Liquid modernity, Bauman's (2000) term for the conditions that prevail under global conditions of neo-liberal economics, requires flexibility, transferable bodies (not skills), a readiness for mobility. They require people who effortlessly and tidily slip in and out of jobs, with a portfolio of passageways. The last thing that this kind of consumer capitalism needs is rooted subjects, loyality, allegiances. These are the passé marks of the heavier times, times that Bauman sees as characterizing the emergence of modernity. Our lean, mean undergraduate pick-and-mix curricula are part of the new, promiscuous reality.

In the context of doctoral education, however, the unimpeded development of transferable, promiscuous beings encounters a serious obstacle: faithfulness.

Faithful spaces

Graduates at doctoral level move into an environment where the relations I have spoken of are wholly different. Far from picking their partners and spaces for each semester, accumulating experiences and skills that 'will', so the default discourse goes, 'serve them well in their futures' and 'enable them to successfully manage their careers', doctoral students sign up to a lengthy, unpredictable commitment to a subject, supervisors, department, and institution. In short, they are required to exercise considerable faithfulness to process, subject and institution.

It is in doctoral students today that we see the university imagine the future of intellectual work. Through our graduate students, we see how the university can be a creativity-monger and how it can sustain itself in and beyond the present. We see that there is hope, there is new intellectual life and the promise of more people who may continue the crucial work of the university as embodied communication, both within and outwith its precincts. It is like gazing into a crystal ball and seeing the university sustain the work of lingering over hard questions, posed repeatedly through the ages. Such work is both an individual and a collective endeavour. It requires the faithful cultivation of love and the space for the events of love to unfold, by all parties. Without love there can be no energy, no 'adding to the world' (Bauman 2003: 9); there can be no stepping out in faith, no taking of risks, no asking of new questions, no failing and falling, from which may come the energy of recovery.

Such work, such a cultivation of faithfulness and energy that can sustain the full cycle of creative practice can occur even within the structures of modern universities and particularly with doctoral students. Indeed, we might argue that it requires the present structures and highly circumscribed conditions for the kinds of energy and tenacity we have spoken of here, to be released. Conditions of abundance do not necessarily produce excellence, and great work has been produced out of conditions of austerity, repression and anguish in the past as well as from riches and patronage. The stifling nature of excessive bureaucratic control may spawn fresh thinking from the margins, though there is, of course, no recipe, no precise sets of conditions, that can automatically determine results.

Mixing the transferable skills discourse with the active development of faithful love is, to repeat, rather like mixing oil and water. At best, we have an office affair that is doomed to end in tears. To gain a doctorate you have to cultivate tenacity, carefulness, discipline and roots. As part of this cultivation, under the present training conditions, you must bend to the powerful, counter-discourses of liquid modernity. Training and transferable skills will teach you, at one and the same time, how to be promiscuous, how to betray your scholarly learning, cut across the discipline, seek out quick fixes and use the language of consumption in place of education.

Listen now again

It is too dark outside to see the rain. It has been dark for a while now, and the semester has dragged us into oblivion. There is a hush in the old Bridie library, a venerable approval from those hanging on the wall. There is much to hear that has not been heard for centuries, but the dust is being blown from the books, the spines crack invitingly and we hear strange words and songs, a lute, a madrigal and a moment from middle earth.

The students are in charge again. The idea came in conversation, as they so often do, at the end of the last creative enterprise the students put in to practice. 'I want to know what it would sound like if my work was performed' said the student. 'Could we put on an event where we hear work performed that we haven't ever heard before, that usually just languishes in libraries?'

Until now our argument has moved along simply enough; the context of graduate education is one dominated by the skills discourse; undergraduates experiences are ones to which the metaphor of promiscuity may be applied, and that align with the conditions of what Bauman terms liquid modernity. Graduate students inhabit a different space, one in which a considerable degree of faithfulness is required of them and yet one which is now subject to the repeated counter-education of transferability training and skills. We could leave it here but to these positions we may add a further possibility. Might it be possible that destiny is spatially and relationally determined; that differing dispositions for creative action grow out of relationships, and that it is through these very relationships that old spaces may be subverted and new spaces created?

Under this line of argument our question – how we make academics? – becomes a question of the kinds of relationships, exchanges and the kinds of spaces that may foster faithful creative practice, faithful, that is to the practices of academic work. Are the relationships ones between teachers as knowledge producers and learners as knowledge consumers, as often characterizes the undergraduate domain, or is the communication of faithful love and its spatial arrangement of an entirely different order? In short, what do we teach postgraduate students to be and become and how do we create the spaces in which this work may progress?

Trust is an event

The graduate students in GSAH are proud of their achievements. From a single graduate school conference on the theme of magic, they have created a host of creative activities that enable them both to make spaces and to forge relationships with scholarship and as scholars in action.

The first conference led to the development of an on-line, student-run, peer-reviewed journal and in the course of five months the students responsible have edited and published 20 articles and pieces of creative writing and received their first positive review (www.sharp.arts.gla.ac.uk). More conferences, study days, seminar series and workshops have followed as other groups of students have been inspired to follow suit and to make their own academic events happen.

HERO Higher Education & Research Opportunities in the United Kingdom

Webworlds

A trio of treats from the clever end of the World Wide Web

THIS month's pick of the world wide web unearths some treasures . . .

e-sharp

Glasgow University's postgraduate writers have united for a new journal, *e-sharp*, the first issue of which is themed around magic. Thus we are offered the metamorphosis of an elderly woman into a bird, spiritual healing in the Mediterranean and an exploration of Glasgow's own enchanted landscapes.

It's an intriguing collection. Last month's Hypertext contributor Jim Ferguson lends his engaging narrative voice to proceedings, with a James Kellman-esque dose of chaotic reality and desperation. Cathy McSporran takes a considered look at the clash of ideologies between CS Lewis's and Phillip Pullman's epic children's stories, of considerable interest to anyone who has read either author.

The economic cost of this has been negligible – a few glasses of wine and some nibbles to celebrate the launch of the journal, lunch at the conferences, fees for a visiting speaker, and permission from myself to have fun around the edges. T-shirts, badges, logos, postcards, posters, web design, trailblazing cakes and fairy wings have been the outward signs of scholarship in progress and the forging of community.

How has this happened? It has happened by bringing the academic community together in relations of trust and responsibility. Staff and students – and this includes trainers, secretaries, catering staff, janitors and administrators – are given a cleared but defined space in which to make scholarship happen between them. They are given some resource, though it is negligible – £1,000 here, £300 there, £20 for a train fare and some bottles of wine from the GSAH cupboard – and they are reassured that the buck will ultimately stop with me, not with themselves. These activities are in addition to their own individual research projects, though experience is telling us that their projects gain energy from such spaces and relations. Their relationship with myself, as initial creator of this space and provider of resource and relation, becomes one of human, collegiate and scholarly accountability, not of an audit trail.

Communities are places which are discernible by their creative practices, by their entrepreneurialism, by their disagreements and struggles and by their energy. What sustains the process of making academics, we are finding, is a commitment to what the anthropologist Victor Turner terms 'anti-structure' – the playful and deliberate upending of the normal hierarchies and ways of being (Turner 1995). We can make academics if we let them *be* academics in their own ways. To do this requires the turning of the tables, the surrendering of resources, power, control and the establishment of a kind of trust in the human creative process *in* community.

This is countercultural work in that it goes directly against the grain of bolt-on training and skills courses. It is costly, even if it can come on the cheap. For the students to make their own academic networks and communities, for them to explore their own ways of being a nascent university, they need to be enabled to make new spaces out of the very fabric of their relationships. Their own disciplines, knowledge, even the rooms available to them and that shadowy network of extra-university relationships that will give them additional support – all need to be brought into new constellations.

This *can* happen in departments and even, in exceptional cases, where a supervisor works to find ways of bringing her students together into a dynamic relationship that complements the practices of supervision. But for a diverse graduate community to be built, that can find its own ways into making academics, then a structured space is required in which the world may be turned upside down and in which others may rewrite the rules.

And this is what this looks like:

Sleeping in

I 'sleep in' on the e-mail discussion group for the student editorial committee of their journal *e-Sharp*. They know I sleep in and maintain that it helps them take risks to know that I will jump in if there is help or encouragement required. This means I am party to the planning and the ebb and flow of activity, to the despondency and to the delight. The students were getting fed up at the apparent lack of response to their attempts to engage someone to add symbolic weight to their call for papers on the theme of borders and boundaries. And then this dropped into my box:

'BINGO! MEP coming to launch!!!!!!!!!!!!'

Hooray!

PS – if attachment isn't attached, it says 'Mr Miller, MEP, will be delighted to attend.'

Suddenly we had an event on our hands, deans and directors making speeches, and another cheap corner of the university transformed with European flags, data projected presentations and the happy chatter of intellectual talk about magic, trailblazing, borders, boundaries and Buffy.

Review: First Annual Graduate School Conference: Magic

So, how was the conference received? A cornucopia of magical terms is required to describe its delights, its enchanting appeal and its magical effect. Its brilliance reflects that its success was much more than mere illusion. What's more, this was achieved without the use of wands – a truly magical feat! It was a spellbinding conference, thoroughly enjoyed by participants and audiences alike. As to the secret of conference success? Well, as we are all aware, good conference organizers, like good magicians, never reveal their tricks![1]

Review: Second Annual Graduate School Conference: Trailblazing

For this, I think, is what I gained from the conference: the knowledge that trailblazing comes from within. As if to demonstrate this, on the Friday night in the wonderful Tchai Ovna we were treated to free tea and stories by our very own university's creative writing students. Here were trails being blazed live as we listened, privileged. It was a humbling experience for me, so used to the comfort of a time lag between composition and reception, to hear pieces fresh out of the minds of some of our most talented individuals. On the Saturday evening in the Glasgow University Union, listening to the relaxing wind-down entertainment by people who I had met over the two days revealing yet more startling colours, I thought about what we had learnt, and what we had shared. Travelling together in the conference, appreciating trails which had been blazed in both the past and the present, I felt very strongly that as we watch the present slip into the past we should think, and smile, and reflect, and appreciate, and never forget that our own creativeness can light a trail for others to follow – the constant transmission of inspiration with which we as human beings can make our mark on the future.[2]

Community is where community happens

It could be argued that the kinds of happenings that we sponsor and the dispositions and qualities that we are helping to elicit in students, in GSAH, bear the hallmarks of promiscuity discussed earlier. Students who can make such things happen must possess, so this argument would go, flexibility, transferability and a readiness for mobility. However, in their work together on these scholarship events the students are never asked to abandon their roots, to unlearn the rules of their disciplines, to keep piling up new experiences and new skills; quite the opposite. The students coming together become more faithful to their practices of academic work, more selective, more astute, more rooted and confident in their relations, more discerning in their trust and in their choices.

According to Turner, the work of anti-structure, of upending the normal operations of social hierarchy and structure, produces *communitas*. For there to be anti-structure, there has to be a pre-existing experience and awareness of structure. Turner uses the Latin deliberately to make a distinction between the place of common living – community – and modality of a social relationship – *communitas*. *Communitas*, he argues, is an inherently dialectical element of any functioning society. In short, work in relation to both

---

structure and to the upending of this structure – anti-structure. Turner makes it possible to identify certain common characteristics pertaining to *communitas* – as being 'of the now', as being 'with one another', as involving 'the whole man [*sic*] in relation to other whole men' and as enacting potentiality. These are the grand narrative claims he makes for *communitas*, but in its particular GSAH manifestations *communitas* has produced certain interesting local modalities:

- It occurs in drab spaces that have been transformed with simple, colourful materials that mix professional design with quirky carnival
- It is openly entrepreneurial and inventive
- It loves a bargain
- It releases new language and a language of love and of laughter into the academy
- It mixes the creative arts with their critics
- It produces e-mail headings that make us smile, such as : 'Why HTML is evil and other things of note', when technology threatens to fail us
- It expresses emotions when the going gets tough
- It drinks and eats
- Its conversations revolve around food, not training events – its renders the default discourses invisible
- It demonstrates mutual respect and careful pride
- It often clusters around technological possibilities
- It is ambitious for the collectivity
- It 'others' the current batch of academics in order to imagine different futures
- It is open and energetic
- It is hard-nosed
- It gives many gifts

Conclusions

The ways in which academic selves were formed for systems of élite higher education no longer appear to serve the massified systems of today. New ways of relating to the subjects of our research and to those we are given to teach, are required. Research, teaching and scholarship are all present, indirectly, in this graduate school context of *communitas*, and their presence is relational; it is about relations between whole people in the full flow of being academics.

At times in their histories, universities have been relatively stable spaces. At the present time, when buildings, subjects, disciplines and the demographic make-up of those who are participating in the work of a university are in radical flux, then previously stable relationships between these entities are also subject to change. This may or may not be a bad thing and we cannot know with any certainty what the outcome may be of changing relationships. We can, however, look at our graduate students in the university, and see what possibilities are offered for the shaping of new dispositions, new spaces and new relationships.

Making academics remains academic business. Making academics – forming, trusting, relating, creating academic dispositions – remains the work of scholarship, research and teaching, in constant dialogue. In the seminars, through careful, critical commentary on texts, in the long-term relationships we develop with cohorts of research students, we have an eye to gatekeeping processes that will confirm that an academic milestone has been reached. Such milestones require a mutual faith, in students and in examiners, that the academic has grown to be a historian, a biologist, a specialist in the nuances of metaphor and motif in an eighteenth-century text, a speaker of Old Norse. They also require a sense of this academic as a confident, faithful, trustworthy, and capable communicator of complex knowledges inside and outwith the institution.

But in the context of the all-pervasive discourse of transferable skills and research training, in a job such as my own, the question posed at the outset – how do we make academics? – goes beyond the directly academic, epistemological business of making historians, or biologists. It is about a trickier, transitory set of spaces and relations, relations which, I have argued, work between the metaphors of faithfulness and promiscuity and into the modality of *communitas*.

What I have presented here is work in progress and work that is growing as more and more students come in to this network of creative action. It is new work, though its principles are as old as the hills. It is make-shift, it is wheeled out as good practice, as quality-enhanced, even, for auditors and assurers of quality visiting the university. It is also ephemeral, it is an event, relying on being begun again with each new cohort of students. It is work that is 'against skills' as an unthinkingly imposed ideology or that is content simply to adopt a dominant discourse for the sake of conforming to external pressure. It is work that struggles in the current performative conditions. It struggles to give up power, to establish trust and not to work to outcomes. It is a work that sees creative practice as neither promiscuity or faithfulness alone, but as the work of trust. It sees trust as a vital, vibrant, relational way of making academics.

The outcome of trust is known. We have all experienced *communitas* in one way or another. We all know that elusive, pleasurable feeling of creative flow shared one to another. But it is also unknown, in that we cannot write the outcomes for the future, we cannot control creative practice when a wrestling occurs in the interstices of promiscuity and faithfulness. But, as Bauman maintains, neither can love be learned. It needs the stage to be set so that we may trust it to occur as an event.

Apostrophe

Improvisers, he thinks
making do with the gaps
in their knowledge; thousands of years
on the wrong track, consoling
themselves with the view by the way.
Their lives are an experiment
in deception; they increase
their lenses to keep a receding
future in sight. In arid
museums they deplore the sluggishness
of their ascent by the bone
ladder to where they took off
into space-time. They are orbited
about an unstable centre,
punishing their resources
to remain in flight.

There are no journeys,
I tell them. Love turns
on its own axis, as do beauty and truth,
and the wise are they
who in every generation
remain still to assess their nearness
to it by the magnitude of their shadow.
                                R. S. Thomas[3]

Web-sites

www.ahrc.ac.uk
www.gsah.arts.gla.ac.uk
www.sharp.arts.gla.ac.uk
www.hero.ac.uk
Set for Success: http://www.hm-treasury.gov.uk/documents/enterprise_ and
_productivity/research_and_enterprise/ent_res_roberts.cfm

---

[3] Grateful acknowledgement is made to the estate of R. S. Thomas and to J. M. Dent, a division of Orion Publishing Group for permission to quote from 'Fugue for Anne Griffiths' (epigraph) and the closing poem Apostrophe in its entirety (from *Collected Poems 1945–1990*, London: J. M. Dent, 1993).

11

A Mise-en-Scène for the Theatrical University

Jan Parker

> All the world is of course not a stage, but the crucial ways in which it isn't are not easy to specify.
>
> (Erving Goffman 1969: 78)

The university as theatre

The university is currently a place governed by performance. As researchers, teachers and administrators, our performance is measured against indicators (journal publications, impact ratings and external funding for national research assessments, and budget management, access quotas and duty points for our administration). As teachers, we are judged by our students' performances and also by our own: the present widespread system of student course questionnaires will in the UK soon be formalized into national student satisfaction league tables. Terms such as 'performance', 'role', 'scenario' are used throughout a managerialist and functionalist discourse within which the university's academic purpose is defined.

But what might our universities look like if the discourse were that of a different kind of performance, if we saw ourselves, that is to say, as part of a theatrical university? If 'performance' could be dissociated from its modern connotations of [pre]scripted, assessed display and acquire again the rich developmental possibilities inherent in a performance culture: a culture in which character is formed, refined and challenged in all kinds of intellectual and other display? (Goldhill 1999: 1–10)[1]. What might the university become if the discourse of performance were again brought into association with a

---

[1] Greece was such a 'performance culture', where character was developed in performance to seniors and to peers; where intellectual mettle was refined in philosophical and political debate and in the sort of delightful and competitive display of ideas preserved in Plato's dialogues (where even those present at the celebratory

theatrical sense of play and of the trying out of temporary yet transformational roles? If the university were to think of itself as an arena where all
participants in their different ways join in deep meaning-making and the
temporary and yet life-changing experience which theatre provides?

That however would involve a different way of thinking about higher education, not least in that the original site of theatre, that of classical Greece,
was a place of licence, a separate and special space where all kinds of discourse and all kinds of questioning were allowed. Partly for that reason, it was
the place of higher education, the place where citizens individually and collectively could reassess their identity and their place in the world. It was a
protected and temporary space for vicarious and alternative experiences,
where norms and beliefs could safely be revisited and perhaps revalued.

Most of all it was a place for what Winnicott called 'serious play': for
trying on values and experiences that are not, yet affect, the 'real' person
(Winnicott 1974). (In Greece all kinds of theatre, comedy as well as tragedy,
romance as well as the absurd were thought to have a serious educative
purpose in moving the audience for a while away from real, norm-bound
situations and inviting them to imagine something challengingly other.) In
the course of inhabiting and sympathizing with others' experiences, others'
constructions about life and values, those in the theatre also experience
other ways of making meanings: through images, resonances, irony, pathetic
fallacy, *coups de théâtre*, through the play text's dichotomies, belief systems,
narratives of cause and effect, of history and destiny; and through other
rhetorics, other affects than those in play in daily debate and analysis.

The roots of theatre are in ritual – a marked-out place where questions can
be asked of the ancestors and gods, whose extreme acts are restaged in front
of a community/audience who both participate in and expiate the act. Both
act and participation are framed by the questions, doubts and demands of
the chorus who stand between stage and audience. This offers a suggestive
model of the space that students enter when they come to university: first,
that the university offers a special space where they are presented with many
different kinds of narrative and of explanation, with any and every possibility, even extreme ones. Second, a role may be open to students like that of
the chorus: the responsibility to themselves and their community to think
about, experience, engage with, and in some way come to internalize complex explanations; to question, contextualize and finally comment on what
they see for the wider community. And, third, it offers them a performance
space in which, trying on various masks, addressing various communities,

---

drinking party, the Symposium, were expected to give fine rhetorical displays!). The
theatre was an especial extension of the sites of such developmental competition,
where the players' presentations were judged by an active, responsibility-taking audience who judged both issues and dramaturgy, and attendance at which was seen as a
key political and educational activity. Where all character is performed – constructed
while being played out in public – theatrical performance is overtly, generally and
immediately educational and character forming.

they develop and distinguish their own persona in a way only possible in performance.

Simple and single views of the world – of cause and effect, of providence and chance, of good and evil, of things turning out right or wrong – can always be overturned in the theatre, which sometimes creates uncomfortable experiences. Johnson said of Shakespeare's plays that they:

> partake of good and evil, joy and sorrow, mingled with endless variety
> . . . and expressing the course of the world, in which the loss of one is
> the gain of another . . . in which the malignity of one is sometimes
> defeated by the frolic of another; and many mischiefs and many benefits
> are done and hindered without design. (Samuel Johnson 1765: 62)

In such theatre, there are competing models of what is right, what is necessary, what is proper, and what is good. Such competing models are played out to watchers now critically distant, now engaged; now willingly suspending critical judgement, now judgemental.

The theatrical university, therefore, would be one which offered the experience of sometimes disorienting pluralism: of roles, of challenges, of explanatory and evaluatory frameworks. This would be, too, a challenging place, for students, researchers and teachers alike: making demands for engagement with potentially alien identities and thought systems that challenge the stability of identity, of knowledge and of normative values.

Multiple voices, plural narratives

Even to posit such plurality, however, posits also the need for plural and different narratives of higher education. And that is also what the theatre can do – show competing and alternative models for characters to inhabit on stage and off. In Greek tragedy, characters sure of their identity and their place in the scheme of things at the start of the play usually find out that the cosmos is not so simple.

Even to open up such a perspective is to open up a debate about the objectives of higher education; to talk of alternative frameworks is to question disciplinary and domain-specific epistemology; to experiment with ideas of persona and identity to disturb the stability of the role of teaching and of teachers' expertise. The terms of any such debate run against much of the single, prevailing, commodified and quasi-vocational discourse of research, teaching and curriculum planning. Such issues may, therefore, be destabilizing but they call up a longstanding matter: the perceived sterility of knowledge and development of the self in the traditional 'liberal' disciplines which underpin liberal education.

Contemporary narratives of higher education, after all, are usually created by those who prize univocality and a narrowness of ambition and definition – that is justified as 'transparency': in mission statements, institutional marketing, open-day brochures, in assessment criteria, job specifications, academic promotion or dismissal criteria, and research council bids. Plotting a course along prescribed axes of development is advisable for students, researchers and teachers alike – literally so with the growth of the metrics of the academy. (The Pedagogical Academy in Lund University publishes the taxonomy on which it bases criteria for assessing its university teachers' progress along the path laid down from 'excellent' to 'expert' teachers to the top of the tree – 'scholars of teaching'.) The problem with this is not the wish that teachers develop but that they develop along such a narrowly prescribed course and are to be measured according to such a definite yet reductive model of what the central encounter in the university, that of student with teacher, consists of.

Likewise, curriculum design has become dominated by what has been termed as 'the ideology of learning and teaching' (Cameron 2003: 137),[2] that is, simple or simplistic ideas of progression and learning outcomes that reduce the educational encounter to a two-dimensional exchange of goods and services. Meanwhile, a discourse of professionalism and training, of expertise and competence pervades university practice. Here, too, we encounter a univocality of narratives, narrowly constraining as they construct the identity of teachers and taught, the multifacets of researcher and researched.

Race track or theatre?

Learning how to live with and cope with complex interpretations or explanatory models – ones that cannot be reduced to a linear explanation or valuation, a simple dichotomy or polarity but need to be complexly responded to, reflected on and engaged with – is the essence of higher education. Or so the Greeks would have thought: the youth trained mind and body for the race track and gymnasium and for war, *and* for the symposium. But higher education was about trying out identity and learning what it was to be human; and the place of education was the theatre.

Today, however, we have taken the racetrack as our model for the modern university; literally so, for that is what 'curriculum' means. We naturally talk of students as 'following a course', of their 'progression' and even, sinisterly, of their 'exit velocity', all metaphors originating in the racetrack. Writing in an Olympiad year, the metaphor of the university as a course with hurdles

---

[2] Quoted in Jones, McLean *et al.* (2005); they continue: 'the field of higher education pedagogic research is currently dominated by one particular perspective: that which defines excellence in teaching as the delivery of measurable outcomes and so which "privileges the efficient transmission of information". . . . "Learning outcomes" are regarded as units of measurement to account for excellence. We might also observe how official discourse about university teaching presents it as banal, simple, technical, uncontentious and apolitical.'

that have to be jumped, a designated series of goals known and prepared for in advance, pride for all who reach the final stage and glory for those whose prowess and training gain them a medal, is especially potent.

But in Greece, the racetrack was the place of training, not education. On the racetrack, the goals were indeed clear and the appropriate training programme demanded discipline and obedience. Education and pedagogy were different: both words mean 'leading, extending' and the context of the youth's development was a site of dialogue, questioning and choice, of listening and performing in philosophic, rhetorical, political and, overarchingly, theatrical debate. Theatre attendance was an active, not passive part of becoming and being a citizen; character formation, on stage and in the audience, seen as honed by competitive theatrical debate where crucial issues were played out in the minds and hearts of those participating. The benefit came from the experience and from engaging in an open-ended process; the questions could become clear but not the answers. Open-ended, but not formless: disciplined, dialogic and dedicated developmental activities in which the students had an individual and collective responsibility to take their part.

This, then, is the fundamental decision to be made by twenty-first-century universities: *Are they to be race tracks or theatres?* Are the goals and course laid down in advance by others, *or* are they to be developed in performance? Are personas and identities to be adopted, adapted, inhabited or created? And, vitally, are we to encourage students in making their own disciplinary, and disciplined, meanings?

Such questions go to the heart of epistemology, to disciplinary hold over research, and to disciplinarity itself. For if academic knowledge is *stably* structured in disciplines and subject areas, then researchers', teachers' and students' roles are all also stably established. The idea of a theatrical university, on the other hand, suggests a model of knowledge being created in an encounter between conflicting paradigms, and maybe even in the encounter between conflicting roles. Such an idea even opens the destabilizing possibility of students themselves creating new disciplinary knowledge.

Knowledge and control: whose learning, whose outcomes?

> We are much less Greeks than we believe. We are neither in the amphitheatre, nor on the stage but in the panoptic machine . . . our society is not one of spectacle but of surveillance.
>
> (Michel Foucault 1977: 217)

But for there to be the possibility of knowledge and understandings created outside the normal disciplinary research channels, from encounters between students and teachers, mechanisms and narratives of control have to be foresworn. Performance, in Foucault's terms, has to become again a site of playful education, not an instrument of assessment and control.

I teach Greek tragedy seminars and sit on curriculum, examination and strategy committees; the discussions are uncannily similar in both fora. In both, we talk about the problematic value of learning from experience, of different ways of knowing (male and female, adolescent and mature, conscious and sensory, experiential and logical). We argue about proper and improper control over others and over others' decision-making and meaning-making, and over the value and interpretation of outcomes. But in the classroom setting, we work with multivoiced narratives and plays with problematic ends whereas in committee we all too often work with a fixed framework (a 'discussion document', benchmarks, criteria) and predetermined goals.

In the Greek theatre, there is no fixed and supravening viewpoint – even the gods can be misguided and malicious and the hero mistaken. The characters explain themselves, the chorus comments but the spectator experiences a series of conflicting viewpoints with mixed emotions and hopes. The end rarely provides a simple closure – the hero survives damaged or dies unvalidated, the future is uncertain and the explanatory frameworks are seen to be insecure.

In 1986, I was the Classics representative on a panel looking to accredit Cambridge University's part-time courses, as part of which we accepted the then radical new idea of specifying learning outcomes. This was despite spirited resistance among some of us on the panel: it seemed to those of us as profoundly anti-educational, education involving – for us – a transformational and therefore unpredictable interaction between the individual and the course. Even then the pressure was for the setting of learning outcomes to be a closing down rather than an opening up of the course's possibilities, to be not developmental but coercive. Since then, of course, the idea that learning outcomes are teleological – that they determine what should be aimed at – rather than commentatory, has become universal. But the 1986 accreditation panel went even further: it recommended that tutors should predict not just learning outcomes but, something that caused a storm of protest and outright refusal to co-operate, also ULOs – Unintended Learning Outcomes. This seemed to us both illogical (if outcomes were unintended, they were by definition, surely, unpredictable?) and, most importantly, improper. It did not seem to us that it was for the teacher to circumscribe, or even enquire into, the various extremely personal and allowably idiosyncratic benefits of studying our material in our classes. The objection was ethical as well as epistemological: the control we were resisting was over the forms of meaning-making the students were to be allowed, and allowed to keep private. It was agreed, in the end, to allow students to fill in the 'ULO' box (a great success – the students loved the opportunity to ascribe importance to all kinds of aspects of the learning experience) but not to have what was entered part of the accreditation process.

The real driving force behind specifying learning outcomes and over much curriculum planning is the desire for univocality – one set of terms in which outcomes could be expressed – and over control of the outcomes themselves.

The theatre, on the other hand, is a place of dialogue. Tragedies, and the discussions of them, are multivocal: different world-views clash and have to be evaluated; everyone's perspective is different because all approach and experience the action differently. When the end (of the course, of the play) comes, there are different understandings of what has happened: the path that leads to the end has to be traced separately and each understanding co-ordinated with that of others.

In such a complex and multivoiced meaning-making process, the out-comes are uncontrollable and unpredictable, the product potentially unorthodox and problematic. Such a model challenges the twenty-first-century university to offer students a similarly richly various, imaginative and question-raising environment and to offer students participation in activities and conversations that challenge the existing structures of understanding. But students have to make their own path through what is on offer, make the conversation their own and come to their own conclusions and they have to do all this through normal, though not normative, practical academic activities. So the participation has to be the kind of temporary engagement and of working out of ideas in practice that belongs not on the stage but in the drama studio and theatre workshop. Owned and directed by students and teachers together, the outcomes of such experimental processes may be disturbingly unorthodox. Troublesome, in fact.

Troublesome knowledge

'What happens at the end?', I ask of a class studying a problematic Sophoclean play. From their answers I divide them into those who see the end as that which happens to the abandoned, wounded isolate Philoctetes and the other those who focus on the fate of the young Neoptolemos, son of the now dead Achilles, the 'greatest hero of them all'. Confirmed in their initial interest and sympathy, the two groups diverge as they firm up their reading of the play. The week ends with a battle royal as the two groups come together to answer that question: what happens at the end. Because the end is troubling and uncertain, closure for one character involves loss for the other and the only compromise is one that fulfils neither's highest aims but keeps the relationship alive. And then there is an [un?] satisfactory intervention of a god on the crane (mechanê) *(the stereotypical god from the machine,* deus ex machina*).*

The week's essays argue from both engagement and detachment; they complexly and variously challenge most current scholarship and identify a strain of bitterness and loss of belief in politicians and war lords which feels contemporary. I check the context of the original production and find striking political resonances.

I could have set them commentaries, works on closure such as The Sense of an Ending *and offered them purchase on academic critical reading. But then I would have received essays from writers primarily exercised by the challenges of scholarship rather than of the text and their own and their peers' appropriations of it . . .*

Two examples of the generation of such unorthodox academic products have recently been published: the Patchwork Texts project, which traced the results and implications of introducing innovative, critically reflective writing assignments into a range of fields (Ovens *et al.* 2003) and a project that resulted in a significant and radical revaluing of student disciplinary meaning-making processes, the 'Threshold Concepts and Troublesome Knowledge' research project (Meyer and Land 2003). In the latter, an inter-institutional, interdisciplinary team based in Coventry University investigated and demonstrated students' often unrecognized and always unvalued constructions of alternative and extra-paradigmatic knowledge. The team investigated students' cognitive development in many disciplinary and some professional areas, looking particularly at the progressive acquisition of 'threshold concepts': concepts that, once acquired, change irreversibly the student's understanding of the disciplinary paradigm. Their interest is in the meaning-making processes of students who are between thresholds: 'liminal' students who appear to their teachers – from the vantage point of possessing all the concepts – to be lost and in need. But students, not yet having attained the requisite disciplinary framework of understanding, make their own, producing an idiosyncratic and extra-disciplinary account of the phenomena. Of course such an account can be seen as simply wrong, but a less judgemental and open reading might see that what is being produced is 'troublesome knowledge'; the sort of meanings that the discipline cannot comprehend.

In theatrical terms, the audiences outside the action are experiencing and representing in terms other than those laid down by the dramaturge or director: taking neither the character's subjective understanding nor the commenting chorus's summation nor some historical or theological viewpoint but rather some understanding of their own. Through the experience, they form their own framing narratives about the large questions by which they have been challenged.

Mediating new narratives, new knowledge to the community

I set the opening writing task as 'Alien[ation] and sympathy: closing and distancing devices in Greek tragedy'. Or rather, I don't, I ask for 'any kind of public writing' and make it clear I don't want the expected weekly essay. Challenged, threatened or liberated according to their personality, I receive a wonderful assortment of texts and txts. One has returned from working with exiles in Tibet: thinking of imprisoned Tibetan nuns she has met she writes on Cassandra and the polluted priestess. Another visualizes the Bacchants on Mount Cithaeron, described in the Bacchae, *as members of a New York transvestite's club; a third rewrites Antigone's speech as a reply to* Trainspotting*'s Renton's monologue 'Choose Life'.*

Creating their own outcomes, making their own meaning, making troublesome knowledge are valuable opportunities that the theatrical university could provide. But there is a further and even more challenging aspect to the metaphor: in the Greek theatre, the city's youths who, it has been proposed, formed the chorus, were charged with standing between stage and audience, their role to experience intimately the action and mediating their experience to the community as a whole. So how could the modern university offer such a role to students, to experience, engage with, and in some way come to internalize complex explanations; to question, contextualize and finally comment on what they see for the wider community?

The students are not just receivers of their 'theatrical' education for they have the right and responsibility to mediate that education to the wider community. For the students to be fully envoiced and for them to contribute fully to the narrative texture of higher education, their processes of understanding have to inform the discipline's understanding of itself. They have to be reflective not in the sense of their own agenda and development, important though that can be, but in the sense of holding a mirror up to the discipline community. For the purpose of theatre, as Hamlet says to the Players is 'to hold as 'twere the mirror up to nature' or, here, to show the discipline community how its concerns, agenda and processes appear from the outside. Students' experience of the disciplinary 'content' may be very different from that of their teachers both because students ask different questions and because they have a different sense of what matters.[3]

Students ask different questions because they have not yet been trained to see with disciplinary eyes – the duckrabbit is still unstable and may even look like some other creature. It is possible that the ways of meaning-making that students come up with in default of the as yet unacquired disciplinary concepts may offer the discipline new ways of thinking. Disciplinary paradigms have been seen since Kuhn to be both the puzzle-setter and the provider of tools to solve the puzzle. However, those outside the paradigm might have both different puzzles and different ways of solving them; and many even have new embryonic paradigms of their own to offer. The teacher can rule such possibilities as outwith the discipline, as signs of naivety and lack of disciplinary tools and understanding and can set herself to correct the deficit. But Kuhn pointed to the inherent controlling and inhibiting function of

---

[3] A recent series of open plenary lectures at Cambridge was called 'What Matters in' . . . theology, genetics, English literature, philosophy, art, etc. (To be published in a 2005 Special Issue of *Arts and Humanities in Higher Education*, (4) 2). Given by luminaries they were indeed illuminating. But I could not help wondering what the priorities and perspectives would have been were they to be given by third- or even first-year undergraduates.

the discipline. Accordingly, and as Kuhn indicated, paradigm shifts necessarily come from without – from the setting of questions that are outside the frame. But, even if such new framework-breaking questions are being asked by students, that knowledge has to be recognized and positively validated as such. For this to happen, the discipline has to imagine itself differently.

Could the analogy of the Greek theatre, where every speech is answered, where issues are debated in alternating line-by-line verbal duels, where the chorus listens and then comments, offer a new model of academic knowledge making? Of knowledge created in communication, in common with others, in performance? I have had the surely not unfamiliar experience of finding that the paper written before the conference changed when performed because the cue cards and bullet points meant something fuller and different in performance. Both the script *and* my identity were actually changed in the encounter with the audience (Parker 2005). A model of knowledge being made in the company of others and in performance wipes out the scholar-researcher-teacher divide: all are performers. And, as such, knowledge is 'encountered' rather than accretive, while research is a process rather than a placing of 'another brick in the wall'.

Revitalizing disciplinary practice

Some of the revitalizing of the discipline community could come simply from exposure to the students' new ways of looking and from new ways of responding: from 'The Shock of the New' – the impact on new students that contact with disciplinary texts and issues can (and should) have. This shock can easily be cushioned by normalizing tasks.

But in the last decade, the hard sciences have pioneered the use of new disciplinary writing tasks designed to focus and deepen incoming students' engagement. Based on the precept that scientists do not 'do' and then 'write up' science, writing-intensive courses across and throughout the students' undergraduate career encourage the development of understanding *through* as well as *in* writing. The resultant disciplinary writing is neither 'creative' nor 'reflective', as those terms are usually used, though the writing sequences are designed to allow full creative expression and demand reflective engagement. The tasks are various and may involve response to such 'literary' science writers as Borges, to biography, to poetry and to journalism. The tasks invite experimental writing and deliberately move away from the traditional lab report, science journal article and essay form and the results can be genuinely new science writing and thinking (Mermin 2002: 15–28).

This example suggests that the university can, as a matter of general principle, in practice enable students *really* to make their own path (given the institutional restrictions); their own meaning (given the disciplinary frameworks) and, moreover, contribute that troublesome knowledge to the community as a whole. For that to happen, more than richer narratives and aspirational models are needed: there has to be institutional change. When Plato set out to describe his ideal state, he asked what one step would start to make the ideal realizable: it feels proper to do likewise here.

So, the one step that would start to bring students' own meaning-making to the wider community is, I suggest, to give them their own voice in the conversation that is higher education. Specifically, to allow meaning-making, and their way of seeing, as valid contributions to disciplinary debate. For this principle to be realized, there have to be two practical changes. The first is that student writing has to be taken away from the current, narrowly focused assessment system; otherwise, students will continue to see writing only in terms of what is required for satisfying and pleasing the examiners and will write conscious of judgement rather than as a means to develop understanding and individual perceptions. The second is that there have to be fora for the disciplinary and wider higher education community to read and enter into dialogue with student writing.

The first proposition is especially radical: our universities' curricula are designed to co-ordinate the teaching, learning and assessment strategy, with the assessment process providing both the carrot and stick, the motivator and the validation. To propose that student writing be taken at least partly away from assessment changes the teacher's role away from that of judge and gatekeeper to one of facilitating the creation and the grafting on to the disciplinary stock of new narratives and new knowledge. It changes the standard, traditional and reproducing attitude to both disciplinary writing and the pedagogical relationship.

Such changes are radical for the student but, also, for the teacher for whom it offers a way of breaking away from the limitations of disciplinary discourse and permitted modes of expressing and indeed making disciplinary knowledge. It also changes the role and identity of the student, from disciple, or disciplinary trainee to *writer* in all the many facets that connotes. For once writing is taken away from assessment, it becomes instead a medium of special performance: it becomes both the product of and the process of understanding. 'Performance' is meant here in a large sense – as in 'performing a role' or 'a piece of music'; a performance that is the result of skill, engagement, worked through interpretation and a greater or lesser amount of investment of the self.[4]

---

[4] This is to go against the current prevailing model of student writing, that of 'New Literacy Studies' (whereby the student is socialized into the institution by learning academic styles and conventions (academic literacy). In discipline-based courses this also takes the form of learning to enter the disciplinary discourse community by learning the permitted forms of knowledge making and the discipline's permitted style and genres of expression. Those who see the discipline as controlling the permitted forms of knowledge construction and expression see student writing development as necessarily learning to conform and, to some extent, to mimic acceptable forms. Only when the students can express their ideas in the accepted form of argument, a form that differs from discipline to discipline, will they succeed. (Lea and Street 1998: 157–72)

Losing, and finding, academic identity

There are implications here for more than the students' writing and understanding; for the students' construction of their academic identity. Those working on academic literacy point to previous identity-forming background and experience that currently have to be *unlearned* in order for the new academic identity to develop (Ivanič 1998).

The university requires that students leave behind previous perceptions and preoccupations but this is particularly difficult if the subject, for instance art, religious studies or popular culture, has been chosen because of a sense of personal engagement. Likewise students with personal involvement or returning and requalifying professionals bring with them experiential knowledge which they have to unlearn in order to 'write what is required'. There is no place in our current university model for troublesome knowledge or for individual meaning-making, and so no place for developing an integrated and inclusive new identity.

But to see instead the discipline as like a theatrical company – a community of practice and of discourse, rather than as a citadel of knowledge – is to open the possibility that writers can contribute directly and individually to that community's knowledge base. If all are allowed to contribute their writing, all become bound together, sharing the common identity of disciplinary writers: students (given licence and channels of dissemination) together with teachers (hopefully inspired and challenged by their new role as mediators of new knowledge) and researchers.

But the student writer has to be allowed to perform in all the different roles and with all the different challenges outlined at the start of this chapter. They have to be able to explore conflicting paradigms, to generate troublesome knowledge and to challenge the discipline community's sense of itself, of its priorities and of work to be done. That entails licence and the Greek chorus's privileged role of answering back.

But less rebarbatively and more radically, they have to be able to write themselves into new personas: new and discontinuous from those developed before coming to university and from those usually seen in the discipline community. Student writing must be taken seriously as contributions to disciplinary knowledge, even if – especially if – the writing does not conform to disciplinary norms. New understanding, new knowledge will be expressed in new ways, though it can be judged by such 'normal' standards as critical engagement, the quality and depth of the argument, and the depth and importance of the issues raised.[5] Such writing could feed into the

---

[5] Experiments, such as that of the Patchwork text (Ovens *et al.* (eds.) 2003), in the UK with alternative writing sequences have so far struggled, though struggled successfully, to have the results acknowledged as disciplinary writing: I have published analyses of my students' writing in the Classics University Departments' journal *Bulletin*. But 'alternative' writing is most often sidelined as developmental, therapeutic,

disciplinary community in a variety of ways: *directly*, as on a par with, though different from, other kinds of contributions to the disciplinary conversation and *indirectly*, by focusing teachers' attention on students' experiences and processes of understanding. Such a richer understanding of the immediate impact and challenges of the disciplinary material could enliven both the teachers' own writing and the research-dominated disciplinary agenda. This would surely offer a welcome teaching–research reversal: it is usually taken for granted that research should enrich teaching but here, teaching may enhance research.

Students, and indeed their teachers, would be free to write with new disciplinary voices, new frames of reference and to write new kinds of disciplinary knowledge.

Towards a performative identity

Such writing demands a fuller and richer kind of performance from the student than the mastering and demonstration of a given package of learning. It demands that the university provide a context in which such rounded and nourishing ideas of performance can flourish. It demands, to borrow the title of a recent, fascinating book on performance studies, that the academy move 'from philology to performativity' (Jackson 2004). Such a university and such writing are both fuelled by and address the wider concerns of the student: her experience and her priorities as a member of her generation, her culture. A colleague showed me a dialogue written in MSN-speak which went to and communicated the heart of the concerns of a Beckett novel; a Durham Classics professor gets her students to translate Greek choruses into rap. Such exercises are not eccentric or attention-grabbing devices but attempts to get the students to bring a greater and deeper range of engagements with the text into focus by asking them to translate into a contemporary, avowedly personal and experiential genre. This kind of writing draws on and draws out deep and personal engagement by students with the discipline's material and with the discipline's challenges.

Academic personae

There is yet a further aspect to this richer idea of performance. To perform – on stage, in teaching, in writing – is to project a persona. Literally, a 'mask that amplifies' the persona is a mask which fits over the face and renders more resonant that which is delivered through it. Different schools and traditions of theatre have different accounts of the relationship between the

self-expressive and creative rather than academic. It may of course be all those things, but it is to be judged and valued as contribution to the conversations forming the academic disciplinary agenda.

actor, the mask and the character s/he plays. But whereas some modern Western theatre traditions hold acting to be an impersonal skill, most would argue that acting draws on and transmutes areas of the actor's self. That acting is transformational – elements of the actor's experience and personality go to creating the 'character' or 'persona', but also can subtly transform the actor's own 'self'. The final claim, therefore, I would like to make on behalf of the theatrical university is that the serious play, the trying on/ writing out of various personas, the temporary adopting/adapting of various value systems, the making of provisional, conflicting and radical meaning in the face of alternative and conflicting systems and signs, all go to creating a multidimensional and humane student.

Graduation

The theatrical performance is not real life, and nor does it prepare the audience for real life experiences. But the sense in which it is not is complex – it is a place that continually offers and relies on recognition based in real life; otherwise, there would be no engagement. Being part of a performance does not involve suspension of belief but it does involve a willingness to enter into complex relationships with others' vision and experience of the world.

Strange things happen at the end of performances in a theatre: coming out from the dark (which is for us the only continuity with the sense of ritual, sacred space), there has to be a transition into the 'real world' – accompanied by emotion, delight, laughter, pity, humanity, a sense of renewal and change. Graduation also marks a distinct change, coming out from a special place into the world of work.

A recent, ominous catchphrase is the need to 'measure exit velocity' at graduation. I take this to mean that we shoot out students (like mortars?) into the world of work. The theatrical university, a place of challenge, identity change and serious play would, I hope, be a difficult place to leave. I much prefer the image in the very last lines of *Paradise Lost*, that great meditation on the price of knowledge and individuation, on human fallibility, adventurousness and growth into wisdom. Hand in hand, the two first humans turn their faces from the garden of dependence newly able to look to the world outside and to see that

The world was all before them.

12

Placing Service in Academic Life

Bruce Macfarlane

Introduction

One could be forgiven for thinking that universities are for only two purposes: research and teaching. The proper balance between these two functions has always concerned the academic community and has recently attracted renewed attention in the UK in the wake of higher education reform proposals (DfES 2003). Some contend that to be considered an institution of 'higher' learning, it is essential that universities and colleges commit to both functions. Further, it is often argued that research plays a key role in informing genuinely university-level teaching (Barnett 1990). Others, notably the UK government, have concluded that there is little evidence that research is necessary to good teaching in higher education (DfES 2003). It is considered better, therefore, to concentrate research funding in élite institutions and let others focus on the teaching of, mainly undergraduate, students. This position, though, undermines the notion of an intellectual link between teaching and research.

In this debate, it is often forgotten that universities have a historic role beyond arguments about the importance of the teaching-research 'nexus'. In this regard universities across the world have three widely acknowledged missions: teaching, research and service (Cummings 1998). While the first two of these missions frequently attract the attention of academics and policy makers keen to shape (and reshape) the higher education agenda, service has become the neglected third dimension of academic life.

I will present an exploration of how academic staff, working in a range of higher education institutions across the world, interpret the notion of 'service' in the modern university. The subsequent analysis will also seek to explain the role of service in relationship to teaching and research, the motivation of staff who perform service activities and the system-wide forces that threaten to further undermine such commitment.

What does 'service' mean?

Where, it might be asked, does the notion of 'service' come from and what does it mean? Many of the UK universities founded during the Victorian era, such as Manchester, Liverpool and Birmingham, were established by philanthropists, local politicians and businessmen. These universities had a founding commitment to serve the needs of their local communities: they were 'civic' universities. They contained a full range of subjects for the first time including science and engineering disciplines relevant to the industrial heartlands they served (Scott 1995). Civic universities though were about more than a modernization of the curriculum and local pride. They were about opening up higher education to other classes in society and to women (Haldane 1913).

In the US, the meaning of service can be traced back to the so-called land-grant universities that were established in the latter half of the nineteenth century (Boyer 1990). Universities such as Wisconsin and Nebraska had a commitment to serve their local communities through applied research to practical problems. They, along with other early state universities, had their 'roots deep in the soil' (Slosson 1910). In common with the English civics, the land-grant universities were about egalitarianism and opportunity as well as vocational relevance (Kerr 1982). The vocational role of the medieval European university in terms of the preparation of men in theology, law and medicine can be dated back much further (Dunbabin 1999). It was not until the nineteenth century that the civic institution as a symbol of the growth, confidence and greater inclusivity of the modern industrial age took root.

But what does 'service' really mean for the twenty-first-century academic? One of the few contemporary definitions of 'service' is provided by Peter Knight (2002). He distinguishes between contributions *within* the institution and contributions to the community *outside* the walls of the university. Knight gives student academic advice and sitting on a variety of committees as examples of internal service roles. His examples of the external service role are public talks, representing the institution on local associations and serving on national professional associations. While helpful, Knight's definition tends to exclude elements of service which bridge the 'town and gown' divide. Service learning, for example, is a well-established tradition where community service is integrated as part of an academic course (Gascoigne Lally 2001). In several disciplines there are specific service traditions: work placements in business and professional disciplines, public exhibitions and performances in the performing arts or alternative dispute resolution in law.

Some writers argue that a distinction should be drawn between service activities that are examples of academic 'good citizenship', such as serving on university committees or volunteering tutorial support to high school students, and applications of professional expertise as 'an outgrowth of one's academic discipline' (Lynton and Elman 1987: 148). Here, the work of members of the academy is about an extension of their scholarship rather than some sort of philanthropic activity. Boyer (1990) develops the notion of the 'scholarship of application' on the back of making the same, sharp distinction between internal and external service as Lynton and Elman (1987). He argues that the word 'service' has become a catch-all term from which serious application of scholarly knowledge needs to be disentangled. Boyer gives examples of the scholarship of application – medical diagnosis, serving clients in psychotherapy, shaping public policy, creating an architectural design and working with the public schools – as distinct from service activities within and beyond the campus not linked directly to the extension of discipline-based academic expertise. Boyer contends that his version of service as the 'scholarship of application' represents 'serious, demanding work' (1990: 22) as opposed to internal service activities such as 'sitting on campus committees, advising student clubs, or departmental chores' and external work like 'participation in town councils, youth clubs, and the like' (1990: 22).

This recasting of the external elements of service as 'scholarship', needs to be seen in a wider context. Boyer, in particular, was concerned with broadening the definition of scholarship in academic life to counteract the historic bias towards reward and recognition for discovery-based research. However, if we are to accept this reclassification, where does this leave the notion of service? It would mean that service is defined as little more than internal charitable activity on campus. Moreover, it would appear to represent, to summarize Boyer, a range of uninspiring and unintellectual 'chores'.

In reality, however, the distinction which Boyer and others have drawn between internal and external service, casting only the latter as scholarly or intellectual, is hard to sustain. It is misleading to regard only those activities that stem directly from someone's discipline-based expertise as constituting scholarship. So-called internal service activities are more extensive and require greater professional knowledge and skills than has been traditionally appreciated. These incorporate service in support of teaching, such as course design or teaching observation; service in support of research, such as mentoring an inexperienced colleague; and other service activities that span the teaching and research functions, such as developing interprofessional teaching materials. The examples cited above are all scholarly in nature. They are vital to nurturing student welfare and the continued learning of both academic staff and students. While the status of so-called internal service activities may be inferior, they are central to sustaining the well-being of the learning community.

In doing justice to the nature of service it is also important to recognize the role of service in relation to wider society. This form of service is concerned with interactions beyond the academic community to contribute to societal development more broadly. There are many examples of this tradition such as extra-mural studies stretching back to the civic universities in the nineteenth century (Scott 1995), service learning, using discipline-based expertise for the benefit of public and private organizations or individuals acting in the role of 'public intellectuals'.

Interpretations of service

While many universities express a commitment to service at the 'macro' level as part of their institutional mission, it is important to consider how this 'translates' at the 'micro' or individual level of understanding and commitment (Becher and Kogan 1992). In seeking to gain a grasp of such perceptions, face-to-face interviews and a short questionnaire were used to illicit responses from 21 academic staff from universities in the UK, North America, Australia, Canada and southern Europe representing a range of disciplines, institutional contexts and levels of seniority. This work resulted in a number of interpretations of the service role.

1. Administration

UK academics, in particular, struggled to define what they understood to mean by the term 'service'. It is a term with which they are largely unfamiliar and, for some respondents it was a term that did not 'translate at all'. In consequence, all activities other than teaching or research are perceived by some academics to come under the general heading of 'administration'. Academics from other countries also connected service with administrative duties but were more inclined to attach a range of other meanings to the term. In an attempt to make sense of this concept in relation to their normal frame of reference, several UK academics argued that service activities were part of the teaching role. Here, 'service as administration' was perceived to entail largely teaching-related duties such as course management, admissions work including student interviewing and preparing paperwork for university committees and external audits of teaching.

Inevitably, this view of service, equating the term squarely with administration, is a largely negative one. Such activities are seen as a growing burden and an unwelcome intrusion into the core aspects of academic life, namely teaching and research. In this sense, administration was described by one American academic 'as making up much of the clutter of professional life' and by a Spanish respondent as 'distractions from preparing classes or doing research'.

However, while there was no sense of pleasure in being asked to carry out administrative tasks, some expressed a sense of obligation that such work was important and necessary for the good of the institution and its students. What one respondent referred to as 'organizational citizenship' implied a responsibility to contribute to the development of the institution. Hence, activities like course management and participation on university committees and working groups are seen by some academics as an integral duty rather than an illegitimate demand on their time. The fact though that there are different perspectives with regard to whether such work should be undertaken or avoided leads to what one respondent referred to as 'the usual suspects syndrome'.

2. Customer service

The massification of higher education in many national contexts over the last 20 years has led to profound changes in the aims of institutions, the curriculum, the composition of the student body and societal expectations more generally with respect to the purpose of a university education. Higher education has become a globalized part of a service-oriented culture analogous with the 'student-as-customer' (Scott 1999) and the lecturer as 'service worker' (Ritzer 1998). While academics have traditionally been uncomfortable with notions of students as 'customers' or 'clients' (Gordon 1997), university lecturers drawn from professional and vocational backgrounds are less likely to be discomforted in applying this lexicon (Macfarlane 2004).

The notion of service as performing for the 'customer' was identified by a number of respondents. The customer was normally regarded as the student with one academic from a Dutch management faculty describing their role, and that of their colleagues, as 'service providers' on behalf of students and business organizations. As another respondent suggested, 'teaching is very much bound up with providing as good a quality of service for students as possible'. Moreover, this customer service perspective was not just limited to staff from business and other vocational disciplines. It was a perspective shared by an educational development specialist who described service in terms of liaison with different schools of the university and 'providing what the school wants'. In these responses, the notion of customer service was positively identified rather than being associated with negative perceptions associated with loss of status, power or autonomy.

Other academics though viewed student 'demands' for service in more negative terms and were concerned that this is resulting in unreasonable levels of expectation being placed upon lecturers. One UK academic argued that, in the context of e-learning provision, there is an 'increasing perception that we provide a service that they (students) pay for and that they deserve, anticipate and require a certain level of "service". They let us know when we do not meet their rising expectations and the work that results adds to my admin load.'

3. Collegial virtue

'Service as collegial virtue' refers to the interpretation of service as a moral obligation of academic life in support of colleagues within one's own institution and more generally across a disciplinary or professional field. This understanding of the concept shares some elements in common with 'service as administration', such as providing references for fellow academics, but it also incorporates broader scholarly activities such as peer review for academic journals, external examining and both formal and informal mentoring of colleagues. This latter example was described by one of my respondents as a 'gift relationship' whereby senior academics help the development of those younger and/or less experienced. Another lecturer described activities such as reviewing papers for publication as essential to the survival of the academic profession. Here there was a frequently expressed sense of duty and responsibility towards more junior colleagues and disciplinary communities in particular. Despite the time-consuming nature of collegial activities, many academics expressed communitarian instincts arguing, for example, that 'each community member has a responsibility to share in the service role which is essential for any functioning community'. Echoing this sentiment more directly another respondent stated that you simply 'owe it' to your colleagues to support them in their academic development.

Despite the sentiment of this collegial ideal, a number of respondents were clear that a harsher reality sometimes underlies the rhetoric. According to this view, while senior academics perform service roles with power and status, such as peer reviewing for journals, newer or more junior lecturers are routinely forced to execute administrative service roles, such as course management, as a 'rite of passage'. As a professor from an American university stated 'realistically, internal service is something that "junior" (un-tenured) faculty are pressed into and find hard to refuse'. While kudos is gained from collegial service roles in relation to wider scholarship, internal service tasks do not attract a similar degree of recognition or reward. This results in a sense of resentment among junior staff and led one of my respondents to state that he felt 'shafted' by more senior colleagues because of his administrative workload. The way that power relations within the academic community impact in shaping service roles is an example of what Hargreaves (1994) has referred to as 'contrived' collegiality.

4. Civic duty

This interpretation of service reflects what is sometimes termed as 'public service', a sense of obligation to serve the interests of the local community and wider society. It represents a further extension of the service role beyond obligations to one's own organization or institution (service as administration) and to colleagues (service as collegial virtue). One academic expressed this sense of wider duty to society when she stated that 'much of value is lost when the "community" is viewed as a mere organization in which individuals just happen to work'.

Service as civic duty entails doing 'voluntary work' or 'outreach' for the benefit of the (often, local) community in a way not necessarily connected with scholarly expertise. An academic at an American university stated that within his institution the concept of service was interpreted as 'being out in the community and helping people in a very tangible way . . . that typically means helping the homeless, working at a soup kitchen or some other "shelter" '. This understanding fits squarely with the modern tradition of 'community service' (Coles 1993). Giving the example of volunteering at a local hospital, a UK respondent saw this type of activity as congruent with his desire to 'put something into those communities from which one derives benefits'.

5. Integrated learning

Service to the community though can mean more than charity. To be made meaningful to students, as well as staff, there is a tradition of integrating service into the curriculum through a variety of initiatives. 'Service as integrated learning' refers to connecting academic study with work and community-based projects and activities. Among North American academics, in particular, there was a strong awareness of 'service learning' whereby students carried out projects, internships and consultancies with individuals and organizations in the community. The learning benefits for students were described both in terms of enhancing their understanding of the link between theory and practice and the development of personal, social and work-related skills. Examples given of such activities included a dispute resolution programme whereby students mediate between parties in civil law suits, 'internships' or work placements where students spend a period working in an organization, a case study of product 'life cycles' with local companies and a 'consultancy module' within a business degree. Much, although not all, of this activity is formalized as an accredited (and assessed) part of the curriculum.

There was a strong sense among those academics involved with some aspect of service learning that this work improves the quality of student learning. Getting learners to reflect on their service learning activities through producing some kind of written assignment was seen as an important mechanism for students to appreciate and comprehend their own personal and intellectual development. The way service learning activity benefits teaching was also articulated. From the teacher's perspective, although time consuming to establish, these were said to provide a number of gains. The use of applied examples in class, the writing of case studies or the building of relationships leading to research opportunities related to their scholarly interests were cited.

Where does 'service' fit?

These five interpretations of service have important implications for the relationship between research, scholarship and teaching. One of the problems with the growing literature focusing on this relationship is the erroneous impression it creates that 'teaching' and 'research' are the only two roles which academic staff perform. Part of the hegemony of the teaching–research debate is the way that all academic activities are supposedly incorporated under these twin banners. A lot depends on definitions, which are rarely made explicit. The term 'teaching', for example, is defined quite narrowly by academics in some institutional contexts as little more than giving a lecture to a group of students. By contrast, staff working in post-1992 UK universities among my respondents tended to associate the term 'teaching' with a broader set of interrelated activities incorporating personal tutoring, the preparation of teaching materials and designing new courses than their counterparts in older institutions.

In all five interpretations there was a clear sense that service is a moral obligation to students and colleagues, regardless of the direct or indirect career benefits. There are tensions though with regard to the willingness of some academic staff to undertake what is perceived as their 'fair share' of service activities, especially in relation to course management and committee work. This is a reflection, to some extent, of the rise of competitive pressures in academic life: to gain tenure, attract research funding, meet targets for growth in student numbers, publish in the 'best' journals and so on. While there has always been competition in academic life, such pressures have been exacerbated in recent years due to the globalization of the higher education market and attempts by governments to audit research and teaching excellence as part of a new culture of accountability and performativity.

Further, it is problematic, as several of my respondents pointed out, to 'measure' the service contribution of a member of staff. This is in contrast with familiar ways of accounting for research success, such as through publications or research grants. In relation to the teaching role, measures of excellence have grown in sophistication in response to calls to raise its status vis-à-vis research. There is now substantial use of student evaluation, a growing emphasis on the training and certification of university lecturers, the development of professional accreditation and the use of teaching portfolios for promotion purposes. By contrast, the performance of 'service' at the individual level fits less comfortably with the measurement of academic activities and achievements via performance indicators.

Increased pressure to meet research and teaching performance measures means that the service role has been 'squeezed'. A large number of lecturers commented that there was simply 'not enough' or 'insufficient' time to devote to service-based activities. Integrated or service learning initiatives are rarely unproblematic to establish and normally highly time consuming for academic staff in building and maintaining community relationships. They are unlikely to be 'tidy' or free from difficulties in supervising students or assessing their learning. Under pressure from modularization, which militates against cognitive integration, and a range of quality review processes, service learning that is not part of the formal assessed curriculum is less likely to survive. Moreover, even formalized elements, such as work placements in UK four-year business studies 'sandwich' degrees, have fallen into serious decline in recent years.

The changing nature of the academic workforce through casualization means that there are fewer full-time and/or tenured faculty able to commit the time and energy outside formal teaching timetables to service activities. In the US, estimates indicate that around two-fifths of university faculty now hold a part-time appointment, double that of 30 years ago (Benjamin 2000). Moreover, audit of research quality, in countries including the UK, Australia, New Zealand and Hong Kong, have put pressure on academics to focus on publication at the expense of other activities, including time-consuming service activities. These forces mean that there is less credit given to service activities with the occasional exception of promotion to a personal chair in certain institutional cultures, such as post-1992 UK universities (Tight 2002).

There was a keen awareness among academics that service work suffers both a lack of status and, further, 'won't get you tenure, promotion or a pay rise'. As an example of this perception, one respondent commented that in developing a school's e-learning platform, there was little understanding or appreciation of the importance of this type of service work among colleagues and a perception that this 'ought to be something IT support staff do'. There was a general feeling that service work went largely unrewarded and unappreciated. Thus, the motivation for performing service activities was mainly expressed in terms of a mixture of altruism and a sense of obligation to students, colleagues, disciplinary communities and wider society. Service, as one academic defined it, is effectively 'any uncompensated (or more correctly, not directly compensated) work related activity'.

A new space for service?

A range of forces endanger the commitment of university lecturers to the principle of service which helps to underpin the workings of academic and institutional life. Other university traditions, in particular the Germanic model of the research university, have placed an emphasis on 'distance' between the academic as a researcher and the world at large (Boyer 1990). The university as an 'ivory tower' does not sit comfortably with the notion of service to the community. To a large extent, the increasingly dominant role of the state in higher education during the twentieth century supplanted the erstwhile influence of civic and philanthropic influences. The modern university, however, is under increasing pressure to convince the state that it deserves such funding (Tjeldvoll 1998). The traditional role of service remains more strongly embedded in many US universities founded as land-grant institutions. In the UK philanthropic and business funding of universities, including the civics, was gradually displaced by government funding, whereas many US institutions have maintained high levels of support from local benefactors, alumnus and regional communities. As a result, it is no coincidence that service learning is much more firmly rooted in many US universities with closer ties to their local and regional communities and less dependence on central government funding than in the UK.

Market forces and the need for institutions to differentiate themselves from their competitors is leading to a shake-up in the definition of the academic job description. This is sometimes referred to as the 'unbundling' of academic work (Kinser 1998) whereby the traditional all-rounder who performs a combined teaching, research and service role is replaced by a series of specialists such as teaching or research-only appointees, instructional designers and assessors. This phenomenon is gathering pace as a result of the expansion of private, for-profit organizations such as the University of Phoenix (eliminating the research role altogether) and e-learning initiatives whereby universities look to compete in large markets on a global basis. This 'unbundling' means that there are now fewer academics employed with the kind of inclusive set of responsibilities which makes service work either a responsibility or a practical possibility.

The concept of 'service' has shifted and been reinterpreted over time. In the UK, the Robbins report (1963) on higher education identified 'the transmission of a common culture and common standards of citizenship' (p. 7) as one of the four objectives of a university education. While this sentiment may have been echoed by the Dearing report (NCIHE 1997) 34 years later, service was, by this time, a word largely defined in terms of its economic utility. Chapter 12 of the report, focusing on the local and regional role of higher education, was given over almost entirely to the economic and business-related impact of universities. The shift to economic utility was completed by the UK government White Paper published in January, 2003. The White Paper contained chapters about research, teaching, access, expansion and 'Higher education and business' (DfES 2003).

As responses from a number of academics indicated, service is now a term more closely associated with business and consumer relations than 'public' service. It tends to be used in relation to building business relationships on the basis of 'quality' and efficiency. Thus, we have 'service quality', 'service delivery' or simply 'service management' – phrases imported from the lexicon of business life. However, it is not just the language of business which has entered university life. The ideals of liberal individualism have supplanted communitarian and collegial values. Competitive individualism has always been a part of academic life but it now imperils the collegiality and co-operation required to maintain the quality of teaching and research activities. Sitting on departmental or institutional committees as part of 'service as administration' is one prime example. Here, academic life is a reflection of society where civic participation has also been in decline for many years. In interviews with academic staff in UK universities, Harold Silver (2003) found very little evidence of a sense of community based on a shared set of institutional norms or values. Altbach (1995) also comments on the decline of community in US universities as a result of the increased size and diversity of the academic profession.

Academics rarely talk about 'service'. They are more likely to identify the demands of 'administration' or 'management'. Performing service roles, such as course co-ordinator, admissions tutor or head of department, used to be conceptualized as part of the *quid pro quo* of academic life. As a member of an academic community one received certain benefits in return for subordinating individual interests. These have traditionally included job security, academic freedom to carry out one's own personal research and a recognition that individuals have different strengths and weaknesses. Academics would take turns to perform administrative roles such as admissions tutor, committee chair or head of department.

Ironically, a study of the mission statements of higher education institutions reveals that nearly all contain some form of explicit commitment to serving regional and/or local communities. However, it is clear that there is growing friction between institutional espousal of such goals and the career survival of academic staff. Service is not a good investment in terms of career advancement (Knight 2002). Research receives the lion's share of status and kudos in academic life, exacerbated in recent years by audits of research quality in a number of higher education systems. Government and university initiatives to apportion some reward and recognition for excellence in teaching are growing. There are now well-established programmes such as the Carnegie scholars in the US, 3M Teaching Fellows in Canada, Awards for University Teaching in Australia and the National Teaching Fellowship scheme in the UK. These initiatives though are unlikely to rapidly correct the historical imbalance between research and teaching in the short term, in the same way that racial or sexual inequality cannot be quickly eradicated through legislation alone.

Service has probably never been so important to the efficient functioning of the university. Auditing of the teaching role by government agencies and professional bodies has added expectations to university life such as peer mentoring, the observation of teaching and continuous curriculum design (and re-design). The thirst for research funding has similarly expanded the range of service demands which support the establishment of new journals, the review of more grant applications and the need to mentor junior researchers to achieve their full potential in a competitive environment. The critical role that service plays in supporting teaching and research needs to be understood as a key 'space' in the academic role. To adapt an analogy from organizational theory (Handy 1981), the academic job description can be likened to an 'inverted donut'. At the formal heart of the academic role are clearly defined expectations in relation to teaching and research, often expressed in metrics such as teaching hours or numbers of publications. This is the 'jam' in the middle of the (American) donut. While these functions may represent the core, formal expectations of academic life, service forms a substantial part of the less well defined periphery or, in terms of the analogy, the outer part of the donut (see Figure 12.1 overpage).

Concluding thoughts

Where does this leave service? What has got lost in the debate about teaching and research is that universities are also about serving the community; not in a purely narrow economic sense but, in the words of Dearing, 'to play a major role in shaping a democratic, civilised and inclusive society' (NCIHE 1997: 72). Part of the crisis of professional life, to which Jon Nixon

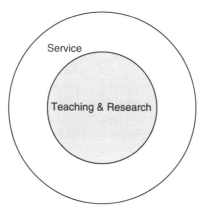

Figure 12.1 Service in the academic role

(2001) refers, concerns the retreat from the service role. It is a demanding, time-consuming and complex activity that receives scant reward or attention. While it would be wrong to suggest that there was ever a 'golden age' in respect of the service role, the twin forces of bureaucratization and individualism are driving it out of academic life to be replaced by the 'burdens' of administration and the 'demands' of students in a consumerist age. While service roles have often been performed with an eye to tenure or promotion prospects their 'exchange value' (Knight 2002) is in serious decline. Arguably, such 'citizenship' tasks have little, if any effect, in the achievement of tenure (Bentley *et al.* 2003).

This analysis might appear to offer little hope for the future of service as a core commitment of universities and academic life. However, there are some grounds for optimism. First, recent attempts to define the notion of 'scholarship' in academic life have received growing attention. Most attention has focused on the 'scholarship of teaching' encouraging academics to research their own practice to bring about better understanding of teaching as an intellectual pursuit. However, service is about a broader range of scholarly activities that forms the surrounding infrastructure that supports both teaching and research.

Finally, most academics do not operate purely on the basis of a rational calculation of personal 'profitability' (Knight and Trowler 2000). Despite the pressures and obligations they face, academics do not always do the rational thing (Coate, Barnett and Williams 2001). They still find space for service in their professional lives. Writing about the characteristics of the academic community over 30 years ago, Robert Nisbet (1971) argued that one of these was a strong sense of *honour*. According to Nisbet, the essence of honour 'cannot be, by the very nature of the attribute, measured or compensated by money or material reward' (Nisbet 1971: 53). Ultimately, service is about taking seriously the obligations of citizenship in the academic community. As one of my respondents commented: 'If I was in it purely for the rewards I wouldn't be an academic in the first place.' Many lecturers and professors see themselves as honour-bound to fulfil their obligations as citizens of the academic and wider community. As Robert Coles argues: 'all service is directly, or indirectly, ethical activity, a reply to a moral call within, one that answers a moral need in the world' (Coles 1993: 75).

13

The Degradation of the Academic Ethic: Teaching, Research and the Renewal of Professional Self-Regulation[1]

David D. Dill

Introduction

The institutional framework of rules and incentives that influences the academic profession's commitments to teaching and research is changing all over the world. These changes are certainly affected by government actions and by market forces. But because of the tradition of collegial governance and academic autonomy granted to universities, the professoriate still retains substantial influence over the conditions of academic work, the priorities of the academic reward system and the social controls that shape academic behaviour. Adam Smith noted this problem in the eighteenth century when he complained of the Oxford professors who 'make a common cause to be all very indulgent to one another, and every man to consent that his neighbour may neglect his duty provided he himself is allowed to neglect his own' (quoted in Kerr 1994: 9). If our institutional framework has structural faults, the academic profession must also accept some responsibility for creating them, for neglecting to notice them, or for making inadequate efforts to correct them (Thompson 1987).

It is important that scholars of higher education study and critique the negative effects of market forces as well as misplaced government efforts at academic regulation on the university. But it is equally if not more important for the continuance of the university as we know it that we look systematically and critically at our own professional behaviour – at our structures of university self-governance, at our processes for peer review and at our underlying academic beliefs. If the professoriate is to insist, and I believe we must insist, on the need for academic autonomy, then we also must offer convincing evidence to each other and to the larger public that our collegial processes for the maintenance of academic standards are vigorous and valid.

[1] This is a revised version of a paper originally presented at the December, 2003 SRHE Conference in London, UK. I am indebted to Ronald Barnett and Martha Dill for useful criticism. I remain solely responsible for the arguments advanced.

In the arguments to follow therefore I will explore the degradation of the academic ethic, which I believe places at risk the academic profession's fundamental social contract with society.

Regulation

First, we need to explore the meaning of the term 'regulation' as it applies to academic work. Perhaps as a result of the reforms in higher education over the last decades in the UK and elsewhere, the term 'regulation' is now immediately interpreted within the academic community as a code word for government 'command and control', that is the imposition upon the university of external standards backed by government sanctions. However, the term 'regulation' can also be understood more broadly as all actions intended to influence social behaviour valued by the public (Baldwin and Cave 1999). It is in this sense that we have traditionally used the term within the academic community, describing collective actions designed to assure academic standards as professional self-*regulation*, obvious examples of which include the external examining system in the UK and voluntary academic accreditation in the US.

Our use of the term 'regulation' in this latter manner emphasizes a crucial point about academic work. That is that academic standards in teaching and learning cannot be maintained by the actions or beliefs of individual professors alone; they also require the supportive bonds of formal structures and processes such as socialization to our academic subject, peer review of proposed new modules or courses and external professional review of academic quality. I use the term 'academic ethic' to refer to this environment of social controls and norms that set the standards for academic conduct and influence our professional choices.

When confronted with arguments for new forms of university regulation, such as improving academic quality through state-sponsored market competition, or regulating academic conduct through government rules and sanctions, we instinctively appeal to this broader notion of the academic ethic as a more effective means of assuring academic standards. But is the contemporary case for professional self-regulation sound? Does it reflect an accurate assessment of the strengths and weaknesses of the academic ethic or is it based largely upon our professional preferences? Any argument that we make for academic autonomy must be based on the proven effectiveness of the academic ethic in fulfilling our professional obligations to society.

Teaching and research

As access to higher education has come to determine the 'life chances' of increasing numbers of our citizens, public concern about the proper balance between teaching and research within universities has grown. Observers in many countries have noted a 'research drift' in higher education in which scarce resources and energy in all types of academic institutions are increasingly committed to research at the expense of improvements in teaching and student learning. While we may perceive this as a current concern, the causes of the problem have existed for some time. In a prescient analysis written in 1970, from which I have borrowed the title of this paper, the sociologist Robert Nisbet (1971) decried the increasing imbalance between teaching and research in the US university. Nisbet attributed this imbalance in part to the loss of deeply and widely held beliefs regarding professional obligations among the professoriate as well as to a weakening of the bonds of structure within universities supportive of these beliefs.

The relationship between teaching and research in the university sector is changing in at least two ways. First, there is increasing concern that resources intended for teaching are being used to cross-subsidize research. This is an issue of long standing in the US and was a stated concern in the recent UK White Paper (DfES 2003). Second, there is concern that professors within subject fields are not as actively committed to improving the quality of student learning as they are to pursuing their own research agendas. How are these issues related to the degradation of the academic ethic as I have defined it and what steps may be necessary to restore professional self-regulation so that it effectively meets our obligation to the larger society?

The cross-subsidization of research by teaching

The cross-subsidization of research by teaching was highlighted in a recent study of US higher education by researchers at the Rand Corporation (Brewer, Gates and Goldman 2002). In field studies of strategic behaviour among representative institutions of higher education, the Rand researchers discovered that most US colleges and universities were actively engaged in a pursuit of academic prestige. Because prestige is earned in the university world not by what students learn but by faculty research reputation and measures of student selectivity, the pursuit of prestige was leading to an academic arms race. All types of institutions, including those most committed in the past to teaching, were investing scarce resources in lower teaching loads for faculty members, in improved research facilities, in matching funds to secure research grants, in merit-based aid for able students and in student consumption benefits such as dormitories, eating facilities, or fibre-optic computer networks designed to help attract high-achieving students. The Rand researchers concluded that while this pursuit of prestige markedly increased the social costs of US higher education, there was little evidence that it was improving the quality of teaching. I note that, in an analysis of higher education reform in the UK, Lindsay and Rodgers (1998) discovered that many UK universities have adopted resource allocation strategies remarkably similar to those identified in the 'prestige-seeking' institutions studied by the Rand researchers in the US. That is, the strategies did not address the educational needs of students, but emphasized increased investment of faculty time in research and 'selling' the institution to attract able students.

Of course, faculty research activity is essential to the teaching responsibilities of universities. I cannot fulfil my professional obligations to teach research doctoral students unless I have an active research programme. But reviews of research on student learning indicate that the correlation between research productivity and first-level instruction is very small and that teaching and research appear to be more or less independent activities (Terenzini and Pascarella 1994). Alexander Astin's (1996) studies exploring the nature of the relationship between research and teaching in the US suggest that a strong departmental research orientation (that is a department whose faculty publishes many books and articles, spends a substantial amount of time on research and attaches high personal priority to engaging in research) is negatively correlated with factors related to teaching including the number of hours spent teaching and advising, commitment to student development and the use of active learning techniques in the classroom. In a national survey of social scientists in the US, Mary Frank Fox (1992: 301) discovered that 'more productive researchers . . . have less classroom contact with students, spend fewer hours preparing for courses, and consider teaching much less important than research'. She concluded that teaching and research are not complementary activities, but different activities that are in some conflict with each other.

Perhaps the more critical consideration in the cross-subsidization of research by teaching is not financial resources, but faculty time. The economist Estelle James (1986) first noted that the university department or faculty could be understood as a non-profit labour co-operative engaged in the production of multiple products. James (1986) argued that faculty members, particularly in universities, value research over teaching, because of its intrinsic interest, because of its clear contribution to departmental reputation and because in competitive research and labour markets, which are becoming more common around the world, time spent on research can lead to increased grant revenue and future earnings for the individual faculty member. In this context, faculty members will choose to 'satisfice' teaching quality (Massy 2003) – to limit their time investment in teaching and to maximize their time investment in graduate instruction and research. In effect, faculty members act individually – and are supported in these actions by academic policies collectively determined at the departmental level – to shift to research activity time intended principally for teaching and paid for by the government and tuition paying students.

National surveys of faculty activity in the US (Fairweather 1996) over the last several decades have confirmed that the proportion of time faculty members reported spending on teaching has fallen and the proportion of time they reported spending on research had risen in all types of four-year institutions, including small liberal arts colleges. As Charles Clotfelter (1996), an economist at Duke University, discovered in a detailed analysis of changes over time at representative departments at Chicago, Duke and Harvard Universities:

> If the [three] institutions examined here are any indication, the period between 1977 and 1992 was one of gradual, but quite perceptive, change. Virtually without exception, average classroom teaching loads, measured in courses taught per year, decreased in the sample departments. Although these calculated loads by no means cover all aspects of teaching, they are suggestive of a significant movement away from teaching and toward research. (Clotfelter 1996: 204)

Aggressive recruitment for prestigious faculty in fields such as economics has only exacerbated the problem. The chair of the economics department at Princeton observed that there is now a 'race to the bottom' in teaching loads, as star professors are awarded with high salaries, minimal teaching obligations and permitted to do extensive work off campus (Steinberger 2001).

The problem of faculty time not only affects teaching, but also the practices of professional self-regulation. Any process of collective action is costly in terms of individual time. As Oscar Wilde reportedly observed, the single greatest weakness of socialism was the number of evenings it wasted. Professional processes of self-regulation such as external examining, academic accreditation and academic audit, not to mention the university-based regulatory processes intended to assure academic standards, all require substantial amounts of faculty time, usually with minimal rewards. A decade ago, Clark Kerr (1994) expressed concern about the observable decline of the academic ethic. Kerr noted the emergence of a 'new academic culture' with less commitment to the local academic community and to citizenship obligations within it:

> All over the United States, it is more difficult than it once was to get university teachers to take seriously their departmental and college responsibilities. They are more reluctant to serve on committees, and more reluctant to make time readily available when they do . . . They wish to concentrate on their own affairs and not that of the institution. (Kerr 1994: 14)

Commitment to improving academic quality in subject fields

The second concern about the relationship between teaching and research is the issue of the commitment to improve student learning within subject fields. Academic programmes are developed, delivered and improved in all academic systems primarily at the level of the department or faculty – what has been called 'the basic unit' (Becher and Kogan 1992). As Tony Becher (1992) noted in developing a quality assurance system at the University of Sussex in the UK:

> [T]he most important consideration in quality assurance must be a

holistic rather than an atomistic one, namely the benefits students derive from the totality of their degree programmes, rather than the satisfactoriness or otherwise of their interactions with individual members of staff. (Becher 1992: 58)

Reviews of research on teaching in higher education confirm the influence of the basic unit on student learning. Students' learning of academic content and their cognitive development are significantly associated with the pattern and sequence of the modules in which they enrol, by programme require-ments that integrate learning from separate modules, and by the frequency of communication and interaction among faculty members in the subject field (Pascarella and Terenzini 1991).

Our public obligation to assure student learning is therefore reflected not only in the commitment and energy we give to our individual courses or modules of instruction, but also in our collective zeal to assure and improve academic standards at the department or subject level.

The managerial theorist Henry Mintzberg (1979) offers a description of how in the past socialization to a discipline supposedly provided the neces-sary regulation of academic standards in universities. Long years of training supplied future faculty members with the standardized skills and knowledge characteristic of their particular subject. Their approach to teaching, to their subject content and to their research was influenced by these ingrained norms. As a consequence, faculty members could teach individually and independently because the professor lecturing on physics to engineering students could successfully predict what the professor lecturing on calculus to the same students was covering. The norms of professional socialization thereby permitted faculty members to co-ordinate their teaching while working autonomously.

But this concurrence on standards, skills and academic content, if it ever existed, has disintegrated with the rapid expansion of academic knowledge and the emergence of multidisciplinary and interdisciplinary subjects. Sur-veys of faculty in the United States (Lattuca and Stark 1994) reveal that disciplinary norms and standards, which used to provide a basis for academic co-ordination, are of declining influence on faculty behaviour. In many dis-ciplines, faculty members no longer easily agree on definitions of subject content, nor are they in agreement that specified sequences of learning are appropriate for students. In several disciplines, faculty members expressed the belief that the field's diversity precluded achieving a consensus on what students need to know.

A national survey of ethical beliefs about university teaching in the US by John Braxton and Alan Bayer (1999), the first relevant empirical investiga-tion of academic ethics that I have discovered, raises further questions about the influence of academic norms.[2] The researchers discovered that the

---

[2] This intriguing approach to the study of academic ethics by Braxton and Bayer (1999) is worthy of replication in other countries. The study was originally published

strength of professional norms with regard to responsibilities for teaching, advising and grading, obligations for the planning and design of courses and commitments for the governance of the department and university were weakest among research universities. They also studied differences in disciplinary cultures and noted that there was greater agreement on ethical standards for teaching and their enforcement in more paradigmatic fields such as the sciences than in the social sciences and humanities. These observed differences in professional norms across disciplines have not received the attention they deserve.

Similar differences in disciplinary cultures have been noted in recent studies of grade inflation in US higher education (Rosovsky and Hartley 2002). Grade inflation or more accurately grade compression in which few low marks are awarded to students, has been increasing over time in the US and is particularly prominent at the most prestigious universities such as Harvard and Yale. Concern about the inflation of marks and academic awards has also arisen in the UK (Yorke *et al.* 2002). One persistent characteristic of grade inflation in the US is that it has occurred primarily in the social sciences and humanities and not in the natural sciences and mathematics.

Disciplinary variation in the awarding of grades transgresses the principal of equal treatment of students that Braxton and Bayer (1999) identified in their survey as a core ethical standard among the professoriate and may also compromise the university's ability effectively to serve the public interest. For example, several studies have suggested that variations in student grading standards across subject fields is one contributor to the observed decline in enrolments in mathematics and the sciences in the US as achievement-oriented students migrate to subjects that award higher grades (Johnson 2003). But few US universities have in place any regulatory process for assuring that academic standards are equivalent across fields and US style accreditation does not examine the issue of marking standards. Even in the UK, David Warren Piper's (1994) informative study of the external examining system revealed that grading profiles vary significantly and in apparently arbitrary ways from subject to subject in the same university as well as between institutions.

Social control and communication

If academic self-regulation as I have suggested is flawed, how can it best be renewed? In discussions with policy makers in a number of countries about

---

in 1999. I suspect other academics will be no more surprised than I that, although I live in an area with one of the highest concentrations of professors anywhere in the US, when I checked out the book in question from the University Library in the summer of 2003 the librarian had to paste a date card on the inside cover because it had never been read before.

means of assuring academic standards, I have always emphasized what we have learned from evaluation studies of the new forms of external quality assurance adopted in the UK, Europe and Asia. The most consistent finding is that processes such as academic audit and subject assessments have increased the amount of discussion among faculty members at the department and university level about teaching and student learning (Dill 2000). When they discover that the primary measurable effect of these policies is to increase conversations among professors, the policy makers have generally been 'underwhelmed'. Nevertheless, I believe that communication is the very heart of the matter. Increased interaction and communication is the essential condition for effective professional self-regulation and is our best hope to sustain our responsibility to society for effective teaching and student learning.

In field research at the departmental level in US universities Bill Massy and his colleagues (Massy, Wilger and Colbeck 1994) suggest why this is the case. They uncovered a pattern of 'hollowed collegiality' in which departments nominally appear to act collectively, but avoid those specific collaborative activities that might lead to real quality improvements in academic programmes. For example, faculty members readily reported informal meetings to share research findings, collective procedures for determining faculty promotion and tenure and consensus decision-making on what particular courses should be offered each term and who should teach them. But:

> Despite these trappings of collegiality, respondents told us they seldom led to the more substantial discussions necessary to improve undergraduate education, or to the sense of collective responsibility needed to make departmental efforts more effective. These vestiges of collegiality serve faculty convenience but dodge fundamental questions of task. This is especially the case, and is regrettable, with respect to student learning: collegiality remains thwarted with regard to faculty engagement with issues of curricular structure, pedagogical alternatives, and student assessment. (Massy, Wilger and Colbeck 1994: 19)

Similarly, in his survey of the UK external examining system, Warren Piper (1994) noted the lack of discussion about marking standards among faculty members teaching in multidisciplinary or joint courses, which even in the late 1980s represented over 30 per cent of degrees in the university sector. As he commented:

> There are some compelling suggestions of the lack of contact among departments . . . Many of the respondents pointed to the need for staff from different disciplines to plan multidisciplinary courses jointly and to get beyond the approach of simply combining lists of subjects to be covered. (Warren Piper 1994: 158)

Major contributors to this observed pattern of professorial isolation are contemporary professorial commitments to specialization and prevailing academic beliefs about academic freedom and autonomy. Faculty members not only do much of their teaching alone, but because academic sub-fields are defined quite narrowly, many faculty members find it almost impossible to discuss their teaching with one another. In a comprehensive analysis of the professional ideal in America, Bruce Kimball (1992) documents the shift during the twentieth century from a belief in service to the public to the active pursuit of individual income and prestige. Reflecting on the academic profession Kimball (1992: 314) asks whether increasing academic specialization has been used 'to deflect criticisms of professionals' power and prestige by disguising their self interest'?

In addition, collective efforts at improving student learning are frequently frustrated by assertions of academic freedom. But does this assertion of autonomy in individual teaching serve the public interest or private needs? Marvin Lazerson (1997) suggests that academic freedom in the US has over time been misinterpreted to mean that individual faculty members have an unchallenged right to determine the content of their courses:

> What professors did inside the classroom had to be defended against external threats . . . The defence of academic freedom had the effect of making the classroom a 'private' domain – as faculty responses to student evaluations often made clear. Any questions about what happened in the classroom, even whether students were learning anything, were viewed as threats to the faculty member's liberty. The transactions of the classroom, teaching and learning, needed to be excluded from serious observation and contention. (Lazerson 1997: 21)

Similarly, Lee Shulman (1993) has observed that unlike academic research, teaching has come to be treated as private rather than community property. In research and scholarship, Shulman notes, academics are members of active communities: 'communities of conversation, communities of evaluation, communities in which we gather with others in our invisible colleges to exchange our findings, our methods, and our excuses' (Shulman 1993: 6). In contrast, faculty members symbolically close the classroom door and conduct teaching as a solitary activity. The timid application of effective peer review to teaching and student learning, which is observable throughout most of the world, is likely traceable to this unexamined assertion of academic freedom. As former Dean Henry Rosovky of Harvard has argued: 'Academic freedom does not absolve colleagues or administrators from assuming responsibility for what are essentially matters of procedure, management, good order and – above all else – legitimate student needs' (Rosovsky and Ameer 1998: 150).

I have already noted the research emphasizing that the amount of communication among faculty members in a department is a significant predictor of student learning. In their study of academic ethics, Braxton and Bayer (1999) also argued that effective deterrence and detection of proscribed academic behaviour is more likely to occur in departments with frequent social contact. Departmental meetings, face-to-face informal interactions and performance reviews related to teaching and student learning provide the social ties necessary for the communication, observation and enforcement of ethical standards.

In his early work on organizations, Henry Mintzberg (1979) similarly noted that where universities place greater emphasis on innovation and creativity, they will form more multidisciplinary groups. In these groups, the standardization of skills and knowledge characteristic of the traditional disciplines will become a less effective mode of co-ordination. Traditional professional norms will need to be supplemented by what Mintzberg termed the process of 'mutual adjustment', by which he meant new mechanisms for communication among the professionals.

Finally, in a related earlier study, *Communication and Organizational Control* (1974), the sociologist Jerald Hage provided a valuable explanation for the role communication plays in professional self-regulation. Hage conducted extensive field studies of the medical profession and concluded that traditional hierarchical methods of co-ordination and control are ineffective in professional settings because of the complexity of professional tasks and the need for individual autonomy. Consequently, he argued that the necessary co-ordination must be achieved through a process of socialization that features high levels of communication and feedback about professional tasks. This communication is not vertical as with administrators, not primarily written as in reports and procedural documents, not episodic and does not focus on the detection or transmittal of sanctions. Rather, the communication is horizontal with respected peers, largely verbal and face-to-face, continuous and focuses on the exchange of information about means of improving core professional tasks.

If we compare these perspectives on the role communication and social control should play in effective professional settings with the reality of how atomistic academic life is lived within contemporary universities, we can begin to appreciate why the academic ethic is being degraded. The traditional reliance on disciplinary norms and collegial processes that accorded substantial autonomy on academic standards to departments and faculties is ill suited to the modern world of research specialization, newly formed subject fields and international competition for scholarly prestige. If we are to sustain the self-regulation of universities, we will need to discover and implement more effective processes for collegial academic governance and the assurance of academic standards. Let me briefly suggest what some of these processes may look like.

Professional regulation for the new age

First, it is unlikely that reforms in professional self-regulation will occur without external pressure. The internal changes in academic quality assurance and the improvements in first-level instruction that have been implemented within universities in a number of countries over the last decade simply would not have occurred without the demands posed by government-mandated external reviews. This 'enforced self-regulation' (Baldwin and Cave 1999) is in my view a necessary condition for rebalancing the relationship between research and teaching. Ultimately, however, as I have suggested, the most effective regulatory processes will be those social controls designed and implemented within universities by the members of the academic profession themselves.

In my visits to universities in several countries as an evaluator of quality assurance practices, I have observed a number of practices, both effective and ineffective, which suggest needed directions for change in academic governance and peer review. The impacts of these and other innovations will need to be verified through independent and objective study, but I believe these practices provide concrete illustrations of the important role communication and feedback play in effective social control in academic settings.

The most influential process I have seen for encouraging teaching and student learning at the department level occurred ironically in one of the most research-intensive institutions I have visited. Within this university, the academic quality assurance process was not in the hands of administrators, but the responsibility of a committee of faculty members elected from across the university and consisting of respected researchers and scholars who were committed to assuring academic standards. It was this committee, not the administration, which was actively pressing each department to demonstrate the effectiveness of its processes for improving teaching and student learning. The committee required initial reports from each department on its quality assurance processes, but followed up these reports with face-to-face meetings with the members of each department to provide criticism and suggest needed improvements. This committee was a formal standing committee of the university, an integral part of the university governance process, with close linkages to the leading administrators. In fact, the committee had identified the academic deans as a particular problem in the improvement of academic standards because they were not actively engaging the departments to improve student learning through their budget allocations and planning processes.

In the newly evolving world of higher education, the incentives and awards for university administrators are increasingly linked to the building of academic prestige and departmental research reputation, not to the challenging and unpopular task of improving academic standards. Comparable questions about administrative neglect and the mismatch between administrative incentives and the need for academic integrity have been raised by researchers studying the problem of scientific misconduct within US universities (Sterneck 1999). For these reasons, I strongly concur with Jerald Hage (1974) who argued that professional self-regulation must rely principally on processes of peer review.

A second example is a university that had developed an innovative award programme for academic quality assurance. The university provided a substantial cash award to departments that could make a convincing case for the implementation of new processes that demonstratively improved academic standards. Each candidate department had to make a written case and then was visited by a committee of faculty peers who interviewed the department faculty and students and assessed the relevant evidence. The activities of the winning department were then showcased within the university as a means of encouraging the improvement of other academic units.

We may note that this award programme in this university is a creative response to two nagging problems for improving teaching and student learning in universities. The first problem is how to provide financial incentives for collective actions to improve academic standards, without punishing students. The second is how to encourage the transfer of teaching and learning improvements developed in one academic unit to other academic units. Transferring good practice is a substantive challenge in university settings (Dill 1999). Those countries that have systematically conducted subject reviews within their university sector have discovered wide variance in the quality of teaching and learning across units within the same university, which I earlier noted. These better performing units have knowledge about improving teaching and learning from which other units could learn if effective collegial processes were developed for identifying best practices and successfully transferring them among academic units. Such knowledge transfer is thwarted by established governance traditions of departmental autonomy and decentralized decision-making.

A third example is a university that had recently reformed its first-degree level programmes, adopting modular programmes and continuous assessment and consequently phasing out its traditional external examiner system. Because of concerns about fairness to students as well as commitments to providing appropriate incentives for student learning, the faculty of the university established a standing committee to develop and implement university-wide marking standards. The committee established and published grade distribution guidelines for the university as a whole and monitored departmental grade distributions for each term. The department chairs of units which varied significantly from the grading guidelines were regularly called before the committee and asked to provide supporting arguments and evidence for the observed exceptions.

These brief examples suggest how academic self-regulation might be better designed to address our academic responsibility for assuring the quality of teaching and student learning in the new academic environment. The examples also illustrate some of the practices of effective social control through communication and feedback previously introduced. These structures and processes help guide professional behaviour, identify deviance and create mutual expectations. As suggested, the good practices cited are clearly collegial, that is, they were developed and implemented by the faculty themselves. They are also continuous in that they are a permanent part of the ongoing academic governance process of the respective universities, not temporary task forces created in response to external demands. Administrators play a supporting role in these cases, but the processes clearly stress peer review. The processes include written reports, but they avoid the danger of empty 'proceduralism' by emphasizing the active practice of professional judgement (Turner 1999). This requires face-to-face communication with academic units as a means of socializing the larger faculty to expected professional norms and responsibilities. Through this communication, there is also the greater possibility of disseminating information on means for improving core academic processes including the transfer of best practices developed in other academic units of the university. Similar to the external quality assurance processes that I mentioned previously, these internal university processes also place collegial pressure on each academic unit continuously to improve its academic standards.

Conclusion

The new processes of academic self-regulation that I have described may appear commonplace in countries such as the UK where substantial institutional investments have been made in academic quality assurance over the last decade. Understandably, some may feel that their universities have successfully adapted to the educational demands of the new environment and that it is now time to invest scarce energy in other challenges. I respectfully disagree. For better or worse, the world is rapidly adopting academic structures that will make higher education around the globe more not less like that in the US (Trow 2000). Taught courses, modular instruction, continuous assessment, merit-based faculty salary systems and the competitive awarding of research grants will likely all become more common in higher education. Many countries are now adopting the US hierarchal degree structure of first-level undergraduate degrees, second-level professional degrees and third-level research doctoral degrees, which will have consequences for both student and faculty attitudes toward grading and academic standards. And, in this process, we are already seeing the emergence of an international academic arms race based upon measures of academic prestige and faculty research reputation. We are not confronting a one-time adjustment in higher education, but an ongoing dynamic change with great significance for the balance between research and teaching.

As I have suggested, many of these changes will likely erode the remaining vestiges of the traditional academic ethic, which has in the past helped us fulfil our academic obligations to society. Greater faculty mobility will decrease the social ties within departments and universities that helped to sustain norms and academic standards. The increasing returns to research and scholarship will affect attitudes toward teaching in all institutions of higher education, as young faculty members attempt to advance professionally. I fear that individual professors, who in the past would have made substantial personal commitments to teaching, to grading with academic integrity and to maintaining the self-regulatory processes for assuring academic standards, will look at the incentives and awards of the emerging competitive system of higher education and conclude that such commitments are now irrational. Our ability to sustain and assure academic standards will be continuously put to the test. As a consequence, we all will be seeking means for renewing the academic ethic.

Scholars and researchers in higher education can therefore make an important contribution to the future of the university by inquiring more deeply and objectively into the academic beliefs and governance procedures that influence the quality of teaching and student learning in higher education. We need to know more about the strengths and weaknesses of new forms of collegial governance now emerging in response to demands for greater academic accountability. We need to discover how peer review can be more effectively utilized to improve academic standards. We need better to understand the extent of the apparent differences in ethical standards between academic disciplines and fields and the causes of this variability. We need to know how academic socialization can be accomplished in a world of rapidly expanding knowledge and new subjects as well as increasing professorial mobility. And we need to know when academic freedom is genuinely compromised by professional self-regulation and when such claims are bogus or conceal faculty self-interest.

But let us not be naive about the reactions to such investigations. Research into the ethical environment of universities will be disturbing. Those colleagues who applauded our attacks on managerialism, our questioning of new government regulation and our concerns about the effects of market forces, will likely sit on their hands when we inquire into professional standards of conduct and the efficacy of self-regulatory processes. As Peter Rossi (1987: 73) so aptly put it, 'no good applied social research goes unpunished'.

But we should be emboldened by the responsibility of our social contract with society. The public has entrusted the academic profession with its future human capital. We have been awarded substantial professional autonomy with the expectation that we will in turn assure in an efficient and equitable manner that our students learn the knowledge, skills and values essential to society. We must, as Bill Massy (2003) has powerfully argued in his book on quality and productivity in higher education, honour that trust.

Concluding Note

This volume has represented 'work in progress' in two senses. First, the application of the spatial metaphors of space itself and shapes to higher education is, I believe, a relatively new approach in our understanding of the field. Clearly, the sense in which such a set of metaphors is helpful – indeed, is more helpful than any drawbacks it may have – has not been tackled in this volume; it has just been largely assumed to be helpful. The contributions to this volume have surely demonstrated that there is a potential in this set of metaphors that is worth pursuing.

At one level, this is hardly surprising. Universities have been with us for eight hundred years and have had a significant physical presence. They occupy much space (to which a standing committee on 'space management' of the UK's Funding Council is testimony, quite apart from a large suite of projects currently in hand for that committee investigating universities' space 'utilization' and 'space needs'). Universities have a definite material existence; and so spatial metaphors are likely to be especially resonant. But if spatial metaphors are to work here, it is because they work on a level other than the material by helping us better to understand and to see into these strange organizations we know as 'universities'.

My view is that spatial metaphors are doubly helpful. First, they help us to conceptualize the current configuration of universities. They invite diagrammatic representations in which the different functions of a university are plotted against each other. Taking a university as the canvas, and depicting it as a set of juxtaposed spaces, not only relationships but also gaps or voids might be more easily appreciated: *this* teaching function in *this* university may be seen to have little in the way of a research endeavour connected to it but *that* research activity, too, is now strikingly also seen as semi-detached, unconnected to any of the teaching activities in the university.

But spatial metaphors also at once, surely, draw us into conjectures as to future possibilities. Could there, for this university, be a different configuration of the shapes that form the university? Could there be alternative patterns? Could spaces open, either for new activities, or even completely new conceptions and practices within present activities? I believe that this volume has at least shown sufficient of the power of spatial metaphors to suggest that they might be taken on seriously as a conceptual tool for further inquiry. In such an inquiry, doubtless, too, other spatial metaphors than those used here – such as Bourdieu's notion of 'field' or Bernstein's idea of 'region' – might also be examined to see if they are helpful additions. The emergence of the 'virtual university' might also be examined through spatial metaphors, although their diagrammatic representation might offer something of a particular challenge.

But this volume, and perhaps more importantly, has been evidence of 'work in progress' in another sense, additional to the development of our conceptual understanding of the university. For this volume, surely, has shown that there are many individuals who are living out hopes of doing things against the currents of the age; not just some of the authors here, but contained in the pages of this volume are all manner of indications – some overt, some implicit – that individuals, whether largely alone or in teams, are working hard to insert, as it were, a wedge that opens a space for new, purposive and fruitful activities. These activities may, for example, be a redrawing of an existing activity (a new way of presenting a thesis) or the insertion of a new kind of activity (a creative student-owned venture which, in the process, happens to meet the demands of an imposed skills agenda, and surpasses that agenda) or a new way of the university reaching out to the community in a spirit of service.

There is surely sufficient in the pages of this volume to show that there is a wide range of ways of reshaping the university. The greatest barrier to positive development may well be not the lack of material resources, or the limited evaluation regimes, or the marketization of higher education or the present challenges to academic identities – all of which are real and significant – but our own imaginations, our energies and our courage to try things out and to keep going. In the end, the question has to be asked: do we have a will to reshape the university?

Bibliography

Adams, J. and Bekhradnia, B. (2004) *What Future For Dual Support?*, Higher Education Policy Institute, Reports and Articles. http://www.hepi.ac.uk/articles/.

Advisory Board for the Research Councils (ABRC) (1987) *A Strategy for the Science Base*. A discussion document prepared for the Secretary of State for Education and Science by the Advisory Board for the Research Councils. London: HMSO.

Advisory Board for the Research Councils/University Grants Commission (ABRC/UGC) (1982) *Report of a Joint Working Party on the Support of University Scientific Research*, Cmnd 8567. London: HMSO. (The Merrison Report)

Altbach, P. G. (1995) Problems and possibilities: the US academic profession, *Studies in Higher Education*, 20 (1): 27–44.

American Heritage Dictionary of the English Language, 4th edn (2000) Electronic version published by Houghton Mifflin Company.

Andresen, L. W. (2000) A useable trans-disciplinary conception of scholarship, *Higher Education Research and Development*, 19 (2): 137–55.

Andrews, R. (2003) The end of the essay, *Teaching in Higher Education*, 8 (1): 117–28.

Aoki, T. (2000) Locating living pedagogy in teacher 'research'. Five metonymic moments. Paper presented at the *International Conference on Teacher Research*. Baton Rouge, LA, April 2000.

Applefield, J. M., Huber, R. and Moallem, M. (2001) Constructivism in theory and practice: toward a better undertanding, *The High School Journal*, 84 (2): 35–53.

Argyris, C. (1999) *On Organizational Learning*. Malden, Mass.: Blackwell Business.

Argyris, C. and Schön, D. A. (1974) *Theory In Practice: Increasing Professional Effectiveness*. San Francisco: Jossey-Bass Publishers.

Argyris, C. and Schön, D. A. (1996) *Organizational Learning*. Reading, Mass.: Addison-Wesley. (Orig. 1978)

Arrow, K. (1962) Economic welfare and the allocation of resources for innovation, in *The Rate and Direction of Invention*. Princeton: Princeton University Press.

Arts of Citizenship (2004) Program statement. www.artsofcitizenship.umich.edu/about/program.html (accessed 13 August 2004).

Ashby, E. (1985) Preface to I. Brewer, *Learning more and Teaching less*. Guildford: Society for Research into Higher Education & NFER-Nelson.

Ashwin, P. (2003) Variation in students' experiences of small group tutorials, in C. Rust (ed.) *Improving Student Learning: Theory and Practice – 10 Years On*. Oxford: Oxford Centre for Staff and Learning Development, Oxford Brookes University.

Astin, W.A. (1996) Involvement in learning revisited, *Journal of College Student Development*, 40 (5): 587–97.

Badley, G. (2002) A really useful link between teaching and research, *Teaching in Higher Education*, 7 (4): 443–55.

Baldwin, G. and James, R. (2000) The market in Australian higher education and the concept of student as informed customer, *Journal of Higher Education Policy and Management*, 22 (2): 139–48.

Baldwin, R. and Cave, M. (1999) *Understanding Regulation: Theory, Strategy, and Practice*. Oxford: Oxford University Press.

Barnett, R. (1990) *The Idea of a Higher Education*. Buckingham: The Society for Research into Higher Education/Open University Press.

Barnett, R. (1992) Linking teaching and research: a critical inquiry, *Journal of Higher Education, 63 (6): 619–36*.

Barnett, R. (1994) *The Limits of Competence: Knowledge, Higher Education and Society*. Buckingham: Open University Press.

Barnett, R. (2000) *Realizing the University in an Age of Supercomplexity*. Buckingham: Open University Press.

Barnett, R. (2003) *Beyond All Reason: Living with Ideology in the University*. Buckingham: Open University Press/SRHE.

Barone, T. and Eisner, E. (1997) Arts-based educational research, in R. M. Jaeger (ed.) *Complementary Methods for Research in Education*, 2nd edn. Washington, DC: AERA, pp. 73–99.

Bauman, Z. (2000) *Liquid Modernity*. Oxford: Polity Press.

Bauman, Z. (2002) *Society under Siege*. Cambridge: Polity Press.

Bauman, Z. (2003) *Liquid Love*. Cambridge: Polity Press.

Baxter Magolda, M. B. (1999) *Creating Contexts for Learning and Self-Authorship*. Nashville, Tennessee: Vanderbilt University Press.

Becher, T. (1992) Making audit acceptable: a collegial approach to quality assurance, *Higher Education Quarterly*, 46 (1): 47–66.

Becher, T. (1994) The significance of disciplinary differences, *Studies in Higher Education*, 19 (2): 151–61.

Becher, T. and Kogan, M. (1992) *Process and Structure in Higher Education*, 2nd edn, London: Routledge.

Becher, T. and Trowler, P. (2001) *Academic Tribes and Territories: Intellectual Enquiry and the Cultures of Disciplines*, 2nd edn, Buckingham: SRHE and Open University Press.

Benjamin, E. (2000) Overreliance on part-time faculty: an American trend, *International Higher Education*, 21 (Fall): 7–9.

Benjamin, W. (1999) *Selected Writing*, Volume 2 (1927–1934). Cambridge: Harvard University Press.

Benjaminson, P. (1992) *Publish without Perishing: A Practical Handbook for Academic Authors*. Washington, D.C.: National Education Association of the United States.

Bennett, N. (1976) *Teaching Styles and Pupil Progress*. London: Open Books Publishing Ltd.

Bentley, L., Robertson, D., Bell, I., Enzmann, D., Lohmann, S., Rhodes, D. and Shih, J. (2003) *Productivity, Collaboration and Citizenship in Academic Departments*, NESCI Complex Systems Course, UCLA, 16–20 June.

Bernstein, B. (1971) On the classification and framing of educational knowledge, in M. Young (ed.) *Knowledge and Control*. London: Collier-Macmillan Publishers, pp. 47–69.

Bernstein, B. (1996) *Pedagogy, Symbolic Control and Identity: Theory, Research, Critique.* London: Taylor and Francis.

Biggs, J. (1999) *Teaching for Quality Learning at University.* Buckingham: Open University Press/SRHE.

Biggs, J. (2003) *Teaching for Quality Learning at University: What the Student Does,* 2nd edn. Buckingham: Open University Press/SRHE.

Biglan, A. (1973) The characteristics of subject matter in different scientific areas, *Journal of Applied Psychology,* 57 (3): 195–203.

Blackmore, P. and Cousin, G. (2003) Linking teaching and research through research-based learning, *Educational Developments,* 4 (4): 24–7.

Bond, C. (2000) *The development of students' experiences of learning in higher education.* Unpublished Ph.D. Thesis, Griffith University, Queensland.

Bourdieu, P. (1986) The forms of capital, in G. R. Richardson (ed.) *Handbook of Theory and Research for the Sociology of Education.* New York: Greenwood Press.

Bourdieu, P. (1988) *Homo Academicus.* Cambridge: Polity Press.

Bourdieu, P. (1996) *The State Nobility.* Cambridge: Polity Press.

Boyer, E. L. (1990) *Scholarship Reconsidered: Priorities of the Professoriate.* Princeton: Carnegie Foundation for the Advancement of Teaching.

Braxton, J. M. and Bayer, A. E. (1999) *Faculty Misconduct in Collegiate Teaching.* Baltimore: Johns Hopkins University Press.

Bredo, I., Foersom, T. and Laursen, P. F. (1993) Student choice: a model, *Higher Education Review,* 26 (1): 64–73.

Breen, R. (2002) Different disciplines require different motivations for student success, *Teaching Forum,* 50 (Autumn): 39–40. www.brookes.ac.uk/virtual/NewTF/50/tf50contents.htm (accessed 18 August 2004).

Breen, R. and Lindsay, R. (1999) Academic research and student motivation, *Studies in Higher Education,* 24 (1): 75–93.

Breslow, L., Drew, L., Healey, M., Matthew, B. and Norton, L. (2004) Intellectual curiosity: a catalyst for the scholarships of teaching and learning and educational development, in E. M. Elvidge (ed.) *Exploring Academic Development in Higher Education: Issues of Engagement.* Cambridge: Jill Rogers Associates.

Brew, A. (1999a) Research and Teaching: changing relationships in a changing context, *Studies in Higher Education,* 24 (3): 291–301.

Brew, A. (1999b) *The Value of Scholarship.* Society for Research into Higher Education Conference.

Brew, A. (2001a) Conceptions of research: a phenomenographic study, *Studies in Higher Education,* 26 (3): 271–85.

Brew, A. (2001b) *The Nature of Research: Inquiry in Academic Contexts.* London: Routledge Falmer.

Brew, A. (2003) Teaching and research: new relationships and their implications for inquiry-based teaching and learning in higher education, *Higher Education Research and Development,* 22 (1): 3–18.

Brew, A. and Boud, D. (1995a) Research and learning in higher education, in B. Smith and S. Brown (eds.) *Research, Teaching and Learning.* London: Kogan Page, pp. 30–39.

Brew, A. and Boud, D. (1995b) Teaching and research: establishing the vital link with learning, *Higher Education,* 29: 261–73.

Brewer, D., Gates, S. M. and Goldman, C. A. (2002) *In Pursuit of Prestige: Strategy and Competition in US Higher Education.* New Brunswick, NJ: Transaction Press.

Brook, P. (1968) *The Empty Space.* London: Penguin.

Brook, P. (1993) *There Are No Secrets: Thoughts on Acting and Theatre*. London: Methuen.

Brown, R. (2004) *Quality Assurance in Higher Education: The UK Experience since 1992*. Buckingham: Open University Press.

Brueggemann, W. (1999) *The Covenanted Self: Explorations in Law and Covenant*. Minneapolis: Fortress Press.

Bruner, J. (1966) *Toward a Theory of Instruction*. Cambridge, Mass.: Harvard University Press.

Bruner, J. (1986) *Actual Minds, Possible Worlds*. London: Harvard University Press.

Bruner, J. (2000) *The Culture of Education*. Cambridge, Mass.; London: Harvard University Press.

Butler-Kisber, L. (2002) Artful portrayals in qualitative inquiry: the road to found poetry and beyond, *Alberta Journal of Educational Research*, 48 (3): 229–39.

Cameron, D. (2003) Doing exactly what it says on the tin: some thoughts on the future of higher education, *Changing English*, 10 (2):133–41.

Carnoy, M. (1994) Universities, technological change and training in the information age, in J. Salmi and A. M. Verspoor (eds.) *Revitalising Higher Education*. Pergamon: IAU Press.

Carrotte, P. (1994) *An action research cycle in the teaching of restorative dentistry: how my students respond to an invitation to take control and involvement in their own learning*. Unpublished MEd dissertation, University of Sheffield.

Casimir, H. B. G. (1973) When does jam become marmalade?, in R. L. Weber (compiler) *A Random Walk in Science*. London: Institute of Physics.

Castells, M. (1996–1999) *The Information Age: Economy, Society and Culture* (3 volumes). Oxford: Blackwell.

Centra, J. A. (1983) Research productivity and teaching effectiveness, *Research in Higher Education*, 18 (40): 379–89.

Chomsky, N. (1983) Interview (with Noam Chomsky), *Omni*, 6 (2).

Clandinin, D. J. and Connelly, F. M. (1998) Personal experience methods, in N. K. Denzin and Y. S. Lincoln (eds.) *Collecting and Interpreting Qualitative Materials*. California, United States: Sage Publications Ltd, pp. 150–78.

Clark, B. R. (1983) *The Higher Education System: Academic Organization in Cross-National Perspective*. Berkeley: University of California Press.

Clark, B. R. (1993) The research foundations of post-graduate education, *Higher Education Quarterly*, 47 (4): 301–15.

Clarke, C. (2003) I am not the 'scourge of historians', *Times Higher Educational Supplement*, 12 May, p. 19.

Clotfelter, C. T. (1996) *Buying the Best: Cost Escalation in Élite Higher Education*. Princeton: Princeton University Press.

Coate, K., Barnett, R. and Williams, G. (2001) Relationships between teaching and research in higher education in England, *Higher Education Quarterly*, 55 (2): 158–74.

Cobban, A. B. (1990) *Universities in the Middle Ages*. Liverpool: Liverpool University Press.

Code, L. (1991) *What Can She Know? Feminist Theory and the Construction of Knowledge*. Ithaca, NY: Cornell University Press.

Colbeck, C. L. (1998) Merging in a seamless blend: how faculty integrate teaching and research, *The Journal of Higher Education*, 69 (6): 647–71.

Colbeck, C. L. (2004) A cybernetic systems model of teaching and research production: impact of disciplinary differences. Paper presented at *Research and*

Teaching: Closing the Divide? An International Colloquium. Marwell Conference Centre, Winchester, 17–19 March. www.solent.ac.uk/r&t_conference (accessed 13 August 2004).

Coles, R. (1993) *The Call of Service: A Witness to Idealism.* Boston: Houghton Mifflin.

Collins, T and Tillman, S. (1998) Global technology diffusion and the American research university, in J. T. Kennedy (ed.) *Research Administration and Technology Transfer.* San Francisco: Jossey Bass.

Comenius, A. (1910) *The Great Didactic,* trans. G. W. Keatinge. London: A. C. Black.

Court, S. (1996) The use of time by academic and related staff, *Higher Education Quarterly,* 50 (4): 237–60.

Court, S. (1999) Negotiating the research imperative: the views of UK academics on their career opportunities, *Higher Education Quarterly,* 53 (1): 65–87.

Cousin, G., Healey, M., Jenkins, A., Bradbeer, J., King, H. and other members of the Learning to Do Pedagogic Research Group (2003) Raising educational research capacity: a discipline-based approach, in C. Rust (ed.) *Improving Student Learning: Theory and Practice – 10 Years On.* Oxford: Oxford Centre for Staff and Learning Development, Oxford Brookes University.

Cummings, W. K. (1998) The service university movement in the US: Searching for momentum, *Higher Education,* 35 (1): 69–90.

Dalum, B., Johnson, B. and Lundvall, B. A. (1992) Public policy in the learning economy, in B. A. Lundvall, (ed.) *National Systems of Innovation.* London: Pinter.

Davies, S. W. and Glaister, K. W. (1996) Spurs to higher things? Mission statements of UK universities, *Higher Education Quarterly,* 50 (4): 261–94.

De Botton, A. (2001) *The Consolations of Philosophy.* London: Penguin.

Deem, R. (1998) New managerialism in higher education: the management of performances and cultures in universities, *International Studies in the Sociology of Education,* 8 (1): 47–70.

Deem, R. (2001) Globalisation, new managerialism, academic capitalism and entre-preneuralism in universities: is the local dimension still important?, *Comparative Education,* 37 (1): 7–20.

Delanty, G. (2001) *Challenging Knowledge: The University in the Knowledge Society.* Buckingham: Open University Press.

Denzin, N. K. (1997) Performance texts, in W. G. Tierney and Y. S. Lincoln (eds.) *Representation and the Text: Re-framing the Narrative Voice.* New York: State University of New York Press, pp. 179–217.

Denzin, N. K. (1998) The art and politics of interpretation, in N. K. Denzin and Y. S. Lincoln (eds.) *Collecting and Interpreting Qualitative Materials.* California, US: Sage Publications, pp. 313–43.

Denzin, N. K. and Lincoln, Y. (2000) The discipline and practice of qualitative research, in N. K. Denzin and Y. Lincoln (eds.) *Handbook of Qualitative Research,* 2nd edn. California, US: Sage Publications Ltd.

Department for Education and Skills (DfES) (2003) *The Future of Higher Educa-tion: Creating Opportunity, Releasing Potential, Achieving Excellence.* London: The Stationery Office.

Devanas, M. (2001) Biomedical issues of HIV/AIDS, *Science Education for New Civic Engagements and Responsibilities Model Series 2001.* http://www.aacu-edu.org/SENCER/pdfs/Models_Print_Web_2004/HIV_Model.pdf (accessed 13 August 2004).

Dewey, J. (1917) *Democracy and Education.* New York: Macmillan.

Diamond, R. M. and Adam, B. A. (eds.) (1995) *The Disciplines Speak: Rewarding the*

Scholarly, Professional, and Creative work of Faculty. Washington: American Association for Higher Education.

Dictionary of Critical Sociology. Iowa State University. http://www.public.iastate.edu/~rmazur/dictionary/p.html (retrieved 11 May 2004).

Dill, D. D. (1997) Higher education markets and public policy, *Higher Education Policy*, 10: 167–85.

Dill, D. D. (1999) Academic accountability and university adaptation: The architecture of an academic learning organization, *Higher Education*, 38 (2): 127–54.

Dill, D. D. (2000) Designing academic audit: lessons learned in Europe and Asia, *Quality in Higher Education*, 6 (3): 187–207.

Donald, J. G. (2002) *Learning to Think: Disciplinary Perspectives.* San Francisco: Jossey Bass.

Dunbabin, J. (1999) Universities c. 1150–c.1350, in D. Smith and A. K. Langslow (eds.) *The Idea of a University.* London: Jessica Kingsley Publishers, pp. 31–47.

Elton, L. (1986a) Research and teaching: symbiosis or conflict, *Higher Education*, 15: 299–304.

Elton, L. (1986b) Quality in higher education: nature and purpose, *Studies in Higher Education*, 11: 83–4.

Elton, L. (1987) *Teaching in Higher Education: Appraisal and Training.* London: Kogan Page.

Elton, L. (1992) Research, Teaching and Scholarship in an Expanding Higher Education System, *Higher Education Quarterly*, 46 (3): 252–68.

Elton, L. (2000a) Dangers of doing the wrong thing righter, in *Evaluate and Improve, Conference of the Humanities and Arts Higher Education Network.* Open University, pp. 7–9.

Elton, L. (2000b) Turning academics into teachers: a discourse on love, *Teaching in Higher Education*, 5: 257–60.

Elton, L. (2001) Research and teaching: what are the real relationships?, *Teaching in Higher Education*, 6 (1): 43–56.

Elton, L. (2001a) Research and teaching: conditions for a positive link, *Teaching in Higher Education*, 6: 43–56.

Elton, L. (2001b) Training for a craft or a profession?, *Teaching in Higher Education*, 6: 421–2.

Elton, L. (2003) Some thoughts on scholarship, *Educational Developments*, 4 (4): 7–8.

Elton, L. and Lucas, L. (2004) University finance – a 'European' norm?, *Perspectives*, 8: 18–20.

Elwes, R. (1955) (trans.) *The Chief Works of Benedict de Spinoza. The Ethics.* New York: Dover.

Encyclopedia Britannica (1929) Article on 'Mendeleyev', 15: 241.

Etzkowitz, H. and Leydesdorff, L. (1997) (eds.) *Universities and the Global Knowledge Economy: A Triple Helix of University Industry Government Relations.* London: Cassell.

Fairweather, J. (1996) *Faculty Work and Public Trust: Restoring the Value of Teaching and Public Service in American Academic Life.* Boston: Allyn & Bacon.

Feldman, K. A. (1987) Research productivity and scholarly accomplishment of college teachers as related to their instructional effectiveness: a review and exploration, *Research in Higher Education*, 26: 227–97.

Feynman, R. P. (1963) Preface to *The Feynman Lectures.* New York: Addison-Wesley.

Foucault, M. (1977) *Discipline and Punish.* Harmondsworth: Penguin.

Foucault, M. (1980) *Power/Knowledge: Selected Interviews and Other Writings 1972–1977.* New York: Pantheon Books.

Fox, M. F. (1992) Research, teaching, and publication productivity: mutuality versus competition in academia, *Sociology of Education*, 65 (4): 293–305.

Freire, P. (1972) *Pedagogy of the Oppressed*. Harmondsworth: Penguin.

Fuller, S. (2000) *The Governance of Science: Ideology and the Future of the Open Society*. London and New York: Open University Press.

Gascoigne Lally, C. (2001) Service/Community learning and foreign language teaching methods: an application, *Active learning in higher education*, 2 (1): 53–64.

Gee, J. (1989) Literacy, discourse, and linguistics, *Journal of Education*, 171(1): 5–17.

Gibbons, M. (1998) Higher education relevance in the twenty-first century. *UNESCO World Conference on Higher Education*, Paris, 5–9 October.

Gibbons, M., Limoges, C., Nowotny, H., Scott, P., Schwartzman, S. and Trow, M. (1994) *The New Production of Knowledge: The Dynamics of Science and Research in Contemporary Societies*. London: Sage.

Gibbs, G. (1988) *Learning by Doing: A Guide to Teaching and Learning Methods*. London: Further Education Unit. www.glos.ac.uk/gdn/gibbs/index.htm (accessed 13 August 2004).

Gibbs, G. (2000) Are the pedagogies of the discipline really different?, in C. Rust (ed.) *Proceedings of the 1999 7th International Symposium Improving Student Learning: Improving Student Learning Through the Discipline*. Oxford: Oxford Centre for Staff and Learning Development, Oxford Brookes University.

Gibbs, G. and Coffey, M. (2004) The impact of training of university teachers on their teaching skills, their approach to teaching and the approach to learning of their students, *Active Learning in Higher Education*, 5: 87–100.

Gleick, J. (2003) *Isaac Newton*. London: Pantheon Books.

Goffman, E. (1969) *The Presentation of Self in Everyday Life*. Harmondsworth: Penguin.

Goldhill, S. (1999) Programme notes, in S. Goldhill and R. Osborne (eds.) *Performance Culture and Athenian Democracy*. Cambridge, Cambridge University Press.

Goodhart, C (1984) *Monetry Theory and Practice*. London: Macmillan.

Gordon, G. (1997) Preparing and developing academics for the needs of effective provision in mass tertiary education, *Higher Education Management*, 9 (3): 67–78.

Gregersen, B. and Johnson, B. (1997) Learning economies, innovation systems and European integration, *Regional Studies*, 31 (5): 467–79. www.business.auc.dk/druid/conferences/winter1997/conf-papeis/birgbjor.pdf.

Grey, C. (2001) Re-imagining relevance: A response to Starkey and Madan, *British Journal of Management*, 12: 27–32.

Griffiths, R. (2004) Knowledge production and the research–teaching nexus: the case of the built environment disciplines, *Studies in Higher Education*, 29 (6): 709–26.

Grundy, S. (1992) Beyond guaranteed outcomes: creating a discourse for educational praxis, *Australian Journal of Education*, 36 (2): 157–69.

Hage, J. (1974) *Communication and Organizational Control: Cybernetics in Health and Welfare Settings*. New York: John Wiley.

Haig, B. (1987) Scientific problems and the conduct of research, *Educational Philosophy and Theory*, 19 (2): 22–32.

Haldane, R. (1913) The civic university: an address delivered to the citizens of Bristol, *The Hibbert Journal*, January: 233–54.

Halsey, A. H., Floud, J. E. and Anderson, C. A. (1961) *Education, Economy and Society: A Reader in the Sociology of Education*. New York: Free Press.

Handy, C. B. (1981) *The Age of Unreason*. London: Business Books.

Hannan, A. and Silver, H. (2000) *Innovating in Higher Education*. Buckingham: Open University Press.

Hargreaves, A. (1994) *Changing Teachers, Changing Times.* London: Cassell.

Harrington, J. and Booth, C. (2003) Rigour versus relevance, research versus teaching? Evidence from business and management studies. Paper presented to Society for Research into Higher Education Annual Conference: Research, Scholarship and Teaching: changing relationships? Royal Holloway, University of London, 16–18 December 2003.

Hartwig, L (2004) The traditional unity of teaching and research in Germany and its consequences for evaluation and university funding, *SRHE International News,* 54: 2–4. London: SRHE.

Hassan, R. (2002) Time and knowledge in the information ecology, *Southern Review, Knowledge Production, the University and the Network Society,* Special Issue edited by R. Hassan 35 (2): 37–54.

Hattie, J. and Marsh, H. W. (1996) The relationship between research and teaching: a meta-analysis, *Review of Educational Research,* 66 (4): 507–42.

Healey, M. (2000) Developing the scholarship of teaching in higher education: a discipline based approach, *Higher Education Research and Development,* 19 (2): 169–89.

Healey, M. (2003) The scholarship of teaching: issues around an evolving concept, *Journal on Excellence in College Teaching,* 14 (1/2): 5–26.

Healey, M. (2005) Linking research and teaching to benefit student learning, *Journal of Geography in Higher Education,* 29 (2) (forthcoming).

Healey, M. and Jenkins, A. (2000) Learning cycles and learning styles: the application of Kolb's experiential learning model in higher education, *Journal of Geography,* 99: 185–95.

Healey, M. and Jenkins, A. (2003) Discipline-based educational development, in R. Macdonald and H. Eggins (eds.) *The Scholarship of Academic Development.* Buckingham: SRHE and Open University Press.

Healey, M., Jordan, F., Pell, B. and Short, C. (2003) The student experience of research and consultancy, SEDA-Society for Research into Higher Educational Joint Conference on The Scholarship of Academic and Staff Development: Research, Evaluation and Changing Practice, Bristol, 9–11 April 2003.

Healey, M., Kneale, P., Bradbeer, J. with other members of the INLT Learning Styles and Concepts Group (2005) Learning styles among geography undergraduates: An international comparison. *Area,* 37 (1)30–42.

Healey, M. and Roberts, J. (eds.) (2004) *Engaging Students in Active Learning: Case studies in geography, environment and related disciplines.* Cheltenham: Geography Discipline Network and School of Environment, University of Gloucestershire.

Henkel, M. (2000) *Academic Identities and Policy Change in Higher Education.* London: Jessica Kingsley.

Herda, E. (1999) *Research Conversations and Narrative.* Westport, Connecticut: Praeger.

Higher Education Academy (undated) Linking research and teaching. www.heacademy.ac.uk/850.htm (accessed 4 May 2005).

Higher Education Funding Council for England (HEFCE) (2003) HEFCE *Strategic Plan 2003–2008,* HEFCE [35/03]. Bristol: HEFCE.

Hill, F. M. (1995) Managing service quality in higher education: the role of the student as primary consumer, *Quality Assurance in Education,* 3 (3): 10–21.

Hindle, B. P. (1993) The 'Project': putting student-controlled, small-group work and transferable skills at the core of a geography course, *Journal of Geography in Higher Education,* 17(1): 11–20.

Hodgson, V. (1984) Learning from lectures, in F. Marton, et al., The Experience of Learning. Edinburgh: Scottish Academic Press, ch. 6.

Hoffman, E. (1989) Lost in Translation. London: Heinemann.

Hughes, C. and Tight, M. (1995) Linking university teaching and research, Higher Education Review, 28 (1): 51–5.

Humboldt, W. von (1810) Über die innere und äußere Organisation der höheren wissenschaftlichen Anstalten in Berlin, in H. Weinstock (ed.) (1957) Wilhelm von Humboldt. Frankfurt: Fischer Bücherei, pp. 126–34.

Humboldt, W. von (1970) On the spirit and organisational framework of intellectual institutions in Berlin, Minerva, 8: 242–67.

Hunt, T. (2004) Goodbye to Berlin, The Guardian, 13 February.

Hutchings, W. and O'Rourke, K. (2001) Introducing enquiry-based teaching methods in literary studies, in Critical Encounters: Scholarly Approaches to Learning & Teaching, Continuing Professional Development Series 6. York: Higher Education Academy. www.heacademy.ac.uk/profdev/case_study6.pdf (accessed 4 May 2005).

Ivanič, R. (1998) Writing and Identity: the Discoursal Construction of Identity in Academic Writing. Amsterdam: John Benjamins.

Jackson, S. (2004) Professing Performance: Theatre in the Academy from Philology to Performativity. Cambridge: Cambridge University Press.

Jacob, M. and Hellström, T. (eds.) (2000) The Future of Knowledge Production in the Academy. Buckingham and Philadelphia: SRHE and Open University Press.

James, E. (1986) Cross subsidization in higher education: Does it pervert private choice and public policy?, in D. Levy (ed.) Private Education: Studies in Choice and Public Policy. New York: Oxford University Press.

Jenkins, A. (1996) Discipline-based educational development, The International Journal for Academic Development, 1 (1): 50–62.

Jenkins, A. (2004) A Guide to the Research Evidence on Teaching-Research Relationships. York: Higher Education Academy. www.heacademy.ac.uk/embedded_object.asp?id=21570&file (accessed 4 May 2005).

Jenkins, A., Blackman, T., Lindsay, R. and Paton-Saltzberg, R. (1998) Teaching and research: student perspectives and policy implications, Studies in Higher Education, 23 (2): 127–41.

Jenkins, A., Breen, R. and Lindsay, R. with Brew, A. (2003) Re-shaping Higher Education: Linking Teaching and Research. London: SEDA and Routledge.

Jenkins, A. and Zetter, R. (2003) Linking Research and Teaching in Departments. York: Higher Education Academy. www.heacademy.ac.uk/embedded_object.asp?id=186334file (accessed 4 May 2005).

Jensen, J. (1988) Research and teaching in the universities of Denmark: Does such an interplay really exist?, Higher Education, 17: 1–26.

Johnson, S. (1765) Preface to Shakespeare, W. K. Wimsatt, (1969). Harmondsworth: Penguin.

Johnson, V. E. (2003) Grade Inflation: A Crisis in College Education. New York: Springer.

Jones, McLean, M. et al. (2005) Investigating the production of university English in mass higher education: towards an alternative methodology, Arts and Humanities in Higher Education, 4 (3).

Kahn, P. and O'Rourke, K. (eds.) (2003) Learning Based on the Process of Enquiry, Proceedings of the 1–2 September 2003 Conference, University of Manchester, Manchester.

Kerr, C. (1982) The Uses of the University. Cambridge. Mass.: Harvard University Press.

Kerr, C. (1994) Knowledge ethics and the new academic culture, *Change*, 26(1): 8–15.

Kimball, B. A. (1992) The 'True Professional Ideal', in *America: A History*. Cambridge, Mass.: Blackwell.

Kinkead, J. (ed.) (2003) *Valuing and Supporting Undergraduate Research: New Directions for Teaching and Learning 93*. San Francisco: Jossey Bass.

Kinser, K. (1998) Faculty at private for-profit universities: the University of Phoenix as a new model?, *International Higher Education*, 13 (Fall): 13–14.

Knight, P. T. (2002) *Being a Teacher in Higher Education*. Buckingham: The Society for Research into Higher Education/Open University Press.

Knight, P. T. and Trowler, P. R. (2000) Department-level cultures and the improvement of learning and teaching, *Studies in Higher Education*, 25 (1): 69–83.

Kögler, H. (1996) *The Power of Dialogue: Critical Hermeneutics after Gadamer and Foucault*. Cambridge, Mass.: Massachusetts Institute of Technology Press.

Kolb, D. A. (1984) *Experiential Learning: Experience as a Source of Learning and Development*. New York: Prentice Hall.

Krahenbuhl, G. S. (1998) Faculty work: integrating responsibilities and institutional needs, *Change*, 30 (6): 18–25.

Kropotkin, P. (1885) What geography ought to be, *The Nineteenth Century*, 18: 940–56.

Kuhn, T. (1962, revised edition 1970) *The Structure of Scientific Revolutions*. Chicago: Chicago University Press.

Larédo, P. (2003) University research activities: ongoing transformations and new challenges, *Higher Education Management and Policy*, 15 (1): 105–23.

Lather, P. (1991) *Getting Smart: Feminist Research and Pedagogy with/in the Postmodern*. New York: Routledge, Chapman and Hall, Inc.

Lather, P. (1996) Troubling clarity: the politics of accessible language, *Harvard Educational Review*, 66 (3): 525–45.

Lather, P. (1997) Drawing the line at angels: working the ruins of feminist ethnography, *Qualitative Studies in Education*, 10 (3): 285–304.

Lattuca, L. R. and Stark, J. S. (1994) Will disciplinary perspectives impede curricular reform?, *Journal of Higher Education*, 65 (4): 401–26.

Lave, J. and Wenger, E. (1991) *Situated Learning: Legitimate Peripheral Participation*. New York: Cambridge University Press.

Lazerson, M. (1997) *Discontent in the Field of Dreams: American Higher Education, 1945–1990*, publication number NCPI-3–01. Stanford University: National Center for Postsecondary Improvement.

Learning and Teaching Support Network (LTSN) (2004) *Linking Research and Teaching*. www.ltsn.ac.uk/genericcentre/index.asp?id=17235 (accessed 13 August 2004).

Le Heron, R. and the Linking Research & Teaching Group (2004) *Geography as a site of co-learning: re-linking research and teaching*. www.gees.ac.uk/iguevent.htm#olps (accessed 15 August 2004).

Lea, M. and Street, B. (1998) Student writing in higher education: an academic literacies approach, *Studies in Higher Education*, 23 (2): 157–72.

Lee, R. (2004) Research and teaching: making – or breaking – the links, *Planet*, 12: 9–10.

Levin, H. (1999) What is clearing technology?, *Free Spirit Journal: Journal of Modern Techniques for Spiritual Development*, XVI (1 and 2).

Lindsay, G. and Rodgers, T. (1998) Market orientation in the UK higher education sector: The influence of the education reform process 1979–1993, *Quality in Higher Education*, 4 (2): 159–171.

Lindsay, R., Breen, R. and Jenkins, A. (2002) Academic research and teaching quality: the views of undergraduate and postgraduate students, *Studies in Higher Education*, 27 (3): 309–27.

Livingston, D. and Lynch, K. (2000) Group project work and student-centred active learning: two different experiences, *Studies in Higher Education*, 25 (3): 323–45.

Long, F. (1994) Research as Living Knowledge, *Studies in Higher Education*, 19 (1): 47–57.

Lucas, L. (2004) Reclaiming academic research work from regulation and relegation, in M. Walker and J. Nixon (eds.) *Reclaiming Universities from a Runaway World*. Buckingham: Open University Press/SRHE.

Lundvall, B. A. (2002) The university in the learning economy, working paper no. 02–06. Danish Research Unit for Industrial Dynamics (DRUID). www.druid.dk/ wp/pdf_files/02–06.pdf

Lundvall, B. A. and Johnson, B. (1994) The learning economy, *Journal of Industrial Studies*, 1 (2): 23–42.

Lynton, E. and Elman, S. (1987) *New Priorities for the University: Meeting Society's Needs for Applied Knowledge and Competent Individuals*. London: Jossey-Bass.

Lyotard, J.-F. (1984) *The Postmodern Condition: A Report on Knowledge*, trans. G. Bennington and B. Massumi. Foreword by F. Jameson. Minneapolis: University of Minnesota Press.

Macfarlane, B. (2004) *Teaching with Integrity: The Ethics of Higher Education Practice*. London: RoutledgeFalmer.

Marginson, S. and Considine, M. (2000) *The Enterprise University: Power, Governance and Reinvention in Australia*. Cambridge: Cambridge University Press.

Massy, W. F. (2003) *Honoring the Trust: Quality and Cost Containment in Higher Education*. Bolton, MA: Anker Publishing.

Massy, W. F., Wilger, A. K. and Colbeck, C. (1994) Overcoming hollowed collegiality, *Change*, 26 (4): 10–20.

May, R. M. (2003) *Managing Creativity*. Anniversary Address, Royal Society. www.royalsoc.ac.uk/templates/search/websearch.cfm?mainpage=/anniversary address2003/about.htm.

McIntyre, M. (2001) *Audit, Education, and Goodhart's Law. Or, Taking Rigidity Seriously*. www.atm.damtp.cam.ac.uk/people/mem/papers/LHCE/dilnot-analysis.html (accessed 23 July 2004).

McSherry, C. (2001) *Who Owns Academic Work: Battling for Control of Intellectual Property*. Cambridge, Mass.: Harvard University Press.

McWilliam, E. (1997) Performing between the posts, in W. G. Tierney and Y. S. Lincoln (eds.) *Representation and the Text: Re-framing the Narrative Voice*. New York: State University of New York Press, pp. 219–32.

Mermin, N. D. (2002) Writing Physics, in J. Monroe (ed.) *Writing and Revising the Disciplines*. Cornell: Cornell University Press.

Meyer, E. and Land, R. (2003) Threshold concepts and troublesome knowledge 1 – Linkages to ways of thinking and practising, in C. Rust (ed.) *Improving Student Learning – Ten Years On*. Oxford: Oxford Centre for Staff and Learning Development.

Mintzberg, H. (1979) *The Structuring of Organizations: A Synthesis of the Research*. Englewood Cliffs, NJ: Prentice Hall.

Moja, T. and Cloete, N. (2001) Vanishing borders and new boundaries, in J. Muller, N. Cloete and S. Badat (eds.) *Challenges of Globalisation: South African Debates with Manuel Castells*. Cape Town: Maskew Miller/Longman.

Montaigne, M. de (1935) *The Essays of Montaigne*, trans. E. J. Trechman. London: Oxford University Press.

Moses, I. (1990) Teaching, research and scholarship in different disciplines, *Higher Education*, 19: 351–75.

Moxley, J. M. (1992) *Publish, Don't Perish: The Scholar's Guide to Academic Writing and Publishing*. Westport, CT: Greenwood Press.

Muller, J. (2001) Return to user: responsivity and innovation in higher education. Commissioned paper for N. Cloete, R. Fehnel, P. Maassen, T. Moja, H. Perold and T. Gibbon (eds.) *Transformation in Higher Education: Global Pressures and Local Realities*. Cape Town: CHEPS/Juta.

Murphy, D. (1995) *Comenius: A Critical Reassessment of his Life and Work*. Dublin: Irish Academic Press.

Naidoo, R. (2004) Fields and institutional strategy: Bourdieu on the relationship between higher education, inequality and society, *British Journal of Sociology of Education*, 25 (4): 458–71.

National Committee of Inquiry into Higher Education (1997) *Higher Education in the Learning Society: Report of the National Committee*. London: HMSO.

Nelson, R. R. (1959) The simple economics of basic scientific research, *Journal of Political Economy* Vol. 27, no 3.

Neumann, R. (1992) Perceptions of the teaching–research nexus: a framework for analysis, *Higher Education*, 23: 159–71.

Neumann, R. (2001) Disciplinary differences in university teaching, *Studies in Higher Education*, 26 (2): 135–46.

Neumann, R., Parry, S. and Becher, T. (2002) Teaching and learning in their disciplinary context, *Studies in Higher Education*, 27: 405–17.

New Zealand Government (1989) *New Zealand Education Act*. Wellington.

Newman, J. H. (1852/1966) *The Idea of a University*. Ed. Frank M. Turner. New Haven CT: Yale University Press.

Newman, S. (2003) *Lesbian Historiography, or A Talk about the 'Sweaty Sheet Fantasies of Certain Modern Tribades'*. Melbourne: Monash University, School of Historical Studies.

Ninnes, P. and Metha, S. (2000) Educational research undone: the post-modern embrace. (book review), *Comparative Education Review*, 44 (2): 205–16.

Nisbet, R. (1971) *The Degradation of the Academic Dogma: The University in America, 1945–1970*. New York: Basic Books.

Nixon, J. (2001) Towards a new academic professionalism: a manifesto of hope, *British Journal of Sociology of Education*, 22 (2): 227–44.

Nolan, K. T. (2001) *Shadowed by light, knowing by heart: Preservice teachers' images of knowing (in) math and science*. Unpublished doctoral dissertation, University of Regina, Regina, SK.

Nolan, K. T. (in press) Knowing/not knowing: Caught in dichotomy or re/siding in slash spaces? *Journal of Curriculum Theorizing*.

Northedge, A. (2003) Rethinking teaching in the context of diversity, *Teaching in Higher Education*, 8 (1): 17–32.

Nowotny, H., Scott, P. and Gibbons, M. (2001) *Re-Thinking Science: Knowledge and the Public in an Age of Uncertainty*. Cambridge: Polity Press.

O'Neill, O. (2002) *A Question of Trust*. BBC Reith Lectures.

Ogborn, J. (1977) *Students' Reactions to Undergraduate Science*. London: Heinemann Educational Books.

Olssen, M. (2004) Neoliberalism, globalization, democracy: challenges for education, *Globalization, Societies, Education*, 2 (2): 231–45.

Olssen, M., Codd, J. and O'Neill, A-M. (2004) *Educational Policy: Globalisation, Citizenship and Democracy*. London: Sage.

Orr, L. (1997) Globalisation and the universities: towards the 'market university?', *Social Dynamics*, 23 (1): 42–64.

Ovens, P. *et al.* (eds.) (2003) Integrating assessment: the 'Patchwork Text', special edition of *Innovations in Education and Teaching International*, 40 (2).

Parker, J. (2005) 'Voice and Academic Identity in "Changing Places"', in M. Tight (ed.) *International Relations*. London: Elsevier Science.

Pascarella, E. T. and Terenzeni, P. T. (1991) *How College Affects Students: Findings and Insights From Twenty Years of Research*. San Francisco: Jossey-Bass.

Paul, J. L. and Marfo, K. (2001) Preparation of educational researchers in philosophical foundations of inquiry, *Review of Educational Research*, 71 (4): 525–47.

Paulsen, F. (1908) *The German Universities*, trans. F. Thilly and W. W. Elwang. London: Longmans Green.

Peters, M. A. (2003) Theorising educational practices: the politico-ethical choices in P. Smeyers and M. Depaepe (eds.) *Beyond Empiricism: On Criteria for Educational Research*. Studia Paedagogica, Leuven: Leuven University Press.

Peters, M. A. (2004) Higher Education, Globalisation and the Knowledge Economy, in M. Walker and J. Nixon (eds.) *Reclaiming Universities From A Runaway World*. London and New York: Open University Press.

Peters, M. A. and Besley, T. (2005) *Building Knowledge Cultures: Education and Development in the Age of Knowledge Capitalism*. Boulder, NY: Lanham, Oxford: Rowman & Littlefield.

Pirsig, R. M. (1974) *Zen and the Art of Motorcycle Maintenance*. London: Bodley Head.

Pocklington, T. and Tupper, A. (2002) *No Places to Learn: Why Universities Aren't Working*. Vancouver: University of British Columbia Press.

Polanyi, M. (1958) *Personal Knowledge: Towards a Post-critical Philosophy*. London: Routledge and Kegan Paul.

Polkinghorne, D. E. (1997) Reporting qualitative research as practice, in W. G. Tierney and Y. S. Lincoln (eds.) *Representation and the Text: Re-framing the Narrative Voice*. New York, NY: State University of New York Press.

Popper, K. (1979) *Objective Knowledge. An Evolutionary Approach*. Revised edn, Oxford: Oxford University Press.

Power, M. (1999) *The Audit Society: Rituals of Verification*. Oxford: Oxford University Press.

Pritchard, R. M. O. (1990) *The End of Elitism*. New York: Berg.

Pritchard, R. M. O. (1998) Academic freedom and autonomy in the UK and Germany, *Minerva*, 36: 101–24.

Prosser, M. and Trigwell, K. (1999) *Understanding Learning and Teaching: The Experience of Higher Education*. Buckingham: SRHE and Open University Press.

Quality Assurance Agency (QAA) (2001) *The Framework for Higher Education Qualifications in England, Wales and Northern Ireland*. Gloucester: QAA.

Radley, A. (1980) Student learning as social practice, in P. Salmon (ed.) *Coming to Know*. London: Routledge and Kegan Paul.

Ramsden, P. (1998) *Improving Learning: New Perspective*. London: Kogan Page.

Ramsden, P. and Moses, I. (1992) Associations between research and teaching in Australian higher education, *Higher Education*, 23: 273–95.

Readings, B. (1996) *The University in Ruins.* Cambridge, Mass.: Harvard University Press.

Richardson, L. (1990) *Writing Strategies: Reaching Diverse Audiences.* California, US: Sage Publications.

Richardson, L. (1998) Writing: A method of inquiry, in N. K. Denzin and Y. S. Lincoln (eds.) *Collecting and Interpreting Qualitative Materials.* California, US: Sage Publications Ltd, pp. 345–71.

Ricoeur, P. and Thompson, J. (1981) *Hermeneutics and the Human Sciences: Essays on Language, Action and Interpretation.* Cambridge: Cambridge University Press.

Ritzer, G. (1998) *The McDonaldization Thesis.* London: Sage.

Robbins, Lord (1963) *Higher Education: Report of the Committee Appointed by the Prime Minister under the Chairmanship of Lord Robbins 1961–1963.* London: HMSO.

Robertson, J. and Bond, C. (2001) Experiences of the relation between teaching and research: What do academics value? *Higher Education Research and Development,* 20 (1): 5–19.

Robertson, J. and Bond. C. (in press) The research/teaching relation: a view from the 'edge', *Higher Education.*

Robertson, J. M. (1935) Introduction, in M. de Montaigne *The Essays of Montaigne,* trans. E. J. Trechman. London: Oxford University Press, pp. xi–xlx.

Robins, K. and Webster, F. (eds.) (2002) *The Virtual University? Knowledge, Markets and Management.* Oxford: Oxford University Press.

Rogers, C. R. (1969) *Freedom to Learn: A View of What Education Might Become.* Columbus: Charles E. Merrill.

Roget's Interactive Thesaurus, first edn (2003) Electronic version published by Lexico Publishing Group, LLC. All rights reserved.

Rosovsky, H. and Ameer, I.-L. (1998) A neglected topic: Professional conduct of college and university teachers, in W. G. Bowen and H. T. Shapiro (eds.) *Universities and Their Leadership.* Princeton: Princeton University Press.

Rosovsky, H. and Hartley, M. (2002) *Evaluation and the Academy: Are We Doing the Right Thing?* Cambridge, Mass.: American Academy of Arts and Sciences.

Rossi, P. H. (1987) No good applied social research goes unpunished, *Society,* 25 (1): 73–80.

Rowland, S. (1996) Relationships between teaching and research, *Teaching in Higher Education,* 1 (1): 7–20.

Rowland, S. *et al.* (1998) Turning academics into teachers?, *Teaching in Higher Education,* 3: 133–41.

Sacks, P. (1996) *Generation X Goes to College: An Eye Opening Account of Teaching in Postmodern America.* Chicago: Open Court.

Savin-Baden, M. (2000) *Problem-based Learning in Higher Education: Untold Stories.* Buckingham: Open University Press/SRHE.

Schatzki, T., Knorr Cetiona, K. and Von Savigny, E. (eds.) (2001) *The Practice Turn in Contemporary Theory.* London and New York: Routledge.

Schön, D. A. (1987) *Educating the Reflective Practitioner: Toward a New Design for Teaching and Learning in the Professions.* San Francisco: Jossey-Bass.

Schön, D. A. (1995) *The Reflective Practitioner: How Professionals Think In Action.* Aldershot, England: Arena. (Orig. 1983, Basic Books).

Scott, P. (1988) Commonwealth universities conference: Worries tended to dominate, *University Affairs (Association of Universities and Colleges of Canada),* 29 (4): 2–3.

Scott, P. (1995) *The Meanings of Mass Higher Education.* Buckingham: Open University Press/SRHE.

Scott, P. (1999) Decline or transformation? The future of the university in a knowledge economy and a postmodern age, in P. Bagge, A. Telling and W. van Haaften (eds.) *The University in the Knowledge Society*. Bemmel, The Netherlands: Concorde Publishing House.

Scott, S. V. (1999) The academic as service provider: is the customer 'always right'?, *Journal of Higher Education Policy and Management*, 21 (2): 193–202.

Sharp, S. (2004) The Research Assessment Exercises 1992–2001: patterns across time and subjects, *Studies in Higher Education*, 29 (2): 210–18.

Sharrock, G. (2000) Why students are not (just) customers (and other reflections on life after George), *Journal of Higher Education Policy and Management*, 22 (2): 149–64.

Shore, B. M., Pinker, S. and Bates, M. (1990) Research as a model for university teaching, *Higher Education*, 19: 21–35.

Shulman, L. S. (1993) Teaching as community property: putting an end to pedagogical solitude, *Change*, 25 (6): 6–7.

Shumar, W. (1997) *College for Sale: A Critique of the Commodification of Higher Education*. London: Falmer Press.

Silver, H. (2003) Does a university have a culture?, *Studies in Higher Education*, 28 (2): 157–69.

Slaughter, S. and Leslie, L. (1997) *Academic Capitalism: Politics, Policies, and the Entrepreneurial University*. Baltimore and London: Johns Hopkins University Press.

Slosson, E. E. (1910) *Great American Universities*. New York: The MacMillan Company.

Smeby, J. C. (1998) Knowledge production and knowledge transmission. The interaction between research and teaching at universities, *Teaching in Higher Education*, 3 (1): 5–20.

Smith, D. (2001) Collaborative research: policy and the management of knowledge creation in UK universities, *Higher Education Quarterly*, 55 (2): 131–57.

Stefani, L. and Elton, L. (2002) Continuing professional development of academic teachers through self-initiated learning, *Assessment and Evaluation in Higher Education*, 27: 117–29.

Stehr, N. (1994) *Knowledge Societies*. London: Sage.

Steinberger, M. (2001) Harvard pulls ahead in economics game, *New York Times*, 27 December.

Stenhouse, L. (1975) *An Introduction to Curriculum Research and Design*. London: Heinemann.

Stenhouse, L. (1980) The study of samples and the study of cases, *British Educational Research Journal*, 6 (1): 1–6.

Sterneck, N. H. (1999) Research universities and scientific misconduct, in J. M. Braxton (ed.) *Perspectives on Scholarly Misconduct in the Sciences*. Columbus: Ohio State University Press.

Tagg, P. (2002) *Conscientious Objections to Audit*. Background document to proposal submitted to the Association of University Teachers (AUT), February. www.mediamusicstudies.net/tagg/rants/audititis/autprop1.html (accessed 23 July 2004).

Talib, A. A. (2002) The Research Assessment Exercise and motivation: a note on the difference in the impact on the active researchers and the non-active, *Higher Education Review*, 34 (2): 51–9.

Taylor, R., Barr, J. and Steele, T. (2002) *For a Radical Higher Education: After Postmodernism*. Buckingham: Open University Press/SRHE.

Terenzini, P. T., and Pascarella, E. T. (1994) Living with myths: undergrduate education in America, *Change*, 26 (1): 28–32.

Tertiary Education Advisory Commission (2001) *Shaping the Funding Framework*. Wellington.

The Boyer Commission on Educating Undergraduates in the Research University (1998) *Reinventing Undergraduate Education: A Blueprint for America's Research Universities*, Stony Brook: State University of New York at Stony Brook. www.naples.cc.sunysb.edu/Pres/boyer.nsf/ (accessed 15 August 2004).

Thomas, K. (1990) *Gender and Subject in Higher Education*. Buckingham: Open University Press.

Thompson, D. F. (1987) *Political Ethics and Public Office*. Cambridge: Harvard University Press.

Tight, M. (1999) Writing in British higher education journals 1993–98: concerns and omissions, *Higher Education Review*, 31 (3): 27–44.

Tight, M. (2002) What does it mean to be a professor?, *Higher Education Review*, 34 (2): 15–32.

Tjeldvoll, A. (1998) The idea of the service university, *International Higher Education*, 13 (Fall): 9–10.

Tobin, A. (1996) Couldn't teach a dog to sit, *Times Higher*, 26 July.

Tomusk, V. (2000) Reproduction of the 'State Nobility' in Eastern Europe: past patterns and new practices, *British Journal of Sociology of Education*, 21 (2): 269–82.

Trigwell, K. and Ashwin, P. (2003) *Undergraduate Students' Experience of Learning at the University of Oxford*. Oxford: University of Oxford, Institute for the Advancement of University Learning. www.learning.ox.ac.uk/iaul/IAUL+3+7.asp (accessed 17 August 2004).

Trow, M. (2000) From mass higher education to universal access: the American advantage, *Minerva*, 37 (4): 303–28.

Turner, S. (1999) Universities and the regulation of scientific morals, in J. M. Braxton (ed.) *Perspectives on Scholarly Misconduct in the Sciences*. Columbus: Ohio State University Press.

Turner, V. (1982) *From Ritual to Theatre: The Human Seriousness of Play*. New York: Performing Arts Journal Publications.

Turner, V. (1995) *The Ritual Process: Structure and Anti-Structure*. New York: de Gruyter.

University of Canterbury (1998, July) *Arts Faculty Newsletter*. Christchurch: UC.

University of Canterbury (2000) *Audit 2000 Portfolio*. Christchurch: UC.

University of Canterbury (2003–2010) *University Charter*. Christchurch: UC.

University of Manchester (1997) Strategic Plan 1997/1998 to 2000/2001. www.man.ac.uk/policies/52.htm.

University of Sydney (1998) Goal 1; Strategic Plan. www.usyd.edu.au/about/publication/pub/stratgic.shtml.

Vassalo, P. (2004) arête, *Philosophy Now*, 45: 7–8.

Victoria, University of Wellington (2004) Charter, 1 January 2004–31 December 2009. www.vuw.ac.nz/home/about_victoria/publications.html#staff.

Walker, M. (2002) Pedagogy and politics and purposes of higher education, *Arts and Humanities in Higher Education*, 1 (1): 43–58.

Warren Piper, D. (1994) *Are Professors Professional?: The Organization of University Examinations*. London: Jessica Kingsley.

Webster, C. (2002) Constructing the teaching-research link in the built environment disciplines, *Exchange*, 3: 15–16.

Webster, D. S. (1984) Faculty and instructional development, *The Pen*, Newsletter published by Division J. Post Secondary Education of the American Educational Research Association.

Webster's Revised Unabridged Dictionary (1998). Version published 1913 by the C. & G. Merriam Co., Springfield, Mass., under the direction of Noah Porter, D.D., LL.D. Electronic version is copyrighted (C) 1996, 1998 by MICRA, Inc. of Plainfield, NJ. Last edit 3 February, 1998.

Wenger, E. (1998) *Communities of Practice: Learning, Meaning, and Identity*. Cambridge and New York: Cambridge University Press.

Westergaard, J. (1991) Scholarship, research and teaching: a view from the social sciences, *Studies in Higher Education*, 16 (1): 23–8.

White, A. (1986) Teaching and research: independent, parallel, unequal, *ERIC Document*, No. ED28150.

Williams, G. (1997) The market route to mass higher education: British experience 1979–1996, *Higher Education Policy*, 10: 275–89.

Windschitl, M. (2002) Framing constructivism in practice as the negotiation of dilemmas: An analysis of the conceptual, pedagogical, cultural, and political challenges facing teachers, *Review of Educational Research*, 72 (2): 131–75.

Winnicott, D. W. (1974) *Playing and Reality*. Harmondsworth: Penguin.

Wittgenstein, L. (1953) *Philosophical Investigations*, trans. G. E. M. Anscombe. New York: Macmillan.

Wright, P. (1992) Learning through enterprise: the Enterprise in Higher Education initiative, in R. Barnett (ed.) *Learning to Effect*. Buckingham: Society for Research into Higher Education & Open University Press.

Yorke, M. (1994) Enhancement-led higher education, *Quality Assurance in Higher Education*, 2: 6–12.

Yorke, M., Barnett, G., Bridges, P., Evanson, P., Haines, C., Jenkins, D., Knight, P., Scurry, D., Stowell, M. and Woolf, H. (2002) Does grading method influence honours degree classification?, *Assessment & Evaluation in Higher Education*, 27 (3): 269–79.

Young, M. (2003) *Curriculum Studies and the Problem of Knowledge: Updating the Enlightenment?* Paper presented to the Education, Policy, Innovation and Change Research Group (EPIC), Education Department, University of Bath, Bath, 14 March 2003.

Contributors

Professor Ronald Barnett, Professor of Higher Education, Institute of Education, University of London. Professor Barnett's main interests lie in the theoretical and conceptual basis of higher education and the university. His most recent books are *Beyond All Reason: Living with Ideology in Higher Education* and (with Kelly Coate) *Engaging the Curriculum in Higher Education* (both McGraw-Hill/Open University Press). He is currently the Chair of the Society for Research into Higher Education.

Dr Carol Bond, Higher Education Development Centre, University of Otago. Her research interests are concerned primarily with university teachers' and students' experiences of teaching, learning and research.

Professor David Dill, Professor of Public Policy, University of North Carolina, USA, where Professor Dill is also the Director of the Public Policy for Academic Quality Research Program.

Professor Lewis Elton, Professor of Higher Education, University College London. He is a Fellow of the American Institute of Physics, a Fellow of the Society for Research into Higher Education and an Honorary Life Member of the Staff and Educational Development Association. Professor Elton's research interests are in different aspects of higher education: innovations in learning and teaching, quality assessment and quality enhancement, and change management.

Professor Mick Healey, Professor of Geography at the University of Gloucestershire. He is Director of the Geography Discipline Network and Senior Adviser for Geography at the Higher Education Academy's Geography, Earth and Environmental Sciences Subject Centre. He was awarded a National Teaching Fellowship in 2000.

Dr Mark Hughes, Senior Lecturer, Organizational Behaviour, Brighton

Business School, University of Brighton. His research and scholarship interests include postgraduate publishing and organizational change in higher education.

Professor Bruce Macfarlane, Professor of Education and Head of Educational Development, Thames Valley University, London. He has published widely in the field of applied and professional ethics with particular reference to academic practice and business education. His latest book is *Teaching with Integrity* (RoutledgeFalmer, 2004).

Dr Rajani Naidoo, School of Education, University of Bath, where she is the coordinator of the postgraduate programme in higher education. Dr Naidoo teaches on a variety of programmes including the Doctorate of Business Administration in Higher Education. Her research interests include higher education policy especially in an international context, the character of teaching in higher education and widening participation and quality. She is a member of the Governing Council of the Society for Research into Higher Education.

Dr Kathleen Nolan, University of Regina, Regina, Canada. Kathleen is Assistant Professor in the Faculty of Education, where she teaches undergraduate and graduate courses in mathematics and science curriculum. Her research interests include mathematics and science epistemologies, integrating technology into the classroom, and critical and narrative research methodologies.

Professor Mark Olssen Professor of Education and Director of Doctoral Programmes at the University of Surrey. Recent articles of his have appeared in *Educational Psychology*, the *British Journal of Educational Studies*, the *Journal of Education Policy*, and *Educational Philosophy and Theory*. He is the author of *Michael Foucault: Materialism and Education*.

Dr Jan Parker, Open University, UK. Dr Parker is Chair of the Humanities Education Research Group (HERG) and edits the journals, *Arts and Humanities in Higher Education* and *Teaching in Higher Education* and the book series: *Teaching and Learning the Humanities in Higher Education*. A classicist, she teaches tragedy to English students in the University of Cambridge and writes on Homer and Greek tragedy.

Professor Michael Peters is Professor of Education, University of Illinois at Urbana-Champaign, USA. He also holds posts as Adjunct Professor of Education at the University of Auckland and as Adjunct Professor of Communication Studies at the Auckland University of Technology. He has interests in educational philosophy and policy and his latest book (with Tina Besley) is *Building Knowledge Cultures: Education and Development in the Knowledge Economy* (Rowman and Littlefield, 2005).

Dr Alison Phipps, Senior Lecturer and Director of Graduate School of Arts and Humanities, University of Glasgow. Her publications include *Contemporary German Cultural Studies* (Arnold, 2002) and (with Mike Gonzales) *Modern Languages: Learning and Teaching in an Intercultural Field* (Sage, 2004). She is Chair of the International Association for Languages and Intercultural Communication.

Dr Jane Robertson, University of Canterbury, Christchurch, New Zealand, where she is Senior Lecturer in the University Centre for Teaching and Learning. She coordinates professional programmes for university teachers including the Postgraduate Certificate and Diploma in Tertiary Teaching (taught on-line with the University of Otago). Her research interests include academics' and students' experiences of the relation between research and teaching in higher education.

Professor Stephen Rowland is Professor of Higher Education, University College London. His books – *The Enquiring Classroom* (Falmer, 1984), *The Enquiring Tutor* (Falmer, 1993) and *The Enquiring University Teacher* (Open University Press, 2000) – aim to place an ethos of enquiry at the centre of educational processes and relationships. He is currently working on *The Enquiring University*. He is also a member of the Governing Council of the Society for Research into Higher Education.

Professor Peter Scott, Vice-Chancellor, Kingston University, Surrey. Previously, he was a Professor of Education at the University of Leeds and from 1976 to 1992 he was Editor of the *Times Higher Education Supplement*. He is also a member of the Board of the Higher Education Funding Council for England. His most recent book, co-authored with Helga Notwotny and Michael Gibbons, is *Re-Thinking Science: Knowledge and the Public in an Age of Uncertainty* (Sage, 2001).

Name Index

Subject Index

The Society for Research into Higher Education

The Society for Research into Higher Education (SRHE), an international body, exists to stimulate and coordinate research into all aspects of higher education. It aims to improve the quality of higher education through the encouragement of debate and publication on issues of policy, on the organization and management of higher education institutions, and on the curriculum, teaching and learning methods.

The Society is entirely independent and receives no subsidies, although individual events often receive sponsorship from business or industry. The Society is financed through corporate and individual subscriptions and has members from many parts of the world. It is an NGO of UNESCO.

Under the imprint *SRHE & Open University Press*, the Society is a specialist publisher of research, having over 80 titles in print. In addition to *SRHE News*, the Society's newsletter, the Society publishes three journals: *Studies in Higher Education* (three issues a year), *Higher Education Quarterly* and *Research into Higher Education Abstracts* (three issues a year).

The Society runs frequent conferences, consultations, seminars and other events. The annual conference in December is organized at and with a higher education institution. There are a growing number of networks which focus on particular areas of interest, including:

Access	FE/HE
Assessment	Graduate Employment
Consultants	New Technology for Learning
Curriculum Development	Postgraduate Issues
Eastern European	Quantitative Studies
Educational Development Research	Student Development

Benefits to members

Individual

- The opportunity to participate in the Society's networks
- Reduced rates for the annual conferences
- Free copies of *Research into Higher Education Abstracts*
- Reduced rates for *Studies in Higher Education*

- Reduced rates for *Higher Education Quarterly*
- Free online access to *Register of Members' Research Interests* – includes valuable reference material on research being pursued by the Society's members
- Free copy of occasional in-house publications, e.g. *The Thirtieth Anniversary Seminars Presented by the Vice-Presidents*
- Free copies of *SRHE News* and *International News* which inform members of the Society's activities and provides a calendar of events, with additional material provided in regular mailings
- A 35 per cent discount on all SRHE/Open University Press books
- The opportunity for you to apply for the annual research grants
- Inclusion of your research in the *Register of Members' Research Interests*

Corporate

- Reduced rates for the annual conference
- The opportunity for members of the Institution to attend SRHE's network events at reduced rates
- Free copies of *Research into Higher Education Abstracts*
- Free copies of *Studies in Higher Education*
- Free online access to *Register of Members' Research Interests* – includes valuable reference material on research being pursued by the Society's members
- Free copy of occasional in-house publications
- Free copies of *SRHE News* and *International News*
- A 35 per cent discount on all SRHE/Open University Press books
- The opportunity for members of the Institution to submit applications for the Society's research grants
- The opportunity to work with the Society and co-host conferences
- The opportunity to include in the *Register of Members' Research Interests* your Institution's research into aspects of higher education

Membership details: SRHE, 76 Portland Place, London W1B 1NT, UK Tel: 020 7637 2766. Fax: 020 7637 2781. email: srheoffice@srhe.ac.uk world wide web: http://www.srhe.ac.uk./srhe/ *Catalogue:* SRHE & Open University Press, McGraw-Hill Education, McGraw-Hill House, Shoppenhangers Road, Maidenhead, Berkshire SL6 2QL. Tel: 01628 502500. Fax: 01628 770224. email: enquiries@openup.co.uk – web: www.openup.co.uk

UNIVERSITY OF WOLVERHAMPTON
LEARNING & INFORMATION SERVICES